THE BRIDGE TO VICTORY

Beth C. Moroney

Paperback ISBN: 978-1-962905-56-5
Hardcover ISBN: 978-1-962905-57-2

Printed in the United States of America

Published by Book Marketeers.com

DEDICATION

The Bridge to Victory is dedicated to all of those who have served and continue to serve in the armed forces of the United States. This inspirational story is a testimonial to the crucial work that all teachers and coaches face daily in the classroom as they strive to mold children into being the next "greatest generation."

Most of all, *The Bridge to Victory* is dedicated to Jay Howard Dakelman, Corporal of the United States Army and dedicated Director of Athletics to Highland Park High School, my father.

Democracy cannot succeed unless those who express their choice are prepared to choose wisely. The real safeguard of democracy, therefore, is education.

Franklin Delano Roosevelt

TABLE OF CONTENTS

Preface 1

Part 1 Bridges 4

Chapter 1 The Ship Sails 5

Chapter 2 Making England Home 12

Chapter 3 The Battle of Normandy 25

Chapter 4 The First Time I Saw Paris 35

Chapter 5 The Battle of St. Vith 42

Chapter 6 Thelma 56

Chapter 7 The Bridge at Remagen 76

Chapter 8 In Enemy Territory 84

Chapter 9 Buchenwald 89

Chapter 10 V-E day 102

Chapter 11 Home 116

Part 2 Victory 138

Chapter 12 Summer Camp With J.B. Nash 139

Chapter 13 Highland Park High School 149

Chapter 14 The Importance of Recreation in Small Town America
.... 161

Chapter 15 JoJo 171

Chapter 16 Thanksgiving 1964: How to Accomplish an Undefeated
Season 185

Chapter 17 1976: The Dream Team 196

Chapter 18 What is the Meaning of Victory?.............................. 221

Chapter 19 A League of Their Own 236

Chapter 20 I Don't Know Anything About Track! 246

Chapter 21 More Track! 260

Chapter 22 Women in Sports 273

Chapter 23 Get Right Down to the Real Nitty Gritty 293

Chapter 24 1982 National Athletic Director of the Year............. 309

Chapter 25 The Last Dance 322

Afterword Legacy... 327

Acknowledgements 354

Bibliography.. 360

Endnotes 369

PREFACE

Jay Howard Dakelman, a proud member of the 86th Battalion Army Corps of Engineers, enlisted in the Army shortly after the Japanese attack on Pearl Harbor. He was barely 20 years old and looking forward to his graduation from the Panzer School of Health and Physical Education, located in South Orange, New Jersey. To this day, Panzer, now part of Montclair State University, is held in the highest esteem as one of the most progressive and elite schools of its kind in the world. Jay's early graduation from Panzer put a temporary cap on his lust for his own education as a student who saw the importance of developing the body and mind to their utmost potential.

The following story about Jay's participation in World War II is thrilling, fascinating, but not unique. As I interviewed children of veterans of the "war to end all wars," it became clear that the men and women who gave of themselves to protect the world from tyranny were, indeed, the greatest generation. Jay's story is a microcosmic representation of all of those who served during World War II, and especially of those who paid the ultimate sacrifice with their lives. For those of us who remember their heroic deeds, we will be forever grateful for every contribution to fight for a world in which democracy can reign supreme forever.

What sets Jay's story apart, however, is how he overcame the bitter memories of witnessing man's inhumanity to man at its extreme worst and molded himself into a leader of young men and women. His ability to motivate, stimulate, and allow young peoples' imaginations to soar and fight to achieve their dreams, whether they were of victory on the football field or track, professional aspirations, familial obligations, or of contributing as moral and ethical members of American society, he never failed at anything that he set out to do.

Aside from being a "master motivator," as so many of his former students and colleagues refer to Jay, he was a visionary. He was committed to equality in educational opportunities. As early as 1947 he encouraged women to work out with male athletes on the track team and pushed for them to compete at meets. He believed fervently that education was the gateway to success in life and advocated for his athletes of color to attend and graduate from college.

After experiencing an early disappointment in the way football championships were awarded in New Jersey, he spent the rest of his career developing a system that would give equity to every school, no matter its size or demographics. His vision led, ultimately, to the championship system that is used in the state today.

He believed in the importance of schools belonging to leagues that enabled fair schedules to be created each year so that there were opportunities within a contained geographic area in which schools could count on equitable competition without having to travel too far. He worked on creating three leagues during his career; the final one led to the Middlesex County Conference, which has grown into one of New Jersey's super conferences.

Jay's unique ability to foresee the future of athletics for all children was one of the key factors that led him to be chosen as the only National Director of Athletics to ever come from New Jersey.

Above all, despite the horrors of war that haunted him until his final days, Jay believed in the ability of humankind to achieve fairness and respect for all. Even though he has been gone for over three decades, the mention of his name still evokes inspirational stories about his impact on the lives of those who knew and loved him.

PART 1

BRIDGES

December 7 ... a date that will live in infamy.
Franklin Delano Roosevelt

CHAPTER 1

THE SHIP SAILS

5:30 a.m. October 13, 1942. The sky brightened slightly as the sun rose in the eastern sky. 20,000 American soldiers saluted silently to the Statue of Liberty as the ship slid by the solemn statue, holding her lit torch in one hand, books in the other. At this moment, tears glistened in many eyes as the men left the New York harbor, wondering if they would ever see their homes and families again. What tricks would Fate play on them once they landed on European shores in the future?

Private Jay H. Dakelman held onto the railing and scanned the crowd of men, wishing that the officers would have permitted a brief furlough the night before sailing. He could have taken the train up to Avon Avenue in Newark to bid goodbye to his grandparents, Bubbie and Grandpa Sholk, and his many aunts, uncles, and cousins, who congregated each weekend at the Sholk home.

Most of all, he would have liked to have shaken his father, Lou's hand and hugged his mother, Ida. He would have looked into his sister's huge, brown eyes and wished her luck as she was going off to the University of Pennsylvania in Philadelphia in just a couple of weeks. Carol intended to study occupational therapy and weighed no more than ninety pounds; Jay had no idea how she would be physically able to handle the weight of most of her patients.

He admired his sister's innate intelligence and drive to learn all that she could about occupational therapy, her chosen field of work, which was still in its pioneer stages. While Jay was obsessed with sports, Carol loved the arts, frequently going to the Metropolitan Museum of Art in New York City to see the latest exhibits. Jay's taste in music vacillated between the swing of Tommy and Jimmy Dorsey's bands and the great fight songs of the big colleges. Jay never professed to have much of a voice, but he loved to belt out, "I'm a ramblin' wreck from Georgia Tech and a heck of an engineer." Carol's passion for music ran to classical chamber groups as well as symphony orchestras. Jay had always been a husky boy, reaching 5'6 at his adult height; Carol's petite frame was adorable but far from fragile. Although the brother and sister were opposites in almost every way, they loved and respected each other immensely.

Out in the distance lay one of Jay's favorite places, the Jersey shore. Practically everyone knew that New Jersey had the most beautiful beaches in the world. His mother's seven siblings, spouses, and numerous children often gathered at bungalows rented in Bradley Beach during the summer months. Jerseyans referred to the beach as "down the shore," a colloquialism drawn from where the ocean was located on the map.

It was his family that Jay thought about as the mammoth ship took him away from the American coastline. He had bid goodbye to them in person three months before when he had boarded the train to basic training in Camp Gordon, Georgia, as an enlisted man.

Jay was proud that he had enlisted during the winter of 1942. Right after the surprise attack on Pearl Harbor, Jay called his best friends at Panzer College to come to his dorm for a crucial conversation about their futures.

"Look," Jay began, "I figure that it's going to take some time for the Army to get enough men and supplies over to Europe to invade. I don't know about you guys, but I don't want to get drafted before I finish my degree. I think that we should go to the draft board and make a deal. With all the pre-med courses we've taken, we can probably go in as medics, which would be a lot better than getting drafted as infantry."

The young men nodded in agreement. They trusted Jay's leadership. He was president of their class as well as being valedictorian. They decided to take Jay's advice and a few days later, they went as a group to the draft office. Having a cadre of medics enlist at one time was a fine idea as far as the Army was concerned and they agreed to let the college students take courses during the summer and graduate in the fall of '42.

Jay was satisfied that his friends had taken his suggestion and ran with it, but he was disappointed and a bit perplexed that his best friend, Jimmy Dow, had been rejected as a 4F status. Jay found this rejection ludicrous. Anyone who had ever seen Jimmy perform on the rings in a gymnastics competition would have to wonder how a specimen like Jim could be turned down by the Army. With his rolling abs and bulging arms, he was quite the image of a Greek god. Later, Jimmy confided to Jay the reason why the Army had rejected him but did not share this information with the other guys. Jay did find it ironic that Jimmy was turned down, while he, who suffered from terrible hay fever and asthma attacks when goldenrod burst forth every August, was welcomed eagerly into the United States Army.

In his senior year at Panzer College, an elite school for physical education, Jay had been Editor-in-Chief of both the school yearbook, *The Olympia*, and the school newspaper. Reflecting on the history of the Class of '43, the book noted, "As seniors, the class was confronted with being the first one to graduate under the accelerated program . . . Now the Senior Class Dinner, the Baccalaureate Service, and the Commencement Exercises are all things of the past. Another class has passed through the glorified halls of PC, a class faced with the cares of a war-torn world. The men will be serving their country in the armed forces, and the women will exercise their knowledge and abilities in a civilian army. Yes, this class is facing the world with one thought in mind--- Let us do our meager part so that the world may once more dwell in peace."[1]

Eleven men from the Class of '43 had left school early to enter the military. Jay was thankful that his education was behind him so he wouldn't have to worry about completing his degree when (and if) he ever came home. Having his Bachelor of Science under his belt gave him a strong sense of accomplishment and purpose because he knew what he wanted to do when he came home from the war. He was determined to become a high school football coach, although his mother had scoffed at the idea. "There is no such thing as a Jewish football coach," she argued stubbornly when Jay turned down the pre-med course at Purdue University. With his photographic memory, Jay would have made a great surgeon, something Ida would have loved to kvell about to her friends and family. But no, Jay was going to teach Physical Education and coach football, basketball, and baseball, and that was that.

Once the ship was on its way, the men headed toward the huge mess hall on the mammoth ship, the Queen Elizabeth. Most of the soldiers had settled into tight quarters as their bunks were stacked five high. It was very cramped, although Jay didn't mind being on the top bunk. A small light shone above his head which enabled him to read deep into the night. Jay was an avid reader and devoured books easily. He enjoyed fiction, but he craved books about historical events.

Aside from being a sports nut, Jay was fascinated by history. One of his biggest worries was how he was going to get reading material while serving in a war. Without books and movies and no Yankee games to listen to on the radio, Jay feared that his mind would stagnate, which might allow the fear of what was going to happen soon seep into his consciousness. He was pretty sure that he would be able to cajole some guys into playing poker, which he was a master at when they had time to spare.

Sailing on the Queen Elizabeth had been an incredible stroke of luck. She was the largest passenger liner that had ever been built and kept that record for fifty-six years. Launched in 1938, she had been intended as a luxury ship for the Cunard line, but her first transatlantic journeys were in military service. Fortunately, although the outside of the ship was complete in 1939, she had not been fitted yet for the lavish interior that was planned for her, so her transformation into a huge transport of military men was relatively simple. Even so, packing in 20,000 men was an ordeal.[2]

Although Jay had seen pictures of the ship in her Cunard line colors, the Queen Elizabeth had been painted battleship gray for the wartime crossings. In fact, he had managed to procure several postcards of the ship in her premature glory before she had enlisted in the Royal Navy. As a student of history, Jay collected postcards and took photographs to document important events whenever he could. He already had his camera loaded with film to begin documenting the odyssey on which he was about to embark.

As the Queen Elizabeth soared through the choppy waves of the Atlantic, there was a great deal of worry about the Germans tracking her whereabouts and sending out a submarine to torpedo the huge ship. Sinking this impressive vessel would be a huge coup for the Germans.

However, the business-like attitude of the British ship's personnel and gun crews gave the men aboard a secure feeling. The liner, being an unanticipated target for any German submarine, meant that her destruction would provide a huge victory for the Germans. Therefore, the QE zig-zagged across the Atlantic to avoid being prey to a predator. Guns were manned 24 hours a day and lifeboats were assigned to the individual units.

During the sail to Britain, each company was assigned a duty. The 86th Pontoon Battalion of the First Army Corps of Engineers to which Jay was assigned, had been appointed as MPs while aboard.[3] With the whole ship open to the soldiers, Jay's job allowed him the opportunity to explore most of the gargantuan vessel. Aside from the fact that the men weren't sure of their immediate destination, they settled in and enjoyed their days at sea.

As a medic, a lot of Jay's time on board was spent overseeing paperwork on the men, recording inoculations that they had, injuries that were being treated, and illnesses that could affect them during the war. Hearing and vision were checked again as well.

Due to her great swiftness in cutting through the ocean, as well as a bit of good fortune, the ship anchored in Greenock, Scotland at 18:30 on October 18.[4] The pleasurable voyage had taken five days, and the men, who had not known their immediate destination, were pleased to learn that they would be spending their time waiting for the inevitable European invasion in the scenic area of England known as the Cotswolds.

How long would the wait in England be until the invasion to free Europe would commence? No one knew right now. But, for the moment, the 86th was safe, comfortable, and ready for the adventure that lay ahead.

The price of greatness is responsibility.
Winston Churchill

CHAPTER 2

MAKING ENGLAND HOME

It wasn't until October 21 that the 86th finally disembarked from the Queen Elizabeth and watched her fade into the early morning fog, disappearing as if in a dream. The men boarded a train for Stroud, England. The trip into England, with plenty of coffee and donuts to eat, was smooth. Spirits were high as the "Yanks" were greeted enthusiastically by the English.[1]

American flags were being waved alongside the Union Jack and mobs of onlookers were shouting, "Welcome, Yanks! It took you long enough to get here!"

Now that the Americans had entered the war, freeing Europe from Hitler's grip was the goal. However, it couldn't happen as quickly as the Allies wanted it to because getting enough heavy machinery, artillery, and troops to a continent an ocean away from battle was a mammoth endeavor.

Unbeknownst to most Americans, Army officers had established a headquarters in London not far from the American embassy in the spring of 1941. Their designation was the Special Observers Group (SPBOS), but they were doing more than being neutral observers. Their function was to organize a military staff to govern personnel, intelligence, plans and operations, and logistics and supplies in preparation for the anticipated American entrance into the war. As early as this point, the importance and involvement of the army engineers was noted and involved in the planning.[2]

Arriving in Stroud, Jay and his comrades were met by the battalion's advance party which represented all three companies of the 86th. Loaded down by their gear, the men struggled up a steep hill and found a deserted poorhouse in which to spend their first night in England.

The building, 1 Bisley Road, was an impressive one, although it was in serious need of repairs. Improvements began on the second day in England, and quickly the old house began to shape up into a manor surrounded by beautiful property. The renovations included a kitchen, showers and sinks were installed, and the lighting in the dingy rooms was updated.[3]

In the workhouse, Jay shared a cozy room with his buddy, Mike Rosario. Both men were thrilled to have a working fireplace in their quarters, a large table, two beds, and considerable wall space on which to hang their favorite pin-ups. A few men had pictures of their sweethearts back home, but for right now, Jay was infatuated with the stunning Rita Hayworth. He admired her waves of red hair, which plummeted to shoulder length.

"I like redheads," he told Mike one night as they were preparing to sleep.

"Did you have a steady girl while you were in college?" Mike queried.

"Nah," Jay replied. "I was too busy with three sports, the dance committees, the yearbook, the school newspaper, and being class president to have time for a steady girl."

"Do you want to get married?" Mike continued to probe.

"Someday, if we get out of this fight alive."

"Me, too," Mike returned. "So, if you don't have a steady girl, who are all the letters from?" Although only a couple of weeks away, it was well-known in the company that Jay was receiving quite a bit of mail.

"Oh, you know, my mom, my sister, and the president of Panzer College, Dr. Brown."

"You get mail from the president of your college?" Rosario gasped, his eyes open in surprise.

"Yeah, well, Dr. Brown and I butted heads quite a bit while I was a student at Panzer, but I think she liked me for the fact that I was strong-willed and wouldn't back down when we were arguing. She liked my stubborn streak." Jay smiled, remembering a note that was deposited in your mailbox stating, "See me. MCB" was enough to make any student in the school quake. A slight woman, Dr. Brown was passionate about sports, most especially gymnastics. She was also feared as a martinet when it came to law and order at her school.

"That's pretty amazing that she writes to you."

Jay nodded with a faint, enigmatic smile.

Living in the Cotswolds of England was about as sweet of an assignment as a soldier could get. The rolling, green hills dotted with thatched houses were charming, and the Brits welcomed the men wherever they went, but especially in the town's 38 pubs.[4] These small bars were homey and crowded due to the onslaught of American military personnel moving in at an astonishing rate.

The pubs enabled the British men and the Americans to bond as the Yanks commiserated with their allies over the daily and nightly bombings occurring in London, Coventry, Birmingham, and nearby Bristol. Plunged into darkness, the revelry went on, with the Brits constantly asking when the Americans would be ready to cross the Channel and force the Krauts back to Germany.

However, the reality was that the anticipated invasion was still nearly a year away as it was taking a huge amount of time to get the supplies overseas that the troops would need to defeat the enemy. As engineers, the 86th needed the materials with which to build pontoon bridges once the invasion began. There were trucks, tanks, guns, and ammunition to come. Also, as the labor of the 86th intensified during the rough work of practicing how to erect the bridges efficiently, the uniforms of the soldiers tore frequently and needed to be replaced. Therefore, bolts of material had to be sent for uniforms to be manufactured in Britain.

The 86th battalion was assigned as the MP detachment in Stroud as they had done on the Queen Elizabeth, and Lieutenant Cullen was the Police and Prison Officer.[5] This was considered necessary in a town of Stroud's size (especially with its 38 pubs). Since the battalion had experience serving as MPs on the crossing of the Atlantic, they had an idea of what was expected of them. There was not a lot of crime in Stroud, and the Americans wanted to make sure that the town remained peaceful despite the rise in its population. Most of the men enjoyed serving as MPs because it gave them an opportunity to meet the town's residents and get to know them more intimately.

One evening, shortly after arriving in Stroud, the company chaplain announced that the local synagogue was hosting a Shabbat dinner and services for the Jewish soldiers in the area. Jay was excited to attend services, especially because of traveling this year; he had missed out on Rosh Hashanah and Yom Kippur, which gave him an empty feeling. Although he was not as devout as his Sholk grandfather who was an Orthodox Jew, celebrating the New Year and atoning on Yom Kippur were important to Jay as his religious obligation.

The synagogue where the festivities were to take place was the Middle Street Synagogue in the center of Brighton, which had been the center of Jewish worship in Brighton for a century. Built in 1874, the handsome edifice was constructed in a Neo-Byzantine style, which was artistically exquisite, especially compared to the unadorned temples in New Brunswick.[6]

Jay was a little anxious about attending the service, but his buddy, Randy Newman, agreed to accompany him. At the Shabbat dinner, Jay sat with the Reisman family, which consisted of Esther, her ten-year-old daughter, Rochelle; Barry, who was only a few months old; and Hilda Miller, who was Esther's sister.[7]

For Randy, the evening was a huge success. He met a dark-haired English girl named Hetty Fine, who was quite shapely to Randy's liking. Jay smiled as he watched the two of them flirt with each other.

On the way home to Stroud, Jay ribbed Randy, "So you found yourself a nice, Jewish girl from Britain. Do you think your mom will be pleased?"

Randy looked dryly at Jay and offered, "Well, you seemed to make a hit with quite a few of the lovely gals at the dinner.

Hopefully, we'll have a place to get some nice latkes when Chanukah comes around." He moved his hands to indicate a shapely woman.

As the months went by, the friendship with the Newman and Miller family deepened, much to Jay's happiness. They spent many pleasant Sundays strolling in Stroud Park. Esther and Hilda thought that Jay was hilarious, whipping out his camera every time they came upon a pharmacy.

"Let's see," Esther chided Jay. "So far, you've got Boots Chemists, Timothy White's, and Smith's Drug store."

"And don't forget Rexall's," piped up Hilda.

"I can't help it that my father wants pictures of every pharmacy in Europe, can I?" Jay responded playfully to their teasing.

In November, Jay and his friend, Eddie Cossart, ventured out of Stroud for the first time and took a quick sightseeing trip to Tortworth Court, referred to as Tortworth Castle. Located near Thornbury, South Gloucestershire, the impressive manor had been built in the Tudor style for the 2nd Earl of Dulcie between 1848-1853.[8]

At this time, the impressive building was being used to house the naval officers who were being trained there.

"Not bad," Eddie said, looking out over the impressive garden from the rooftop of the manor. "I wouldn't mind staying in this joint for a few weeks myself."

"I'll bet those guys get better meals than what Lucacino and Woodard cook up for us," Jay said snidely.

Jay and Eddie enjoyed their brief sojourn to Tortworth Castle, which whetted their appetites for their next furlough in December. They were to have 24 hours of leave to visit London. It was 90 miles away, and Jay knew that time would be measured while they were there. Of course, some historical attractions that he yearned to see were not open due to the war. However, as a Charles Dickens fan, Jay just wanted to experience the fabled city.

"If we only get to see Big Ben, Parliament, and the Tower of London, I will be happy," Jay told Andy Sorenson and Randy Newman, his two buddies who were counting on Jay to lead them around the city.

"I want to go to a pub in London," Eddie declared exuberantly.

"We'll get to one before we have to take the train back," Jay replied. "I have one picked out for us already."

"Leave it to Jay; he thinks of everything," Randy laughed.

Being December and bitterly cold, the men had worn their heavy coats, which weighed them down considerably. The famous London fog enshrined Tower Bridge as the men made their way to see the Tower of London, constructed in the time of the Normans.

As the men drew closer to the Tower, a bridge took them near a metal gate, which was at the level of Thames water. In the dense fog, it appeared eerie.

"That," Jay said, pointing to the gate, "is Prisoner's Gate, which is where the accused were brought to wait for their trials, torture, or beheadings."

"How do you know all this stuff?" Andy chided Jay. "Did you memorize a tourist guide?"

"Well, I read a lot and I enjoy history. I studied quite a bit about the kings and queens of England," Jay responded.

As they neared the entrance of the Tower, the men spotted a Beefeater, dressed in heavy, woolen cape with brass buttons and a tall, black hat. The mustachioed Beefeater was ignoring a curious dog, which was sniffing around his boots. However, the Beefeater didn't flinch as the pooch explored his feet.

"Pub, Jay," Andy ribbed. "I need a beer."

The men made their way over to the Tiger Tavern, which fortunately was right across the street from the Tower of London. Jay snapped Andy's picture in front of the rustic pub, capturing the sign atop the entrance, which read, "This tavern was honored by Queen Elizabeth I."

When Jay approached the bar to place their orders for three fish and chips platters, two beers, and one coke, he asked the bartender about the sign.

"Oh yes," he replied, "Old Queen Bess herself was a regular patron of this place," he nodded at the burnished, wooden beams of the Tudor architecture.

"I hope the fish and chips haven't been around that long," joked Andy when their platters were delivered. "I can't wait to have an authentic British meal."

There weren't many tourists these days in London, but the trio enjoyed the light banter of the English, who had stopped in for a pint.

On the train back to Stroud, Jay searched the fading London sky for a look at the enemy planes that might be coming to strafe the city again. All around the streets, the rubble of houses and businesses that had been destroyed by German bombs angered the soldiers and intensified their eagerness to start their offensive to free Europe from Nazi domination.

"It is going to take a long time to rebuild what's been destroyed," Jay observed sadly.

As Andy and Randy dozed comfortably on the rocking train, Jay's thoughts took him to that dark place, where he tried not to go very often. "It won't be long now, will it?" he thought. Rumor had it that the invasion might take place in early May. "Then we'll be in it for real."

There was a letter for Jay from his good friend, Dorothy Klockner, Jimmy's girlfriend, when they got back to the Poor House. In it, she assured him that her family was fine, as was Jim, who had landed a job at Cranford High School, teaching Physical Education and Health. He was Head Gymnastics coach and an assistant in football and baseball. Jay envied Jim for getting a teaching job so easily. Once all the men returned home after the war, Jay had no idea what the teaching situation would be like. Right now, with so few young men at home, it had been a cinch for Jim to nail down a position.

The days rolled by quickly, and there was always plenty to do. There were classes to attend in aircraft identification and how to use and maintain gas masks. The men regularly visited the shooting range and practiced how to aim at the enemy and be successful in their shots.

The vehicles were designed especially for the job of getting personnel and equipment to a site, building the proposed bridge, and staying there to maintain it. Every conceivable task was accounted for in their construction, and the care and maintenance of the bridges was part of the rigid daily routine. The maintenance and repair were assigned to be handled by the H & S company. To them went the complete checks, the repairing of broken parts, and the ordering of items that they were unable to repair.[9]

On the highways a correct distance was kept between trucks and between companies timed down to the precise second. According to long-tested statistics, this distance offered comparative safety from the enemy's strafing or low-level bombing attacks. All of this was stressed continually on maneuvers, but within the flying range of Germany's airfields, the men remembered easily what they had to do if attacked by surprise.

To offer actual protection during convoys, the trained AA gunners were assigned to vehicles. The machine guns were mounted atop the truck cabs, and a constant vigilance was maintained by the gunners. This meant a big job in maintaining the machine guns, so it was vital to be able to identify the planes that flew overhead.[10]

This created massive work for the motor pool, but on the highways, the company was an easy target to spot, and every man was aware of that fact. The arduous task of keeping the equipment in shape was of no use if the men were not conscientious on the roads. The justification for these maneuvers was easily apparent as the men prepared to fight.

On days when the company practiced bridge building and demolition, Jay and the rest of the medical detachment spent time keeping up with records and tending to men who were injured during the continual training or sick from the miserable English weather.

There were constant inventories of every item, no matter how small, to keep the battalion up to its proper strength. There were guns to be armed, gas masks to be kept in perfect condition, and the vehicles had to be kept in tip-top shape, as they were the most important feature of the battalion. Without the trucks, the Army could go nowhere.

Despite all the effort that was going into the training for action, there was quite a bit of time for recreation. Jay enjoyed going to the movies with his friends, the Millers, as well as day trips to see some of the legendary sites in the Cotswolds. Hikes were a common pastime as well. Jay loved the breathtaking view from Redborough Hill and the old fort that was there. He took many pictures of the scenery and sent the film back to the states where his dad's pharmacy could send the pictures to be developed. Louie sent some of the photos back to Jay so he could see how his photography was improving, but a lot of them remained at home as well so that the family could see what was happening in England.

An athletic program, including daily calisthenics, hikes, fast marches, and runs kept the unit physically fit. The hills of the country reminded the men of their days in basic training back in Georgia. Jay, an early riser, called the men for morning exercises by tweeting on his favorite silver whistle from his Panzer days. Leading the squadron in calisthenics was great practice for coaching in the future.[11]

Another training issue that was becoming increasingly important was the detection and neutralization of hidden mines. What made this chore so challenging was that the Germans continually came up with new types of mines. The company practiced assembling, arming, and disarming their own individual mines. They were fully aware that neutralizing these dangerous weapons was a vital component to their survival.

Although each company had its own mine crew, led by an officer, which went into a proposed bivouac site to sweep the area for mines, each member of the company had to go out at night, in the dark, and during the day to sweep out mines and booby traps. All personnel had to become familiar with the use of the mine detector as well.

Despite the rigorous physical training, Jay had an opportunity to play his favorite position in baseball, catcher, on the Stroud Yankee team, which they played for a civilian audience. On one occasion, a charity game was held, with the benefits going to the Stroud Red Cross.

In April, B company moved to the 1115 Engineer Combat Group. This meant that they had to bivouac in new sites, sleeping in tents that tended to be damp, especially at night. The purpose of the move of B company was so that they could join with the 82 NS and 1295th Engineer Combat Battalions as they constructed 15 twenty-five-ton, reinforced pontoon bridges.[12]

One challenging problem was an assault landing under tactical conditions. The entire battalion received training for this possibility, and the securing of a bridgehead was achieved. The training schedule demanded that maneuvers were rehearsed day and night. Building bridges at night-time was especially challenging because no light was permitted to be used. The men had to memorize the feel of bridge parts so that they could recognize them in the dark.

Having mastered the building of pontoon bridges, B company was transferred twice more, once to Buckinghamshire and then to Misterton, Somerset. B company imparted their knowledge of bridge building to these other companies to help more men be ready to construct a pontoon bridge even in their dreams.[13]

While at Misterton, B company received their alert that the long -awaited invasion would be happening soon. One vital chore that still had to be accomplished was the waterproofing of every vehicle that would be making the crossing. The process of applying the special material to the trucks made it possible for them to be submerged in water and still run.

Back at Stroud, the A company was continuing its bridging 24 hours a day. H & S company, another division of the 86th, was practicing launching storm boats. The camouflage nets were garnished according to a new pattern that they had been given and it took some time to master covering the boats adequately.[14]

May came and went, and still no orders had been given to move. But Jay could feel it in his bones, which were damp to their core due to the rainy British climate. It was coming. The drumbeat of his heart let him know their days of fun in jolly, old England were coming to an end.

The most vital quality a soldier can possess is self-confidence.
General George S. Patton

CHAPTER 3

THE BATTLE OF NORMANDY

To cross the English Channel and begin the assault into France, certain conditions had to occur for the chance of a successful landing. First, there had to be a full moon on the night of the crossing, and second, the tide needed to be rising at dawn. These conditions could be met in only a few days in June 1944. If the invasion was postponed until July, that meant an entire summer month of fighting against the Germans would be lost, a circumstance that must be avoided at all costs.

By the beginning of June, H & S and A companies returned to Stroud, where they were conducting final preparations for the invasion. Excitement was high as the company prepared for combat. By the middle of May, all equipment had been checked out and the men were ready to go. However, the wait dragged on.

Finally, on June 6th, 1944, the men of the 86th heard over the radio that the Allies had landed on the European continent.

"Watch out, Krauts! Here we come!" yelped the eager soldiers as the news spread throughout the encampment.

On June 14th B company was ready for overseas shipment, and they proceeded to Southampton for actual assigning to crafts.

The men were given rations of candy and cigarettes before leaving the sweet shores of England.[1]

B company headed for Omaha Beach on June 17, eleven days after the initial landing, in the vicinity of Vierville and St. Laurent, France. Their channel crossing was smooth and not even one of their vehicles got wet.[2]

On June 21st, the rest of the battalion marched down the long hill and waved farewell to Stroud, which had been their home for eight months. During those months, the English and Americans had forged lifelong friendships, and a few had even found their brides. Leaving the peaceful hamlet, with its welcoming pubs, was sad, but the blood was coursing through the veins of each soldier as he imagined that at last, he would be making his contribution by saving the world from Nazi terrorism.

For Jay, whose passion in life was football, he realized that to capture territory (gain yardage), strategy was the key component. Therefore, he listened to the radio whenever it was possible and thought a great deal about where his unit would be headed as the Allies had to push back against the encroaching German army. Whenever he could have a moment with Colonel Haas, he tried to get any information that he could glean from the officer about their future trajectory.

On July 1, Company A loaded aboard LCT's and ultimately landed at Omaha Beach on July 3. The LCT's did not seem large enough to be able to transport all the heavy equipment that they had to carry, but somehow, the eager soldiers managed to cross the rough English Channel without incident. Company A was joined by H & S Company on July 5th and the entire battalion moved on to Colleville-sur-Mer, where the vehicles were de-waterproofed.[3]

After taking care of the trucks, the men moved into a temporary bivouac at Longueville. As they settled into their tents, the booms of heavy fire could be heard. With enemy planes buzzing above, all of the men, including the medics, grabbed shovels and began digging trenches in which to protect themselves.[4]

"It sure didn't take long for this war to get noisy," Slabicki said, putting his newly calloused hands over his ears.

Over the next few days Jay and his medical associates were busy tending to minor injuries and complaints that the men had as they dutifully scoured the trucks, paying particular attention to those that had been touched by sea water.

However, as that task slowed, many of the men began to relax on foreign soil and tried to converse with farmers whom they met along the way. Even with the assistance of French dictionaries, most of the men were thick-tongued as they attempted to speak in the lilting language of the French. They playfully teased a few country girls and handed out candy bars to make friends. Jay pulled out his camera and took pictures of the men enjoying a little female company, and someone snapped his photo surrounded by a gaggle of pretty mademoiselles.

On July 10, A company began unloading equipment to start hauling telephone poles from Omaha Beach to a signal dump that was under fire. As the men struggled to establish the equipment in place, a huge blast shook the ground under their feet.[5]

"Jeez, what was that?" one of them asked.

At that moment they were unsure of what was happening, but learned a little later that an ammunition dump was burning. Although it was a mile away, fragments of metal began to rain in the vicinity of where the company was toiling. Fortunately, none of the men were injured, but all felt the first inklings of fear in their bellies. Welcome to combat, men of the 86th.

Jay and his buddies took a little time out on Bastille Day to celebrate with a young boy whom the company had "adopted." Nicknamed "Frenchy," the boy liked to assist the medics when he could, running errands for them, waving their medic flag above his head, jauntily wearing Jay's cap.[6]

Once on the move toward St. Lo, Jay enjoyed riding his motorcycle with his buddy, Fred Lamberson, a large man who hailed from Michigan. The two of them liked to talk about Big 10 football and debated about which school in the conference would have the best offense in the upcoming season. Of course, Lamberson felt irrefutably that it had to be Michigan State, although Jay was leaning toward the Buckeyes of Ohio State.

Just anticipating news of the upcoming football season took the men's thoughts off what dangers might lie ahead as they zoomed across the countryside on their mud-covered bikes. Impressive hedgerows loomed near the roads as the Army trekked through, heading toward St. Lo.

Strategically, the battle of St. Lo is regarded as one of the key moments in the history of World War II on the European front.

The famed German General Erwin Rommel and his 7th Panzer Division had entered Normandy in 1940 with the goal of capturing Cherbourg Harbor. On June 17, 1940, the town of St. Lo had been overtaken by the Germans. Much of it lay in rubble from the onslaught that had occurred tragically.

Because of its strategic importance as a crossroads, the Americans needed to recapture St. Lo. Of this pivotal moment, historian Ted Neill wrote, "What seems inevitable in hindsight often isn't in the present moment. Such was the case 43 days after the D-Day landings. Even as American, British, and Canadian forces were slogging their way inland through Normandy's hedgerows, in some places losing a man for every yard gained, the outcome of the Allied invasion of France still hung in the balance."[7] Hedgerows are a maze of earthen embankments that are exceedingly dangerous to advancing soldiers. A heavy bombardment of the town focused primarily on the power plant and railway station, began on the night of July 6 and continued into July 7. The objective of this assault was to cut off German reinforcements in Brittany from the front.

Leaflets warning the civilians of St. Lo of the ensuing danger were dropped by American planes on July 5, telling them to evacuate to safety. Unfortunately, due to high winds, the leaflets missed their mark and residents of neighboring towns received them, thus leaving the residents in extreme danger. In the relentless bombing by the enemy, over 200 prisoners were killed at the local prison, including 76 French, who had been imprisoned by the Nazis.[8]

The actual task of the taking of St. Lo fell to the XIX Corps of the First United States Army, under the direction of General Charles H. Corlett. The Corps was composed of soldiers from the 29th Infantry Division, the 30th Infantry Division, and the 35th Infantry Division.[9]

The Germans had two divisions trying to keep St. Lo under their control: the 352nd Infantry Division and the 3rd Division of the 2nd Parachute Corps.[10]

Through the heavy line of hedgerows, the 29th Infantry Division attacked to the northeast of St. Lo, causing heavy casualties among the Germans. On July 15, the 1st Battalion of the 116th Infantry Regiment, led by Major Sidney Bingham, advanced ahead of the other divisions and was left isolated 1000 yards east of St. Lo for the entire day, leaving them without ammunition or K rations. Twenty-five of their men were wounded, with only three medics to attend them, and they were surrounded by German forces. Planes were summoned to drop plasma while the Germans bombarded the area continuously.[11]

Finally, on July 17, the 3rd Battalion, 116th Infantry, under the command of Major Thomas D. Howie, located the 29th. Hidden by dense vegetation, the 3rd Battalion was ordered not to fire their weapons but only to use their bayonets. Although the mission was successful, Major Howie was killed by a mortar shell explosion. Following Howie's death, the troops were subjected to such a heavy attack that they could advance no further that day.[12]

Major Howie's executive officer, Captain William Puntenney, requested artillery and air support to help disperse the German troops. The 115th Infantry Regiment and the 116th were both on the move, establishing positions along the Madeleine. Overpowered, the Germans retreated west to Rampan.

The Battle at St. Lo was the first major ground battle in Europe following the Allied Invasion at Normandy. Although Jay's unit was several miles away from the heavy fighting, the sight of the Allied bombers, 3,000 aircraft of every description including R.A.F. planes that had swung over the Marigny—St. Lo Ridge were shelling what was left of St. Lo. The noise was deafening, and the ground shook as if experiencing a significant earthquake.[13]

When the battle for St. Lo was finally over, the United States had lost two of its leaders. One was Major Howie, whose body was laid across on the hood of the lead jeep as it entered the ruins of St. Lo, making him symbolically the first American to enter the city. His body was then placed on some rubble and draped in an American flag, a reminder of lost leadership. Also killed during the Battle of St. Lo was General Lesley McNair.[14]

Following the retreat of the Germans, the 86th had much work to accomplish, establishing a new Master engineer dump, a job that took five days to complete. The battalion was then able to load all its bridging equipment from Longueville to the new bivouac area south of St. Lo, 28 miles away from the original site.

Once this job had been accomplished, the exhausted men were able to enjoy a brief respite in which they could wash their filthy clothes, write letters, read, play cards, and one of their favorite pastimes, explore the wreckage of German equipment that had been left behind. Jay snapped a lot of pictures of his friends posing in front of the ruined tanks.

"Hey, Jay," Slabicki called after posing, "let me take one of you."

Although not one for being the center of attention, Jay stood near a bombed-out Jerry tank. His gaze was somewhere off in the distance, and the expression on his face was not hard to read. Having had his first taste of being in a combat zone, with bombers flying overhead and the earth quivering under his boots, he didn't much like it. Then he realized that this was only the beginning. He couldn't begin to predict what more he and his pals were going to experience, but this he knew. None of it was going to be pretty.[15]

The casualties of the Battle of St. Lo proved to be some of the heaviest on both sides during the war. Between July 3 and 22, more than 11,000 American GIs lost their lives, with enemy casualties rising to nearly the same number.[16]

Jay documented the extreme devastation of St. Lo in stunning and tragic photographs. The town was leveled. According to Ted Neill, 95 percent of its buildings were destroyed. He imparts that "even to this day, a shell, emptied of charges, remains lodged in the wall of a church, one of the few buildings left partially standing."[17]

For the rest of his life Jay relished going to movies about World War II. When *The Longest Day* was released in 1962, he packed his three children and wife into his 1960 Buick, affectionately called "the tank" by the Dakelman family due to its green hue and monstrous size and took the family to the drive-in to watch the film. With the tinny speakers blaring into the car, everyone tried to make out the dialogue of the film. But Jay didn't need to hear the dialogue to know what was being said. After all, he had lived the story and the "bombs bursting in air" stayed with him forever.

When the hauling was completed, Jay watched the battalion load all its bridging equipment from Longueville to the new bivouac area 28 miles south of St. Lo. It was incomprehensible and fascinating to watch the bridge pieces being moved, and Jay was inordinately proud to be associated with such fine, hardworking soldiers who had a vital job to accomplish for the army to march safely across European terrain.

The next day Jay was in the medical tent when he heard shouting.

"Medic! Medic! We need a medic, pronto!"

Jay grabbed his equipment bag and darted out of the tent. Men were rushing toward him and pointing in the direction of the forward engineer depot where supplies were being unloaded.

When Jay arrived at the site of the accident, he halted and gaped. The body of Private Norris P. Stanley, a quirky young man with a gentle Virginian accent, could barely be seen, crushed under a crane near where he had been working. Jay dropped his medical bag and ran to Stanley. Kneeling by the body, he felt for a pulse and shook his head while a crowd of men watched.[18]

Jay shook his head. "He's gone," he mouthed, and the onlookers shook their heads in disbelief.

Later, Colonel Howe informed the men that Stanley would be buried at the American Military Cemetery in Blazville, France.

"He'll never get home," Jay mused sadly and then wondered if he and his other friends might have the same fate if they were killed on foreign turf. The idea was too upsetting to ponder for long.

It was time for A and B companies to be on the move again. This time, they headed to a new bivouac at Fervaches where equipment maintenance was conducted. Each time the units moved; their new station had to be swept for land mines before they could settle in a spot.

The next move was 147 miles away to La Madeleine. A few days after their arrival, the forward echelon and two bridging companies were ordered to move to the XIX Corps engineer dump in Aigremont. Orders came to build a bridge one mile south-east of Poissy on the Seine River.

On August 29, the proposed bridge site was reconnoitered, swept for mines, and an approach was prepared. A 36-ton reinforced pontoon bridge was constructed by A and B companies, assisted by two companies of combat engineers. The 590-foot bridge was completed in an incredible four hours and 25 minutes.[19] While crews from A and B companies stayed behind to maintain the bridge, the semi-trailer drivers immediately moved out, heading toward the next engineer dump. It was during this trip that most of the men got their first glimpse of Paris and were astounded by the warm welcome that they received from the crowds of relieved and ecstatic Parisians, who rejoiced in being freed from Nazi oppression.

Defend Paris to the last, destroy all bridges over the Seine and devastate the city.
Adolf Hitler —August 1944

CHAPTER 4

THE FIRST TIME I SAW PARIS

The occupation of Paris by Germany had been accomplished on June 22, 1940, with the signing of the Second Compiegne Armistice. Since the city had been under German domination, it had not undergone the relentless blitzkrieg that London had experienced. The glorious "City of Lights" was still intact, but the citizens of Paris longed to be free of the nemesis that kept them prisoners in their own homes.

After the Allies invaded France on June 6, 1944, Supreme Allied Commander General Dwight D. Eisenhower had to decide how to continue pushing the Germans back without destroying the irreplaceable landmarks in one of the world's most impressive cities.[1] Eisenhower felt that there was no advantage to be gained by engaging with the Germans in an urban confrontation; it would slow down the advance toward Germany and require significant resources to assist the French who remained in the city.[2] With Paris isolated, the German army would be cut off from its means of outside support.

However, pressure from the French people, who would not consider their liberation complete until their capital was restored, and the detested Vichy government overthrown, led to two labor strikes and increasing violence within the city.[3] On August 14, a rebellion was led by the Communist faction of the resistance.[4]

General Charles de Gaulle arrived in Europe on August 20 and convinced Eisenhower that the Germans stood a good chance of defeating the Communist rebels, and therefore, the Americans were forced to seize Paris to complete the mission of liberation.

On August 22, Eisenhower ordered General Omar Bradley, commander of the 12th US Army Group to take the city. Eisenhower had promised de Gaulle that it would be free French forces that would liberate Paris in a ceremonial onslaught that restored French pride; however, General Philippe Francois Marie Leclerc de Hauterclocque's armored division, the group assigned the job of freeing Paris, quickly ran into trouble while trying to accomplish its mission.[5]

The Second French Armored Division finally made its way into Paris on the evening of August 24, 1944, and was joined the next morning by the US 4th Infantry Division and the 2nd Armored Division. Within hours, the Germans surrendered to the French at the Hotel Le Meurice, the newly established French Headquarters. General Charles de Gaulle of the French Army arrived to take control of the city as the head of the Provisional Government of the French Republic.[6]

During this tense period, the 86th was busy maintaining its equipment and preparing to cross the Seine River. On August 29th, a site for the all-important bridge was located and swept for mines. "A 36-ton reinforced pontoon bridge was constructed by A and B companies, assisted by two companies of combat engineers, records Lt. Col. Haas.[7] It was during this time that most of the men of the 86th saw "the City of Lights" for the first time.

Infuriated by the loss of Paris to the Allies, Hitler gave orders to Cholititz, commander of the German garrison and military governor of Paris, to bomb the city to smithereens as well as all the bridges leading into the historic city. However, Cholititz surrendered instead, and Paris was set free.[8]

Following the liberation of Paris, the 86th had a week to enjoy being tourists in the City of Lights. While the bulk of the army was marching on toward Belgium, Jay and his friends were staying at the former estate of Mr. Stern, brother-in-law to the famous Rothchilds. The once posh home had been taken over by the American Red Cross and was called "Columbia Club," located on the Rue de Elysees.

Those who were not medics were put up in the many vacated hotels that abounded in the city. Having real beds for a few days was an appreciated boon for men who had been living in mud for most of the summer. The quality of the air was shifting from hot summer days to the cooler autumn wind, ideal for cramming site seeing into the few precious days that the men had before facing the most bitter fighting of the war. The Germans were on the run now, sure, but sooner or later, a final confrontation would have to be faced.

Jay and some of his buddies wasted no time in getting out to see the emblem of Paris, the Eiffel Tower.

"Hey, Pete," Jay called to his buddy Pete Churak from H & S company, "Give me a big smile!" Jay snapped a picture with his recently acquired German camera and said to Churak, "I'll try to get these developed before we move on. If I can't, I'll send you a copy when we get home."

At the Arc de Triomphe, the men watched solemnly as a young French woman placed a posy of wildflowers on the Tomb of the Unknown Soldier. Having seen so many dead bodies strewn over brush at St. Lo, the idea of an unknown soldier had taken on much greater significance for the men.

A monument of marble stood in Place La Concorde near the Egyptian Obelisk. Dedicated to the city of Strasbourg, the edifice was surrounded by floral wreaths, which had been placed there on the day of liberation by the Parisians.[9]

Jay was awed at the site of the magnificent cathedral at Notre Dame. He snapped pictures of the historically significant building from all angles, never acknowledging that he had enough pictures of this wonder of medieval architecture.

Of course, keeping to his promise of photographing every pharmacy that he came upon, Jay took pictures of every drug store with which he came in contact. He knew that his father would get a kick out of seeing the evidence that Jay had made it to the famous city.

Several evenings during their stay in Paris, the men traveled to the nightclubs in town, including the Folies Bergere. The soldiers rejoiced with the jubilant Parisians, enjoying lots of booze and the company of beautiful French women, still stylish despite the privations of war.

All too soon, it was time to get on the move again and track down the retreating German Army. The bridge at Poissey was removed and loaded onto the trailers and trucks on September 4th.[10] The following day, the entire battalion moved to a temporary bivouac area about eight miles northwest of Mezieres, 155 miles from Paris. Simultaneously, the light equipment section was being shuttled to the Master engineer dump at Meaux under the supervision of Lt. Anderson of the H & S Company.

The battalion arrived in the vicinity of Mezieres at about 6:00 p.m. and waited for instructions from the commander of the 1171st Engineer Group of V Corps. Several hours later, the men learned that a bridge was needed to cross the Meuse River as soon as possible. A site was selected south of Mezieres at Mohon and construction started about 2:00 in the morning. Time was of the essence.[11]

Captain Stearman of B company supervised the construction, and the bridge was built by all the available men from B company as well as one platoon of A company. They were joined in the effort by a small group of combat engineers. The bridge, of class 41 type, reinforced with steel pontoons, was finished four hours later. It was in operation for six days, allowing for one infantry division to cross it, as well as many armored and mobile units.

Jay stood, arms crossed, leaning against a tree with his buddy, Stan.

"It makes you proud, doesn't it, Stan," Jay said, "to see those men marching across that bridge. It's like we are all really a part of the action now."

Pontoon bridges were relatively easy to erect. They had been used as far back as ancient times to transport light loads with pedestrians aboard the trucks. Also known as floating bridges, pontoon bridges were buoyant in the water.

The men had been practicing the construction of the much newer Bailey Bridge, which could support the weight of tanks and heavy artillery, something that the pontoon bridges could not do. Conceived in 1940 by Sir Donald Bailey, an English engineer, the men of the 86th rehearsed building these prefabricated and portable bridges often so that they could be constructed easily in an overnight operation, out of sight of the watchful enemy. Needing no heavy equipment such as cranes or special tools to put them together, the Bailey Bridges were advantageous in many ways compared to the pontoon bridges.[12]

Bailey Bridges consisted of three main parts. Made of steel and wood, the sections could be transported easily in trucks and lifted into place with as few as six men working at a time. The strength of the Bailey Bridge was provided by the ten-foot-long panels that rested on either side. The bridge floors consisted of transoms that were 19 feet wide and ran across the bridge with ten feet long stringers running between them on the bottom, forming a square. Clamps were used to hold the transoms together and stringers were placed on top of the transoms to provide a roadbed for the vehicles.[13]

Once a section of the bridge was complete, it was pushed across rollers on the bridgehead and another section was constructed behind it. The two sections were then connected with pins that were pounded into holes in the corners of the panels.[14]

With three panels across and two high, the Bailey Bridge could support tanks over a 200-foot span. Pathways for pedestrians were installed on the outside of the side panels, allowing soldiers to cross the bridge safely along with the heavy equipment. Jay never ceased to be awed by how quickly the skilled men of the 86th could put one of these miraculous bridges up and just as easily, take them down. He frequently took his trusty camera to the bridge sites to document the construction of the bridges that later were deemed "the bridges that helped win World War II."

Two days after the Mohon bridge was put into operation, another bridge was constructed at Sedan by A company assisted by one platoon of B company and another attached company of combat engineers. The bridge was about 200 feet long and was completed in four hours.[15] During the five days this bridge was in operation, elements of the 5th Armored Division crossed over it and several other mobile units were about to use it.

On September 12th, both bridges were removed and loaded onto the trucks. The battalion prepared to push on, leave France, and move ahead into Belgium. It wouldn't be long, they hoped, before they would put their feet down on German land.

What they didn't see coming, however, was six of the most bitter weeks of frigid cold, fighting the enemy in blizzard conditions without winter coats, boots, and very little to eat. The battle, which was later to be called "The Battle of the Bulge" was coming closer, a battle that would determine the fate of this terrible war.

The object of war is not to die for your country but to make the other bastard die for his.
General George S. Patton

CHAPTER 5

THE BATTLE OF ST. VITH

(Also known as The Battle of the Bulge)

As the 86th moved from their bivouac at Prix and proceeded to Sedan, they were hailed as heroes as they drove through the towns of Belgium. Crowds thronged into the streets, waving and cheering, so glad were they to see the Yanks with their own eyes.

By October 4th, 1944, the troops wound up in a thick forest near Elsingham, Belgium where the men hastily began constructing small huts to protect them from the rain and wind, which whipped around relentlessly. Some of the more industrious men grabbed loose lumber and constructed crude huts. Everything felt wet and clammy. At night the temperature plummeted, making the men even more miserable.[1]

Jay looked up at the tall evergreens, searching for a ray of sun. The woods were so dense that he was reminded of the streets of New York City, where the skyscrapers always blocked the sun. Even in the summer, walking up Broadway was cool. He shuddered with a chill. To make matters worse, winter uniforms had not arrived yet, and the heaviest coat that he had was his wool Eisenhower jacket, which didn't even cover his hips. Although

42

his boots were in good condition, they were not waterproof. Therefore, if the snow started as early as the officers were predicting, many men could succumb to frostbite. However, the 86th didn't plan to stay in the forest for a long time. The men were eager to march all the way to Berlin, the sooner, the better.

Jay was bunking with his buddies, Stan, Medak, and Sacks. He and Medak scrounged up some logs and began to build a rather irregular-looking hut. Sacks and Stan were fooling around with Sparky, a cute little terrier, who had been trailing after them for a while. Sparky provided a great diversion from the boredom that was setting in during this period of waiting. The men were surrounded by soldiers who were following their lead in constructing the lean-tos. Before long, there were so many shaky shanties that the forest resembled a small city in the long-ago Wild West during a gold rush.

The men enjoyed movies every night provided by the Special Services. A small schoolhouse in a nearby town served as a cinema. Jay loved films, but at least one medic was required to be in the tent each night, so he missed a few of the pictures that he had been hoping to see.

There was no prediction of how long it would be before they moved again. A training area was set up at Robertville Lake, which was nearby. The Engineers of V Corps conducted classes in operating outboard motors, personnel ferries, heavy pontoon rafts, infantry support rafts, and treadway rafts. Members of five different battalions partook in the classes. The importance of being prepared for the major invasion of the war could not be emphasized enough.[2]

The tedium of keeping equipment in working order was relentless, given the amount of rain that had been falling. The mud was difficult to navigate, and the soldiers continually slipped and injured ankles, shoulders, and knees, keeping the medics busy.

On October 21st, a demonstration of working the rafts was held by V Corps as the grand finale to the school. Approximately 200 officers attended, nodding at the prowess that their fine men were showing despite the challenging terrain.[3] The men of the 86th understood that ferrying men and equipment across the rivers necessary to invade Germany would be just as vital as constructing the bridges. Every available method of passage would be needed . . . and fast.

By this time, the snow had begun to fall. In the thick of the forest, it was silent and 18 inches deep already. It was far from peaceful, however, as the German planes had begun dropping buzz bombs with annoying frequency.[4]

The battalion, minus A company, which was out experimenting with a trail ferry with the use of a 1350 "1" steel cable, moved to Camp Elsenborn, abandoning their home-made shacks for more comfortable billets. The camp had been a former German site, and it was large and complete. In fact, it offered a few luxuries, such as a shower room.

However, even living in a more civilized situation didn't stop the continual drone of the buzz bombs, which shook the buildings each night. The airplanes tended to come alone, but occasionally they traveled as a pair, day and night. The bombs were a nuisance but fortunately did little damage to their cozy domicile.

Thanksgiving, Jay's second away from home, was particularly rough for him. He recalled the thrill of the New Brunswick football game, played against their meanest opponent,

South River. The game was not played in Memorial Stadium, their home field, but at the impressive Rutgers University Stadium in Piscataway, allowing for larger crowds as enthusiastic spectators streamed in to see the Zebras take on the Rams. Somehow, despite how stranded they were near the forest, the chefs whipped up a dinner of wild turkey with all the trimmings to make the holiday seem a bit more like home.

Hitler, who fancied himself a great military strategist, was about to make a final error in judgment that coupled with the disastrous opening of the Eastern Front in Russia, would cost him everything. The Allies were getting too close to the Belgium/Germany border, and the Axis needed to push them back. Therefore, the Fuhrer devised a nearly perfect plan to surprise attack the Allies in the thick forest of Ardennes.

Quietly, he amassed 13 German divisions, 200,000 soldiers, and 1000 tanks to attack in three areas of the Ardennes. Part of his plan included inclement weather so that the American airplanes would be unable to fly in defense of the Allied troops. Hitler's goal was to divide the British troops from the Americans and push them back through Belgium. Once the two armies were cleft from one another, he would then try to negotiate a peace treaty, more humiliating, of course, than the Treaty of Versailles had been.[5]

At 5:30 a.m. on December 16, the deafening attack began. A heavy fog hung over the forest, making visibility impossible. To make matters even trickier, the Germans wore white uniforms, which blended in with the snow and made the encroaching troops even more difficult to see in the dense fog.

Many of the American fighting forces were brand-new soldiers who had little training and no combat experience. Being so unprepared, many of them turned and ran upon the first attack.[6]

Sleeping in a lean-to shack had been one thing, but attempting to sleep in a foxhole in subzero weather provided a nightmare of extraordinary proportions. This is where Jay and his buddies found themselves in late December of 1944. No matter which way Jay turned his body, he couldn't get comfortable. Sleep had never come easily to Jay; he often stayed up half the night reading because he found it impossible to turn off his brain. Reading at least gave him sufficient focus until his mind finally succumbed to the demands of his weary body.

He lay awake, shivering, trying to wrap himself in a thin blanket. "This is a sure way for me to get pneumonia," he muttered. He recalled a serious bout of the virulent disease that he had suffered when he was 13, just before his Bar Mitzvah. The wracking cough had gotten so bad that his parents finally had to put him in the hospital for a week. The experience had left him physically drained as well as susceptible to bouts of bronchitis every winter, no matter how hard he tried to stay healthy. In his soul, he believed that pneumonia was the nemesis that would one day conquer him and steal his life. With little medication on hand, many men in the company were suffering from terrible coughs and fevers.

What does one think about in the middle of a frigid night, squished into a hole in the ground, hiding from one's enemies? At first, Jay thought about his pals at Panzer and how they hadn't realized how fortunate they had been at the time to be young and carefree. At Panzer, there had always been a lot going on, and Jay had been so much a part of student life. He especially loved dancing and going to concerts in Newark and New York City to hear his favorite bands, like Jimmy Dorsey and Glen Miller. Gene Krupa could really go to town on the drums. In his head, Jay pictured his best friend, Jimmy Dow, dancing in the aisles with his girl, Dotty, to the best swing music in the world.

Jimmy and Dotty Klockner had been together since their early days at Panzer. Jimmy was about as tall as Jay, which wasn't much over 5 '5, but he had a near perfect physique. He was an outstanding gymnast, graceful yet powerful, especially on the rings. His performances just took one's breath away. Jay wondered what Jimmy and Dotty were up to that night. He figured that they were preparing for the holidays. Jay wished that he could be home for the celebrations of Chanukah with his extended family.

Dotty had mentioned in her last letter that her best friend and neighbor, a Jewish girl named Thelma, had agreed to write to Jay. After all, the more mail a guy received, the better. Jay had always been too busy in college to have a steady girl, but Dotty knew that he had a penchant for redheads, and Thelma had the most beautiful, auburn hair. Dotty hoped that maybe Thelma and Jay would click. She had reminded Jay that he had met Thelma once at a skating party their freshman year, but Jay didn't recall anything about the girl. He had been busy ruling the rink with his acerbic jokes and antics on wheels.

At three o'clock in the morning, Jay was still awake and thinking. Sleep just wouldn't come in the air that was so frigid it even tasted bitter to the tongue. His mind dissolved into its favorite exercise: designing plays for the gridiron.

For eight glorious years, Jay had played center on his high school and college football teams. Those were the moments in his life when he felt truly alive. He loved the feel of the oval pigskin ball as he squatted to hike it to his quarterback. The center was far from the most glamorous position on a football team, but Jay believed that center had to be the most intelligent guy on the squad. After all, the center is the core, the heart, where the play begins, and a mistake by the center could cause the q.b. a world of heartache.

Thinking about football reminded him of Dr. Margaret C. Brown, the formidable president of Panzer college. She and Jay were often at odds about their views on athletics, but Jay suspected that this dynamic pioneer in women's sports enjoyed their philosophical repartee. Of course, everyone at Panzer quaked if they went to their school mailbox and found a note that read, "See me. M.C.B." Inevitably, such a note meant that a student was in some sort of trouble.

Jay had been scheduled to begin his student teaching in the fall, just after football season ended. In the final game of the season, Jay got kicked in the face during a play. His mouth bloodied, he spat and two of his front teeth were ejected along with the blood and mucus that was dripping down his battered face.

"Holy shit," he thought, "my mother is going to kill me."

Losing his teeth meant that he would have to suffer hours in the chair of Dr. Leo Mindel, the multi-millionaire dentist who practiced on Elm Row in New Brunswick . . . to say nothing of what a repair was going to cost. Oh no, his parents were not going to be happy about this.

On Sunday morning, Jay looked at his reflection and didn't recognize himself. "I look like Quasimodo," he thought. He had called his parents on Saturday night to tell them the news about his injuries. His mother had instructed him to take a bus down to

Avon Avenue in Newark to his grandmother's house, and she and Dad would pick him up there to take him to Dr. Mindel first thing on Monday morning.

Jay went down to his mailbox and there it was . . . the dreaded note. "See me. M.C.B."

Even though it was Sunday, Jay knew that Dr. Brown would be waiting in her office to have a word. He knocked on her door, and she bade him in her strong voice to enter.

"Whoa!" she exclaimed. "Worse than I thought."

Jay tried to grin, but his mouth wasn't working much. He had two black eyes, but thank goodness, his nose was intact.

"Do you honestly think that I can send you out to teach looking like that, Jay?" She barked at him as if the injury was his fault.

"I hadn't really had much time to . . ."

"We are going to have to postpone your start for at least a week until you get some teeth in that mouth and your skin is less purple. My God, if you go into a school looking like that, you will scare the children to death."

And so, Dr. Mindel had devised a most uncomfortable metal plate that sat on the roof of his mouth with two teeth that fit into the gaps left by where his own had been shattered. Eventually, he got used to wearing the device, but it took quite a while.

As he lay in the mud, knees propped up, teeth chattering, his brain was a mass of Xs and Os as he thought about plays that he would one day like to teach his teams, that is if he lived long enough to become a football coach. The comfort of the game that he adored warmed him more than a down comforter or a cozy hearth. Finally, his brown eyes drooped, and he fell into a stupor.

On December 17th, ordered by the Army Engineer, the 86th prepared to move to the rear. These orders were given due to the German break-through at the Ardennes, which hour by hour was gaining ground all around them. Intermittent shell fire endangered the bridge equipment and the few truck-trailers on site were dispatched to the rear with all the load that they were able to carry. The ground was muddy from the constant rain and snow, and created hazardous conditions, overcome due only to the quick thinking of some of the men. The semi-trailers, on their individual missions, were ordered to return to pick up their loads. Under fire, the men worked brilliantly in remaining to load the equipment at both Elsenborn and Robertsville.[7]

H & S company and the medical detachment moved out and proceeded to Swister, near Spa, Belgium. There, loaded and waiting in the streets of the town, they awaited further orders. The semi-trailers came in one at a time to Swister and were then ordered onto Huy, Belgium.[8]

General orders were issued to the 86th on December 13, which guaranteed the men the important Normandy Campaign Award, one of five that they would achieve during the war.[9]

For a while it was looking dire for the American fighting men, as is reported by Lt. Colonel Haas, "December 17th, ordered by the Army Engineer, our battalion started preparing to move to the rear. This was due to the German breakthrough at Ardennes, which hour by hour was gaining ground all around us. Intermittent shell fire endangered the bridge equipment, and the few trailers present were dispatched to the rear with all the load they were able to carry. The ground made muddy from rain and snow was a hazard that was only overcome by quick thinking on everyone's part. The semi-trailers on their individual missions were informed of the breakthrough and were ordered to return, if possible, to pick up their loads. Under fire the men worked brilliantly in remaining to load the equipment at both Elsenborn and Robertsville."[10]

Back at B company, which was in the most immediate danger of being shelled, loading went on as the trailers pulled in. Three truck tractors with an empty trailer returning from a logging detail on December 17th in the vicinity of Waimes, near Malmedy, ran into a German roadblock. One man was wounded in the leg in the process of escape but was assisted by some of the others and made it back to safety.[11]

However, much to the distress of the men of B company, several of the troops witnessed Private First Class Clymire as he was captured by the Germans. There was nothing they could do to free him from his captors, and when they returned to Elsenborn, they were distraught about his fate.

Within days, the 86th learned about the German murder of 84 American prisoners at Malmedy. Soldiers of the Waffen-SS had grouped the U.S. POWs in a farmer's field, assuring the prisoners that they would be taken care of well by their captors. Instead, soldiers of Kampfgruppe Peiper wielded machine guns and cut down the prisoners in a blood bath, all shot in the head.[12]

43 American POWs who survived the massacre made it back to the city of Malmedy, where they sought medical aid. On their way to the city, they encountered a patrol from the 291st Combat Engineer Battalion, where they reported the bloodbath that they had witnessed only hours before.

It did not take long for an unofficial order to make its way through the American warriors to take no SS men as prisoners but to shoot them on sight.

Anger bubbled through the men of the 86th when they learned that Private First Class Clymire had been one of the assassinated prisoners. The news of his death left them all chilled and disheartened, and it foreshadowed that the worst was yet to come.

In the meantime, Company A's trucks trickled in one at a time, loaded their cargo, and headed out again for Spa. Once there, they learned that the unit had moved to Huy, Belgium and that they would now have to travel to Huy. However, driving on these roads became riskier by the minute as information concerning the battle lines was unclear due to breakdowns in communication. Finally, the trucks were packed up and ready to continue despite the dangerous situation that lay ahead.

When the trucks arrived in Huy, Belgium, the men received the order that they were to build a bridge at Vise. However, once on the road, the convoy was intercepted and directed to go to Waremme where the new battalion area was to be. The rest of the 86th arrived late in the evening on the 19th, leaving the men to knock on the doors of civilian homes, seeking a warm place to shelter.

On the morning of December 20th, a billeting party was organized, and comfortable quarters were located for all the men. The town's school provided shelter for H & S company as well as B company. Civilians continued to house the men of A company so that everyone was relatively comfortable and safe, giving the men a respite from the hard work of loading and transporting the heavy equipment under the most stressful of circumstances.[13]

The people of Waremme were kind and eager to share the holidays with their American friends. In fact, the entire battalion was beginning to build lasting relationships with the townsfolk.

As the men enjoyed the hospitality of their hosts, there was time to play a little catch-up. An inventory of bridging equipment shortages was necessary, as was the constant maintenance and repair of the trucks, which had been rattled in the weeks of journeying over rutted roads.

The men finally had an opportunity to get new uniforms, which would be far warmer than what they had been wearing. It had taken a while for the uniform supply trucks to locate them, but now they were all a bit toastier than they had been in the foxholes of the Ardennes.

On Christmas Eve, when so many of the men were blue, thinking about what they were missing with friends and families at home, a memorable thing happened. While in the forest, snow began to fall and from not very far off came the sounds of Christmas carols being sung in German. Despite their philosophical differences and the crazy Fuhrer named Hitler, the German boys were homesick just as they were. Jay found the experience surreal, and for that moment in time, there was no hatred. There seemed to be a kindred spirit for the 24 hours of the loneliest holiday ever experienced by either side of the war.

Christmas Day provided a brief respite from the cold and depression of the ongoing battle. The entire battalion was forming ties with the civilians of Waremme, who were deeply grateful for their presence and prepared a small feast for them.

During their time in Waremme, the guys had time to play a little basketball. Although Jay was height-challenged, especially compared to most of the other men, he was an excellent shot. He loved the game and had been the manager of the Panzer basketball team for four years.

While the battle in the Ardennes continued to rage until late January, repair work on the trucks continued despite the freezing temperatures. An order was given for the trucks to begin hauling logs again. The massive vehicles were coming in for repairs and substitute trucks were leaving during the time the company stayed in Waremme.

One of the first details to be addressed was the moving of a Bailey Bridge dump near the German's new lines at Modave. This hauling was a twenty-four-hour detail, and the entire dump was moved near Namur. The intense cold during these hauling jobs in insufficiently warm vehicles caused a lot of problems. All through these operations, the men were left to their own devices to find food and shelter for the night.[14]

The trucks continued to haul every item that was possible on their specially constructed trailers. Scattered over half of Belgium, they moved Engineer Depots forward and Bailey Bridge dumps, usually near a siding. B company hauled 72-foot I-beams which was a precarious job with the roads being such a mess. This long load was only possible by adding a special pole-type trailer to 30-foot pontoon trailers.

Negotiating huge vehicles on the narrow streets in the small towns of Belgium with difficult, twisting turns, the men did a phenomenal job at managing their movements. The hauling of lumber also continued from the forest to the finished product stored at E-7 near Aachen. The men passed through the same area of the Ardennes breakthrough and were shocked at the destruction that had occurred in the area.

The Battle of St. Vith as the Battle of the Bulge was originally called, ended with the Germans on the run. The Americans were heartened. They knew that it wouldn't be long now before they would step foot onto German soil. And when that glorious day would come, they would celebrate like no celebration had ever occurred before.

Photo by Jay Dakelman
The Battle of St. Lo (The Battle of the Bulge)

A pessimist is one who makes difficulties of his opportunities, and an optimist is one who makes opportunities of his difficulties.
Harry S. Truman

THELMA

From: Cpl. Jay Dakelman 12702157
Med. Det. 86th Engr. Bat.
APO 230 Postmaster

New York, NY
Miss Thelma Jacoby
97 Columbia Ave.
Newark, New Jersey

Dear Thelma,

I received your swell letter, and I must say I want to thank you for it very much. I did not know whether you remembered me or not, but I most emphatically remembered you. In fact, do you remember the night another Panzer fellow and I went with you girls roller skating?

I do not know why my first letter never got to you. I'm not good at writing; in fact, if you do not believe me, Dotty can verify that, I'm sure.

56

There are some questions you asked me. I'll try to answer them as best I can. I am a member of the First Army, and for more information, read your daily newspapers (Newark Eve. News or the Star-Ledger) or listen to your favorite news broadcaster or radio program. I'm sure you'll learn more that way.

I certainly remember the good old basketball and football games at Panzer; how could I forget? I was too much in them, body and soul, to forget. Unfortunately, this is war and the time, place, and situations do not permit me to partake in any of the activities that I indulged in while at college. Rather this is a different life, one of which I am tired and disgusted, one that I know is a job to do and none of us can quit until this job is finished and completed to the best of our ability once and for all.

I know Lenny Kordansky very well and I'm glad to hear that he is doing so well. I am very interested in the type of work that he is doing and would give anything to be doing the same kind of work, but unfortunately, I am not that fortunate and am just giving my best here on the continent. Someday, I hope to be able to see him and talk to him again about all that he is doing.

Last week I was lucky and received a two-day leave to Paris. It was my first pass to anyplace in about 6 months and it was a real change and break. I had a very long trip by truck to get there and I was happy to even go like that. I had 48 complete hours there and I took in as much as I could in that time. I went on a sightseeing tour and saw all the historic things that one reads about in the papers and history books. I took many pictures and have plenty to show all of the folks when I get home again. The women are very beautiful, but I would still like to go out again with an American girl. I think that every other store is a perfume shop, and that the city simply reeks of perfume. The fashions and the hats and coiffeurs are marvelous and strictly French. I went to the Place Pigalle or the Montmartre section of Paris in the night and that is the French floor show with the Apache dancers in the real French Cabarets, taverns, and nightclubs. Money is valuable and goes like water. I spent my entire two months' salary in only two days. However, I had a wonderful time. I stayed in the home of Mr. Stern who is the brother of the famous Rothchilds of the banking firm of the same name. Need I say any more as to the type of house it was? The Red Cross has now taken it over and most of the boys stay there when they come over on rest leave to Paris. I have so much to tell you that I cannot include it all in a letter and it would make a better narrative than can be done in writing, so most of my stories will have to wait until I get to Newark again and I come to see you and Dotty, that is, if I may? How about it?

Well, I guess I have said too much for the first time, but do not think so badly of me for that as Dotty will tell you sometimes I talk too much. I want to say all my best to you and to your folks. Do let me hear from you again, and soon; anything you want to know, just ask and I'll try to tell you. If I'm not too rash, how about sending me a picture for a pin-up for a lonely foxhole?[1] It would be greatly appreciated. I must really say so long.

Sincerely,

Jay

Thelma Jacoby, a petite, young woman with wavy, auburn hair, put down the magnifying glass that she had borrowed from Pa to read the letter from Corporal Jay Dakelman,[2] sent in V-mail by the War and Navy Departments. The Armed Forces shrank the text so small that it couldn't be read without the aid of a magnifier, but in a way that was nice. It meant that reading a letter took longer, and Thelma had to admit that receiving this first letter from Jay Dakelman tickled her in a pleasant way. With the war on, there weren't many young men around to talk to, even at the Red Cross events held in downtown Newark.

Dotty Klockner, who had grown up across the street from Thelma on Columbia Avenue in the Vailsburg Section of Newark, was close friends with Jay from their time at Panzer College in East Orange. Dotty's boyfriend, Jimmy Dow, was one of Jay's best pals while they were in school, which meant that Dotty had spent a lot of time in Jay's company during their college days. She raved about how intelligent he was, having graduated first in their class, even though he was modest about it. Dotty knew that Jay loved to read, and when he wasn't doodling with Xs and Os on every scrap of paper that he could find, he had his nose stuck in a book.

Jimmy and Dotty made an odd couple, Thelma mused momentarily. Jimmy, with his ruddy complexion and pert nose, was always the life of the party. In his boisterous voice, he loved to tell jokes, drink plenty of beer, and do handstands and backflips whenever asked. His prowess as a gymnast at Panzer was legendary, even though he had been out of college for a little over a year.

Dotty was a string bean, tall and freckled, with bouncy, strawberry blonde curls, which she kept short to make her life as a female gym teacher easier. Dotty's sense of humor was droll to Jimmy's crass stories and jokes, but they complemented each other perfectly. Jimmy was the lightning to Dotty's being the grounding rod.

Dotty and Jimmy talked a lot about their buddy, Jay, who had been shipped overseas just months after their mid-year graduation from Panzer. It was always, "Remember when Jay did . . ." or "Did you hear from Jay lately? How are things going? Has he beaten the Axis back yet?" (One had to be careful about what was said in front of Dotty since her family had German roots). The Klockners tended to be sensitive when people shunned those with German backgrounds.

One day, Dotty approached Thelma with a brilliant plan. "Why don't you start to write to Jay overseas?" she proposed. "I know that getting mail from home makes our boys over there a lot less lonely."

"Oh, Dot," Thelma sighed. "What would I possibly have to say to him? After all, I'm not college-educated like the three of you. I would probably bore him to death."

"Tell him about the music that you are studying. Jay likes music," Dotty said. "Or talk to him about the Yankees!"

Thelma scoffed, "What do I know about athletics or the Yankees?" she quibbled. "And I hardly believe that he is an opera fan."

However, Dotty didn't give up and eventually, Thelma broke down and struggled to write a two-page letter about how things were going in the city of Newark since the war had become full-blown. Jay's family had roots in Newark and Dotty encouraged Thelma to tell Jay what was new in town. Dotty had provided Thelma with Jay's address and Thelma had posted her first letter to the corporal in early November.

Of course, she had no idea what Jay had been doing during the first few weeks while she was waiting for a reply. From the way that Dotty had encouraged her to write, she had expected some reply from him before two months had elapsed. She could not have fathomed that his unit was fighting in one of the bloodiest battles of the war in the forest of Ardennes.

One evening, Dotty phoned Thelma. "Why haven't you answered any of Jay's letters?" she probed.

"Because Jay has not written back to me yet," she replied.

"He wrote to me and said that he had sent you two letters and hasn't heard back from you. I checked that he had the right address, and he did.

"This is a mystery," Thelma admitted. "I'll talk to Pa and see what he says."

Sam Jacoby, Thelma's father, was in his "studio" at 97 Columbia Avenue. A small bedroom off the front parlor had been converted into a storage room for the piles of sheet music and a vast collection of instruments that Sam owned. As a member of various orchestras in New York City as well as Newark, Sam had amassed an enviable collection for his trade as a professional musician.

Having graduated from the Conservatory of Vienna at the age of 18, Sam had mastered every instrument an orchestra employed during a performance. Although his two primary instruments were the trumpet and the violin, Sam had been called upon to play everything from the piano to the timpani when various colleagues had been unable to perform.

During the Great Depression, while many of his neighbors had been out of work and suffering, Sam had still been able to provide nicely for his family. No matter how bad things were in those years, the wealthy still could eke out the admission for great music and Broadway shows, which helped the downtrodden escape their troubles for a few hours. Sam was quite proud of the fact that he had been part of the famous Ziegfeld productions and had played trumpet for Miss Fannie Brice.

For Sam, though, music was always about the melody. Thelma, who had been studying piano and voice since she was a little girl, loved to hear Pa hum classical melodies around the house. She was aware that music was always inside his head, bubbling out of his mouth in short phrases, "Da, Da, Dee, Dum, Dum, Da Da, Da Da," she would hear and guess at what piece he was humming.

Thelma had dreamed of going to Italy to study opera with the grand maestros of Europe, but the war had killed that dream. Besides, although Pa encouraged her music lessons, he would not give his approval for a career onstage.

"All opera singers are who——-rrrrs!" he would yell as he gave his definitive "No!"

As a native of Austria, Pa had a sharp demeanor as a parent. A slight man, he carried himself with military stature. His shoulders were always straight, his back ramrod stiff as he marched down the street. He was a proud man, a man of authority, who had escaped Austria rather than be conscripted into Kaiser Wilhelm's army. Sam arrived in America at the age of 20 with his younger sister, Annie, to seek a life of freedom to play the music that he wanted to play rather than the military marches that the Kaiser wanted to hear.

It took a short while to make enough money to establish himself and start his career in the most exciting city on the planet. Though he missed his mother and four half brothers and sister, life in the United States was good.

Thelma sought out her father when she arrived at their second-story home. With his lucrative career as a musician, Sam had been able to purchase a modern, three-story house that had ample apartments for his wife, Fannie's, parents, Wolf and Dora Reiter to live upstairs, and Fannie's sister, Mollie and her husband, Dave Kordansky, to take the quarters downstairs.

Dave and Mollie's two sons, Leonard and Jerome, Thelma's first cousins, were close in age to Thelma, and the three of them had grown up like siblings. Although Thelma had a brother, Milton, and a sister, Lillian, they were much older than she was. Both were married and had their own families already. Therefore, Thelma didn't know her siblings as well as she knew her cousins, but she was very proud of all their achievements, particularly those of her movie star handsome brother. Not only was Milton an accomplished lawyer, he had his own orchestra, which played at weddings and Bar Mitzvahs on the weekends.

Leonard Kordansky to whom Jay had referred in his letter to Thelma was the very same guy who lived downstairs from the Jacobys. Talk about a small world! Lenny had attended Panzer with Jay which automatically did give them something to talk about in subsequent letters.

"Pa," Thelma called in her loud voice, "where are you?"

"In the studio," he returned.

Thelma pushed back the brocade curtain that separated the studio room from the large living room where the baby grand piano sat.

"I have something to ask you," Thelma began. "Have I gotten any mail from a United States soldier?"

Sam turned toward his daughter and replied, "Why, yes. Why do you ask?"

"Where are those letters? They were addressed to me, weren't they?"

"Yes, daughter, but I threw them out."

"You threw them out!" she gasped, incredulous at her father's actions.

"The name on the return post vas Deckelman, a German name. I am not going to allow you to correspond vit a German, even if he is American!"

"Pa," Thelma was exasperated, "those letters are from a friend of Dotty Klockner's and her boyfriend, Jimmy. The soldier's name is Jay Dakelman, and he is JEWISH!"

"Ja, but the name is German," Pa Jacoby argued. "I vas protecting you."

"Well, don't protect me, and the next time I get a letter from Jay, please make sure that I get it."

Relieved to have solved the mystery of the missing letter, Thelma went into her bedroom to look for a suitable photo or two to send to Jay. She wanted something from last summer at Brighton Beach, perhaps one of her doing a handstand in her white two-piece bathing suit, which showed off her bare midriff.

January 31, 1945

Dear Thelma,

I received your letter of January 4, and I was indeed happy to hear from you. So, you think I have a good memory? Well, if you think you have changed as much as you say, and what I can see from the picture you have sent, I don't think I'll recognize you when I get the chance to see you. I haven't changed that much and so perhaps you'll remember me. I want to thank you for the picture very much and I want to tell you I like it more than very much. Do you have to ask if I want any more? Of course, boy, if there is anything I like to get over here, it is letters that have pictures in them. So, send them bathing suits, furs, all ways.

I took some pictures in Paris and while the weather was miserable, I managed to get some good shots. It is very hard to get extra prints done and I'll have to send them back to the States. However, when I get some back, I will be sure to send some to you. There may only be ten or twelve, but I promise that when I get back home and before I get to come to visit you, I will have a complete set of pictures for you of all our activities over here. How is that? I hope it will be soon.

Thanks for thinking of me enough to tell Lenny to drop me a few lines. I do hope that he comes around so that you can give him my address. I sure would like to hear from him and what he is doing. Get him on the ball.

You think it is such a pleasure to see all these foreign lands, well I must admit it has given me a kick, but honestly, Thelma, it is not as picturesque or beautiful as it sounds on a travel poster. See America first or just stay around New York and Broadway and that is enough to satisfy anyone. Anyway, Thelma, there isn't a hell of a lot standing here in Europe left to see.

You want to know how we spent Christmas and New Year's Eve. Well, it wasn't any fun as we had been used to in our former days. We didn't have any drinking or the likes, but there was some excitement. But I don't enjoy that kind of excitement. Perhaps next year we will have things like the old days.

Believe it or not, I received a letter from Dr. Brown today. She writes to me quite a bit; why I don't know, but she was always okay with me in school. I guess I was the teacher's pet; anyway, that is what Dotty would say. And incidentally, speaking of Dotty, she wrote to me of her engagement to Jimmy. Of course, I had been expecting it for a long time and was very happy to hear that it came off. I hope I get home in time for the wedding.

Well, it is kind of late and I want to write a letter to my mom, so I will close this letter. Don't forget to write to me when you get the chance and I will be looking forward to that picture in the bathing suit, wasn't it? So, take care of yourself and regards to everyone at home.

Sincerely,

Jay

By the time that Jay wrote the third letter to Thelma, the terrible Battle of the Bulge was over, and the 86th was preparing in earnest for the most important push of the war yet: the thrust into Germany itself.

A and B companies moved to Cheratte and trained on the Meuse River. The training involved the erection of a cable across the bridge used in conjunction with a ferry. The ferry traveling along this cable utilized the river's current for power. The operation was successful, but the Meuse River current was not swift enough and thus, the ferry did not move quickly.[3]

The trucks continued to haul every possible item to be placed on trailers that were built for the purpose of storage. Scattered over half of Belgium, they moved engineer spots and Bailey Bridge dumps, usually near a siding. B company hauled 72-foot I-beams which was a precarious job, the roads being in such a sad state of disrepair. This long load was made possible by adding a special pole-type trailer to the 30-foot pontoon trailers.[4]

Among the small towns and challenging turns that were encountered, the men did a phenomenal job. The hauling of lumber continued from the forest to the finished product stored at E-7 near Aachen. The men of the 86th passed through the same area where they had broken through the Ardennes and were saddened to see old familiar sights in ruins.

In preparation for the future battle to enter Germany, classes in booby traps and aircraft recognition were held for personnel stationed in Waremme.[5] This continued through the 86th's stay. B company furnished trucks to haul the Navy's Sea Mules to the vicinity of Nameche for the 329th Harbor Craft Detachment. Men were sent from the three companies to assist in assembling the boats that recently had arrived. Combat engineers learned how to use the new boats, and after preliminary training, the men began to turnkey what they had mastered to the other soldiers.

At Nameche, B company operated five boats to transport personnel. The battalion was then alerted for their next bridging operation. The trucks were recalled from their hauling missions to re-load. This venture had to be canceled, however, and again, the equipment was unloaded as future hauling operations were imminent.

While the entire battalion was together, a firing range was acquired in Liege and one platoon at a time practiced firing. At Waremme, a gas chamber was set up temporarily in a tent so that each man could test his gas mask. It was vital that the gas masks were checked frequently, and every soldier took careful measures to protect that precious piece of life-saving equipment.

B company was stationed at Duren, awaiting possible orders for a bridge operation to be conducted over the Roer River. The Germans were resisting strongly along this river; thus, other bridging units were under extreme pressure from the enemy so that they could not complete the job.

On February 7th, the Roer River alert was canceled and the entire company's bridge equipment was unloaded in preparation for hauling lumber. However, that evening the orders were reversed and the equipment had to be reloaded, which took all night.[6]

On February 14th, a group of men with five storm boats left for Stolberg, Germany with instructions that they were attached to the 12th Engineer C Battalion. They were to train assistant operators at a lake near Weisweiler for the pending operations.

On February 16th, Lt. Cullen left Waremme with the remainder of the storm boats and proceeded to Eschwieler to report to the 1120th Engineer C Group. This group was divided, and half went to the 12th Engineers and the others were attached to the 297th Engineer C Group.[7]

The final problem was a night operation on February 21st with the 13th Infantry assisting. After three alerts were called for the actual crossing, it was not until February 23rd that the final jump-off was scheduled into Germany.[8]

The boats and equipment were carried to the shore early on the morning of February 23rd by infantry personnel and operators. The storm boats were dispersed at five sites along the riverfront for the crossing in groups. To aid in the crossing, a heavy artillery barrage was laid down prior to the jump-off. By 0315, the boats were in the water and the actual crossing had begun.

There were some incidents that occurred that led to dangerous delays at all five of the crossing sites. The swift current swamped the small half-boat, the banks were littered with barbed wire. All these complications slowed the river assault, which disrupted the planned schedule.

A Bailey Bridge was erected after the enemy had been pushed back, and the 8th Infantry Division, which was brought across by the men of H & S company, was able to reach the far shore.

Terrible lessons were learned by the soldiers at these five crossings, but the men were still proud of the work they had accomplished, especially since they were under fire through the entire endeavor. Several men from H & S company were wounded during the counter-battery firing, and the Infantry suffered many casualties.[9]

The storm boat crews returned to Waremme, loading the remaining equipment. They were exhausted from several sleepless days, no food, and the stress of enemy fire. While at Waremme, the equipment was assessed and repaired, with requisitions being put in for equipment that had been lost.

A Company, who was stationed at Waremme, disassembled the bailey bridge at Amay. The equipment was loaded on the trucks and headed for the E-7 and E-8 bridge parks.

During this stressful and amazing period, crossing into Germany, Jay was occupied frequently by treating the wounded. Being busy was a good thing, but some of the images that he had seen lately were difficult to erase from his mind. To triage the men without vomiting at some of the extreme injuries, Jay put himself on autopilot and did what he could to ease the pain of the writhing wounded.

In the following letter to Thelma, a tinge of weariness crept into his writing, and he was beginning to ponder how he would excise the nightmarish visions in his brain when (or if) he returned to civilization. He was beginning to think about continuing his education but wasn't sure that he would be able to concentrate on studies after the experiences that he had endured during the war.

March 1, 1945

Dear Thelma,

A few spare minutes and nothing to do so what more worthwhile thing can I do than to answer your letter. Yes, we had a surprisingly good time and arrived here in eight short days. I do wish they would all arrive like that.

Thelma, I really liked those pictures that you sent me. They really are swell. Boy, what have I been missing all these years? It is a new face to look at and for that question mark which you inserted in the letter, let me fill it in . . . lovely to look at. And Thelma, I don't go in too much for a collection of pictures, only those I really want.

I am sorry I don't have the pictures to send you of Paris as yet as they aren't ready. But in my next letter, I hope to have not only the photos of Paris to send you but the same of Belgium or Liege. Until that time, I want to offer a few substitutes---as you can see, it is a picture of me; it isn't too good but all I have to

offer of myself. The picture is good but I'm afraid I ruined it!!
Anyway, I hope it will be a peace offering until the better ones
come around.

Saw a couple of motion pictures lately. We had Hollywood
Canteen, Hedy LaMarr and Paul Henreid in The Conspirators,
and Ann Sheridan, Dennis Morgan, Alexis Smith and others in
Animal Kingdom. They were swell pictures and we all enjoyed
them. If it weren't for the movies, we would go nuts. You ask
about dances, tell me, what are they? Here is the truth: I haven't
done any dancing since we left England last June. Time sure goes
fast. As for the girls here, well, in Germany there is no
fraternization, and you are not allowed to talk to Germans. In
Belgium, who wanted anything to do with the women there? I can
tell you something but on paper, it wouldn't be so good, so I'll
tell you all about it when I see you. Anyway, women here are out.

I am glad to hear that Jimmy and Dotty are so happy. I
wonder if they realize how lucky they are. Oh, I'm not griping but
they have been able to get started in life, success, and the future.
I am so happy they are taking their Masters. If I ever get back to
being a civilian, I hope to go for my Masters and Doctoral degree
---that is if I'm able to concentrate on books anymore.

Glad to see you give so much blood; it is really put to good
use here and if you only knew how much good it really does. Who
knows, someday, I may even be the recipient of some of your
blood. But you are right when your resistance is down, you can't
afford to give too liberally and too often.

God, you say you have a gift of gab; look at me, five pages
and I haven't said anything yet. So, I better close before I go on
forever. Write soon, and if I don't answer promptly, don't worry,
I'll get a letter to you sooner or later. Just excuse it but please
write. Regards to all at home.

Good nite now,

Jay

April 20, 1945

Germany

Dear Thelma

Again, I must start with an apology; it seems that I am forever doing that now because it is most unavoidable aside from being embarrassing at the same time. I am very sorry for not answering your letter sooner, but truthfully, I assure you for the past weeks I have been too busy to wash myself or better yet to find a place to wash. Now or rather at the present time, things are better, and I am taking advantage of these precious moments.

You talked quite lengthy about the sun and weather. I will tell you, here, the weather has been lovely. The past few nights, we have also had such a lovely moon---big, bright, surrounded by beautiful stars and in a big blue sky. Boy, what a setting and for it, what an inadequate situation was I.

You asked me about music---well, I like it, or course it isn't to me what it is to you. But then physical education (mostly football) is the essence of my life. But I also like music, not only modern swing but believe it or not, I love to listen to records of opera and light opera. I have quite a large collection of records---Dotty K. can testify to that. Of course, I don't know too much about it. I took violin lessons for a couple of months, but I just didn't like it. I would rather listen to music and play football than play music and watch football. I think you can understand what I mean. But I'm willing to learn more about music.

I didn't know you sang or even dabbled (as you say) professionally. I would love to hear you sing and if you sing anything like your pictures look, well, watch out---I'll probably end up buying your Columbia records!!

I'm afraid I'll have to be careful what I write to you and Dotty if you compare notes so carefully. So, you two decided for me to shave my mustache---well, that's nice, but I don't know, perhaps, when you see it in the flesh and not in a photo, you'll think differently.

Speaking of you and Dotty reminds me. A buddy of mine went to Paris on a pass and he got a bottle of perfume from that fair city for me. So, I am going to wrap it and send it to you. I hope that it suits you and you like it. When it comes, please let me know. And say in the package is a whistle and key chain which I made. It is made from German parachute trooper wire---it is just something I did in some spare time---Please, it is for Dorothy so would you give it to her? Thank you!

I want to thank you for your pictures very much---they are my favorite pin ups. I would like to reciprocate, but at this writing I do not have any to send you. In fact, I should think you'd like the scenery more than mine, and why waste film, I figure, so I don't take many pictures of myself. However, I think I'll have some pictures for you in my next letter.

Say, do you ever go roller skating anymore? Remember the last time---you know how many years ago that was? Well, it was 5 years in September---

Believe it or not!!

Well, Thel, I'm afraid it is getting late, and I owe my Mom a long letter. So, I'll have to say goodnite to you for now---take care of yourself---Be good and let me hear from you soon. Regards to all.

Love,

Jay

Thelma

Thelma in a park near her Columbia Avenue home in Newark, NJ

Photo from Jacoby family archives
Sam Jacoby, third from left, with his band in Austria.

There is no such thing as luck, merely opportunity meeting preparedness.
General George S. Patton, Jr.

CHAPTER 7

THE BRIDGE AT REMAGEN

Hitler's dreams were crumbling. The boast of a 1000-year Reich was circling the drain, and the bastard knew it but refused to acknowledge this truth. The Americans were approaching Germany with one million freshly trained soldiers, not the old men and whiskerless boys who didn't wear the snappy uniforms that the German army had donned when their future seemed dazzling and assured. At all costs, the Americans could not be permitted to cross the Rhine at Remagen, which would allow them to attack Central Germany and reach Ruhr, the heart of industry in the Vaterland.

The floundering Fuhrer gave a crucial order in a desperate attempt to keep the encroaching Allied forces from a fatal invasion. The remaining bridge that crossed the Rhine, the Ludendorff Bridge, had to be destroyed so that the Americans would be blocked from a lightning-speed landing at Remagen.

Built during World War I to help deliver reinforcements and supplies to the German troops on the Western Front, "the railroad bridge, constructed of steel, connected Remagen on the west bank and the village of Erpel on the eastern side." It was a steel arch bridge, a little more than a thousand feet long and wide enough to carry two railroad tracks. Two castle-like stone towers with windows guarded each end. Beyond the towers on the far side, the two railroad tracks entered a tunnel cut into a rock cliff. By the morning of 7 March 1945, the last train had gone over. The Germans had covered one side of the bridge with wooden planking, allowing a procession of soldiers, trucks, horse-drawn wagons and guns, civilians, and cattle to cross over it.[1]

After the enemy's supplies had arrived on German soil, they wanted to eradicate the bridge to prevent the Allied forces from being able to use it. Designed by Karl Wiener and constructed by Grun and Bilfinger, the 1,066-foot bridge continued to withstand continued German attempts to destroy it. Like a cat with nine lives, no matter how many charges were detonated on it, including underwater charges set by German frogmen, the Ludendorff Bridge refused to fall.[2]

On March 3, 1945, Lt. Gen. Courtney Hodges, the commander of the American First Army, directed his III Corps with Maj. Gen. John Leonard's 9th Armored Division acting as a spearhead, to drive down the valley leading toward Remagen from the west. Although resistance appeared to be disorganized at this point, the Germans planned to detonate explosive charges once again to destroy the Ludendorff Bridge before the Americans could capture it.

At this moment, the 86th Engineers entered Stolberg, their first German town. Part of A company unloaded its trucks for prospective hauling, and the following night, the battalion was put on alert to be ready to move. The Ludendorff Bridge had been seized for the First Army's 9th Armored Division to cross into Remagen, and the 86th was called upon to construct and operate two ferry sites, as they had often rehearsed.[3] This bridgehead had been a pipe dream for a long time, but the Germans were not about to just hand it over to their enemies without a sizzling brawl.

En-route to Sinzig, the town closest to Remagen, B company fell in with the convoy and proceeded, reaching the site by 6:00. This town had been cleared the day before and the utmost caution had to be taken lest snipers shoot those who were guarding the heavy equipment. Enemy aircraft buzzed overhead continually, strafing and bombing Sinzig and the bridge site, while the 86th watched and waited. Hundreds of anti-aircraft batteries were set up along the highways leading to Remagen. Guns were mounted atop vehicles to fire at enemy aircraft. The men waited nervously for the onslaught of Allied air power.

The German planes didn't stop coming throughout the day and night, still intending to destroy the bridge. From the hills above Sinzig, American shell fire pounded relentlessly, aiming at the German planes.[4] The onslaught of enemy planes was so constant that Jay ignored the steady drone and listened instead to his hammering heart.

German engineers blew a charge near the western span of the bridge, but once again, the charges failed to detonate. A second charge blew, and the bridge seemed to lift in the air before settling back onto its original structure. In their haste to accomplish the job, the German engineers had placed the detonator incorrectly, and the well-built bridge refused to crumble.[5]

This was the most stressful time that Jay and his companions had experienced since the Battle of St. Vith. In some ways, this experience was even worse, although certainly not quite as frigid as it had been in the Ardennes. When the bombs hit human targets, blood and brains rained down on Jay's helmet, marked with the identifiable red cross insignia on the front. The experience was so surreal that his legs shook as he ran toward the injured. Each time a bomb whistled through the air, he ducked his head and prayed that it wouldn't be his brains splattered next on the dark earth.

Once the Americans secured the Ludendorff Bridge, A and B companies were able to begin installation on the two ferry sites, one at Kripp and the other at Remagen. Both companies continued to work under spasmodic ground fire; plus, they frequently were forced to dive for cover due to the constant strafing of the German airplanes. Jay thought of them as persistent wasps which did not want to cease their pesky drone.[6]

The American soldiers were driven to work harder than they had ever done before, despite the perilous conditions, understanding that the work they were doing was the critical key to the end of the Germans for once and for all.[7] This bridgehead was the final German hope, but when daylight broke, the enemy's fierce and continual shelling nearly dashed the spirits of the Allied forces. The Germans were as determined to keep the Americans from crossing the river as the Americans were to march more deeply into the Fatherland. They would not be deterred until they reached Berlin.

On March 9, in a torrential downpour, the 86th arrived to assume its duties running the ferry service. Five boats were lowered into the water. Planking was laid over the boats after which three five-boat rafts were built and the approaches at Remagen and Erpel were prepared. It was reported that, "At 11:00 on 9 March in a cold wind and lashing rain, without waiting for a cable to be emplaced, the first ferry chugged across the Rhine, propelled by two outboard motors and two powerboats — a 22 horsepower motor fastened to each of the end engineer boats and a powerboat lashed to the second and fourth. Headed upstream at a 45-degree angle because of the swift current, the ferry took less than eight minutes to reach the far shore."[8]

With the ferries finally ready, necessary supplies such as gasoline, ammunition, and rations were able to be loaded onto German land. The wounded were ferried back to the other side to be treated for their injuries while the engineers and the medics toiled relentlessly for 36 hours without rest. In his account of the battle, Colonel Haas wrote, "The future did not look too bright."[9]

Although the battle was fierce, and Jay was overwhelmed with the number of men whom he had to triage, he managed to take a few incredible photographs of the Battle of Remagen. Under the photos, the captions that he scrawled, "A new Pershing tank gets ready to cross the Rhine on our 86 English ferry at the Remagen bridgehead," "Two inflated rubber floats ready to be inserted into the Rhine at Remagen bridgehead," "Ack-Ack gunners and guns mounted on a half truck with another air raid at the Remagen Bridgehead," and "Bringing the wounded up the bank from the ferry at Remagen Bridgehead." There are numerous photos of the enemy planes as they strafe the area as well. Jay states, "Another plane over the bridgehead, of course. We all got sick of planes at Remagen," and "Another damn plane down the river."[10] It is interesting to note here that the photos that Jay took furnished the pictures for Lt. Colonel Haas's important book on the exploits of the 86th. Unfortunately, Haas did not include photo credit for Jay in the book.

B company attempted to establish another ferry site at Unkelbach, but the area was under scrutiny by the enemy from the high hills above it. Constant gunfire kept the site from becoming usable, and other challenges arose due to the swift current. Since a heavy pontoon bridge was being constructed at Kripp, the ferry site at Unkelbach had to be abandoned.[11]

During the brief time that the ferry at Kripp did operate, one raft was hit directly with a jettisoned bomb from an enemy aircraft. Two men on the raft were wounded, but not badly, and the raft itself managed to reach the shore for repairs. Enemy aircraft were still trying to knock out the Ludendorff Bridge, but the screen of AA fire that spiraled up to them kept the bombing from destroying targets.

Heavy traffic over the two ferries was relieved approximately the 13th of March by the completion of the heavy pontoon bridge upstream from the B company ferry site. This bridge was constructed under the most horrific conditions. Any activity of the cranes or motors assisting in the construction brought immediate enemy shell fire, which led the 86th to believe that radios were assisting in directing this fierce attack.[12]

Led by the infantry and several members of the 86th, both sides of the river were inspected, and other than snipers, a few radios were uncovered on barges in the vicinity. The area was seized in such a hurry that the troops had not had time to do their usual "clean up" following such an operation.

Several men from the 86th were wounded, but miraculously, none were killed during this valiant effort to cross the Rhine. Regarding the episode of this historic arrival into enemy territory, Colonel Haas concluded, "The tiresome work with the added danger meant the men were under continual strain. The job as a whole was done brilliantly; the companies, as a team of long years, functioned in support of one another. On March 13th, the ferry sites were turned over to the 299th Engineer C Battalion."[13]

Although Jay had time to take photos of the Battle of Remagen, there had been no time to write letters to his family and pen pals back home. However, on the night of March 24, 1945, in his graceful cursive handwriting, which was much easier to read than the scrunched typing of the V mail letters, he sent Thelma a pensive letter that revealed the exhaustion that he felt after what he and his buddies had just experienced.

He wrote:

My Dear Thelma,

I have tried to write this letter for a few days but have been unable to do it. I have a few minutes and while this won't be as long as I'd like it to be, it will have to do until I can do better. Besides, I'm writing this in candlelight, which is not good.

The weather this past week has been lovely and has enabled us to accomplish a great deal toward finishing the job we came to do. But no doubt you have been hearing all about that.

You know, we hit one place that has been quite prominent recently. But, to continue we got to a wine cellar recently evacuated and I'm telling you we went to town. Plenty of wine, cognac (real stuff), champagne, rum, and whiskey. Boy, we really had plenty. As I rule, I don't drink but because of the place I was so scared, I certainly had my share of whiskey. Every time an 88 would drop in, I'd take another swallow. Using good sense though, I didn't get drunk —when I see you, I'll tell you the entire story; it really is a pip.

Oh, yes—I finally got a few pictures of Paris made for you and enclosed in this letter are these pictures. On the back of the pictures is the explanation of where they were taken and what they are. I sure hope you like them. When you get this letter, please let me know immediately because I'll worry until I know they have arrived safely.

To tell you the truth, I have pages and pages more to write to you, but just can't right now. Please excuse me —o.k.? Take care of yourself, give my regards to all in Newark. I hope I'll see you soon.

Love,

Jay

In this poignant, brief note that Jay is able to write to Thelma at the end of the Battle of Remagen, a battle that was waged over a brutal 18-day period, several shifts in his tone are noticeable and continue in the forthcoming missives. For the first time, he addresses Thelma in an endearing way, "My dear Thelma," and he signs "love" as he closes the letter. Having come through his confrontation with death, Jay's emotions are raw and beginning to show signs of bitterness. He speaks of the fear that he experienced over the last few weeks, and although he promises to tell her the stories of his near misses when he comes home in the hopefully near future, it is noteworthy that he never did tell her about his battle experiences.

Like so many of the men of "The Greatest Generation," once home, he was unwilling and unable to return to those dark days and bottled up the images of blood, dismemberment, hatred, and loss in the depth of his being. Being an extremely intuitive and intelligent young man, Jay was aware that one day he would have to confront his memories, but for right now, the worst was yet to come.

We make a living by what we get, but we make a life by what we give.
Winston Churchill

CHAPTER 8

IN ENEMY TERRITORY

For the duration of March 1945, the 86th Engineering Corps frantically built ferry sites and bridges. The vision of victory was so close now that it drove the men to work ceaselessly. A company went to Oberwinter on the Rhine where they constructed a five pontoon ferry for use by VII Corp. The following day, B company dispatched six pontoon loads to Oberwinter and waited for instructions to construct another ferry at an undisclosed site. Two days later, orders came for B company to cross the nearby treadway bridge and proceed to Konisinter to construct the ferry at an abandoned civilian ferry site. Both ferries operated for several days, busily transporting heavy armor, supplies, and artillery until heavy-class bridges could replace the flimsy bridges.[1]

On March 19th the battalion, in support of VII Corps, was ordered to move equipment to Lannesdorf and assist in the construction of a class 36 heavy pontoon bridge. Assisting in the construction and furnishing of equipment were the 181st and 552nd heavy pontoon battalions. Captain Stearman, Head of Operations, oversaw the construction of an 1170-foot bridge, which was completed in 16 and a half hours. Construction started under the cover of darkness and was finished by using artificial fog to keep the enemy from knowing what was occurring. Happily, not one casualty was suffered during this operation.[2]

Battalion Headquarters, in which H & S and A companies found comfortable billets in Mehlem, was close to the site of the new bridge, which they dubbed The Jackpot Bridge. The men bivouacked in hotels and private homes, allowing them to enjoy a few conveniences that they had been lacking for months. Real showers allowed them to scrape off the mud and grime from their fingers and feet, encouraging the men to feel half-human again.[3]

During the next few weeks, A company was put in charge of protecting and maintaining the Jackpot Bridge, with a squad from B company assisting them. The rest of B company remained at Odekoen, using their pontoon trailers for hauling. The first assignment on this detail was to move the bailey bridge park from near Namur, Belgium, forward to a point east of Duren, Germany, where a new bridge park was established.[4]

This enormous job took five days, moving 175 loads at 165 miles round trip. After completing this assignment, the company trucks were dispatched immediately to E-7 at Aachen to start moving that dump to a new site at Bonn. Long hours were spent on the crowded highways, hauling the immense amount of engineering equipment between these two points, which were 76 miles apart.

The trucks rolled continually as the soldiers dug deep to complete the job with renewed fervor. Drivers would stop whenever they arrived at a company area for meals and repairs on their vehicles if needed. The hauling lasted three weeks, and many tons of equipment were moved to the new dump, E-10 in

Bonn. Besides establishing this dump, six pontoon trailers were used for three days to haul steel I beams for the repair of bridges at various points on the Cologne-Frankfurt Autobahn.

March 26, 1945

Dear Thelma,

No, the army food here isn't that good and when you get around to seeing me, you'll have a different opinion, I'm sure. So, Dotty thinks I've changed. Well, in regard to what you saw in the yearbook, what do you say? Of course, now I have a mustache and more wrinkles.

It has been two years since Dotty last saw me and as far as the fellow she knew at Panzer, well, he is left behind there. Tell Dotty she'll meet a new friend, Jay Dakelman, someday soon.

The good weather continues, thank God!! I only hope it keeps on— In a day, it will be the Passover Holidays. I want to wish you and your folks a very happy holiday. Well, I think I must close now. Write soon. Regards to all.

Cheerio,

Jay

Whenever Jay thought about the eternal seders conducted by his stern grandfather, Bernard Sholk, a smile passed his face, remembering some of the more comedic moments that had been recounted over the years as the children of Bernard Sholk tried to get their father to "lighten up."

There was one story that stood out in Jay's mind: that of a prank pulled by his two youngest uncles, Davey and Johnny. Jay had been too young to remember the incident, but his Aunt Ceil recounted it each year. Somehow, just before the oldest boy, Sam rose to open the door to invite Elijah in for a sip of wine from a special cup designated for the venerated prophet, Davey and Johnny had slipped away from the table. When Sam opened the door on his father's cue, two apparitions draped in white sheets whirred into the seder, scaring their mother half to death.

While most of the family howled with laughter at the antics of the two youngest Sholk boys, Bernard scowled but then finally relented and started to chuckle because the prank was simply too irreverent not to laugh. Jay's eyes crinkled in mirth when he thought about this family lore. How was he to know that the seder of 1945 would be the last that Bernard Sholk would ever officiate for his clan? Sadly, Jay's grandfather died suddenly of a heart attack on May 9, 1945, and neither Jay nor his cousin Herbie were home for the funeral, both still stationed overseas.

Warburg was the next location for a new dump site, E-11, 140 miles deeper into Germany. Once there, the pontoon trailers were used to transfer engineering equipment from Bonn up to this new site. Many loads of materials were hauled to this area before the trucks were summoned to return and load up with their own bridge equipment at the old bridge site at Lannesdorf. A company dismantled the bridge and loaded it onto their trucks. The bridge had been in use for 20 days and had carried 48,499 vehicles over the Rhine, a truly incredible military accomplishment.[5]

One must pause at this feat, made possible by the tenacity and courage of the Army Corps of Engineers. When thinking about war, most people consider bloody battles without pausing to ponder how the soldiers were able to get heavy equipment like tanks, trucks, and other armored vehicles onto foreign soil. The men who built the portable, yet stable, bridges over the rivers in

France, Belgium, and Germany were miracle workers, who often toiled around the clock to meet the necessary deadlines so that the fighting men could force the enemy back, deeper into their home territory. Jay loved watching the men at work building the bridges and was fiercely proud of the work that they accomplished. He felt honored to be part of the 86th Corps of Engineers, and he carried that pride with him for the rest of his life.

On April 11, most of the 86th traveled 135 miles from Mehlem, where they had built The Jackpot Bridge, to Bad Wildungen. Once there, maintenance of equipment and vehicles was carried on until B company caught up with the rest of the unit. The entire unit then marched on to Nordhausen.[6]

The very next day, on April 12, 1945, the men were called together to hear the somber news: their beloved President, Franklin Delano Roosevelt, only months into his unprecedented 4th term, had succumbed to a brain aneurysm. All the men knew that their Commander-in-Chief had been failing for almost a year; the pressures of the war, the Yalta Conference, and his fight against polio had taken their toll. Tears glistened in many eyes as they contemplated the end of the war without their leader to exult in the glory of their great victory. How hollow would that day be without President Roosevelt to see it?

We must always take sides. Neutrality helps the oppressor, never the victim. Silence encourages the tormentor, never the tormented. Sometimes we must interfere. When human lives are endangered, when human dignity is in jeopardy, national borders and sensitivities become irrelevant. Wherever men or women are persecuted because of their race, religion, or political views, that place must —at that moment become the center of the universe.
Elie Wiesel
From the Nobel Peace Prize Acceptance Speech
12/10/1986

CHAPTER 9

BUCHENWALD

Stanley Slabicki, Mike Rosario, George Medavich, and Jay Dakelman were wedged in, shoulder to shoulder, on truck benches, traveling in Southwest Germany toward the town of Weimar. They needed to stretch as they had been cramped for hours, and the air was getting stale. The date was April 11, 1945.[1]

Jay remembered learning about Weimar in his high school German class. It had been renowned as a cultural center in Germany, home to great authors like Friedrich Schiller and Johann Wolfgang von Goethe, recognized as writers of the "German Enlightenment." Aside from being a haven for literature, Weimar appealed to many of Germany's finest artists.

In recent days, however, Weimar had traded "Enlightenment" for the darkest period in German history. Following the humiliation of World War I and the Treaty of

Versailles, the Weimar Republic was established, Germany's first attempt at a democratic government, which quickly crashed and burned, leading to the rise of the Nazi party.

Suddenly, Jay noticed an acrid burning in his nose. The air, which had been redolent with pine forests and spring blossoms, quickly turned into a dense mist, with a stench that deepened with every mile closer to Weimar they came.

"Phew," George turned to Jay. "What stinks?"

The medics looked from one to another. The odor was one with which they were too familiar: decaying flesh. But how could that be? They were arriving at the center of Weimar, a large town. Surely, there were no battlefields nearby, at least none that the Americans had heard of in their travels.

The trucks halted and the men waited to be told when they could disembark. They seemed to wait for quite some time when Sergeant Seymour Block poked his head in and called out to Jay, "Corporal Dakelman, I need you to come with me. Captain Spade needs you to do some translating."[2]

Jay climbed down from his perch as the other men grabbed their knapsacks and started to disembark from the truck. Jay and Sgt. Block arrived at a large building, not too badly bombed out, but the windows were covered with misshapen planks of wood. Wordlessly, the two men climbed the stairs and were met by Captain Spade.

"Corporal," Spade said, "we need you to go in and ask that asshole who is the mayor of this berg if he knows what is causing that stench in the air. Can you do that?"

"Of course," Jay agreed. His German, which had been good to begin with after listening to his mother speak Yiddish to her parents while he was growing up, followed by four intensive years of study at New Brunswick High School and Panzer, was polished now after being in the country for several weeks.

Jay entered what had been a stately office at one time. The absence of an apparently huge desk was marked by indentations on the remnants of a once elegant carpet. The huge stone fireplace bore a large crack that ran through the marble mantlepiece, and shards of a crystal chandelier crunched under the heavy boots of the officers in the room.

Aside from Captain Spade, Lt. Colonel Robert O. Haas stood, waiting for Jay to begin the interrogation of Mayor Erich Kloss. Jay avoided pleasantries and demanded simply, "Was gerucht?"

Mayor Kloss shrugged his shoulders and replied in crisp German, "I have only been in this office for a few days. Burgermeister Otto Koch, who was here for a long time, fled recently, and I was appointed to this position only days ago. I don't have a clue as to what is causing that smell." He planted his feet solidly on the wood floor and put his hands behind his back. His head tilted back; his prominent nose raised arrogantly in the air.

Jay did not accept that as an answer. "Come on," he probed. "You may not have been the mayor, but surely the smell bothered you and your family as citizens of this town."

Kloss brightened for a moment as if having a brainstorm. "Ah, yes," he said. "The smell is from the pig farm up the hill." A smarmy smile spread over his protruding lips as he spat out these words. "Diesen Hausschwein gerucht," the mayor said to his aides, and they all laughed. His dark blue eyes crackled as if he had just had a bit of good news. It seemed that despite the dire circumstances in which he found himself, he and his associates were sharing an inside joke.

Jay translated the conversation back to Colonel Haas, who shepherded his group back towards the convoy. "Come on," he said. "Let's go see this pig farm for ourselves."

The troops were rounded up quickly and reloaded into trucks. As they bounced further up the hill, away from the town of Weimar, the stench intensified. Men began to pull their jackets across their faces, attempting to protect their noses from the nauseating smell, and then peered gingerly out of the trucks, trying to see what was happening. They clutched their rifles tightly in case of an unsuspected ambush ahead.

Slabicki was the first to catch sight of what looked to be a wire fence that obscured what was going on beyond it. Although there had been rumors of Jews, as well as the infirm, mentally disabled, political dissidents and homosexuals, vanishing all over Europe, no one in his right mind could have ever imagined what the American soldiers were observing for the first time in this place of filth and decay. The trucks halted and men hopped down to inspect more carefully what they were seeing and trying to find out why skeletons were clinging to a barbed wire fence surrounding the perimeter of this place.

"Hey guys," he said, "am I having a nightmare? What the hell is that?" He pointed to the corpses clinging to the taut wire.

The truck passed through a broken gate, stopping in front of wooden buildings that resembled poorly built barracks. Stacked up against the building were piles of bodies, stiff as planks, crawling with lice, stinking of urine and feces. The bones of those unfortunates stuck up through gray skin at odd angles, like sharp limbs on dying trees.

Horrified, Jay looked at his comrades and mouthed, "What the hell is this? Who are these people?"

"Juden," he heard someone whisper among the walking dead.

"Juden?" Jay thought. "It's not possible. It's just not possible."

The fact was there was little, if anything that they could do to help these few poor souls, who were stumbling, with huge, vacant eyes, reaching out to the men, whispering, "Chocolate? Where's the chocolate?" These staring creatures didn't know much about their saviors, but they did know that the Americans carried Hershey bars in their pockets.

Several of the men whipped out pieces of chocolate and began to dole them out to those whose outstretched hands begged for the candy. Jay watched as one of the skeletons, impossible to tell its gender, wolfed down the rich candy, fell to its knees, vomited, quaked, and then lay still. Death by Hershey bar. How could this even be possible? With his medical knowledge, Jay realized that these dehydrated and starved inmates needed intravenous fluids to even have a chance of survival, not Hershey bars. He shuddered, watching the dance of the macabre as they wandered among the soldiers, grabbing at their uniforms, tears leaking out of their eyes.

Holding handkerchiefs over their faces, the men searched the camp and learned quickly that the Germans called this place of horrors Buchenwald, named for the beautiful beech trees that grew on the perimeter of the wire wall. They peered into the wooden buildings and saw the living and the dead piled together on wooden bunks. Their skin showed boils and open wounds, rancid with puss. Buckets of waste that seemed alive with the buzzing of engorging flies overflowed in several places in the hut. It was impossible not to gag, absorbing the horror.

It was the eyes of the prisoners that haunted Jay the most. Dark, bruised eyes, crusted with dirt and mucus, impossible to tell which were the eyes of the living and those of the dead. Because they were medics, Jay, George, Stan, and Mike's first impulse was to try to tend to the living, but with what? They were not equipped to help those clinging to the remnants of life, even though this is what they had been trained to do.

The four young men stumbled out of the barracks, struggling to keep from vomiting. Of the 21,000 survivors left in Buchenwald, only a few were well enough to speak.[3] Colonel Haas learned from them that on April 8, just days before the arrival of the American army, the Germans had forced most of the remaining Jews of Buchenwald to march 100 miles southeast to the camp at Flossenburg. A few Jews had managed to stay and hide in Buchenwald, knowing that they would die on the long trek east without shoes and only rags on their emaciated bodies. Their final hope of survival was to stay behind.

Without thinking about what he was doing, Jay fingered his dog tags, which identified him as a Jew. As he looked around at the carnage, this hell on earth, he looked skyward and asked, "Why?" He knew that his family had immigrated from Russia at the beginning of the 20th century, but what if some of these dead were distant relations, lost after the Diaspora? As a Jew, he understood that he was a mishpachah (family) to each of the dead lying on the still-frozen ground of early spring. He realized also that at this moment, absorbing this morbid picture, that something in his soul had broken and changed forever.

On April 11, 1945, something important was taken from Jay Dakelman, as well as the other liberators of Buchenwald, and nothing, no joy or success in life, would ever bring it back. The dreams of these young soldiers were to be tainted for the rest of their lives by the responsibility of bearing witness to man's most heinous inhumanity to man.

After spending a couple of hours in Buchenwald, the men were called to return to their vehicles and head back to Weimar for the night. Before they boarded the truck awaiting them, Jay took a final look into a pit with bodies piled high. Tears fell from his eyes, but words stuck in his throat. Suddenly he felt a bony hand grab onto his shoulder, sucking strength out of him.

"Ich bin eine Juden," was whispered in his ear hoarsely, followed by the words, "Yisgadal v yisgadal . . ."

Without turning to look at the person holding on to him, Jay joined in the holy words of the prayer in remembrance of the dead."

Yisgadal v 'yis-kadash 'sh 'may rabo. Omayn.

B' 'olmo di vero chiru say, v 'yatz-mach pur-konay 'viko-rayn m 'shi chay Omayn.

BCha-yay-chon uv 'yomay-chon uv 'cha-yay d 'chol bays yisro-ayl, Ba-agolo uvize mn koriv. V 'im 'ru omayn. Y 'hay sh 'may rabo m 'vorach l 'olam ul 'ol may ol 'ma-yo. Yis-boraych v 'yish-tabach, vispo-ayr, v 'yis-romom, v 'yis-nasay, v 'yis-hador, v 'yis-aleh, v 'yis-halol, sh 'may d 'kud-sho b 'rich hu. L 'aylo min kol bir 'choso v 'shi-roso, tush-b 'choso v 'neche-moso da-amiron b 'olmo, v 'im 'ru omayn. Y 'hay sh 'lomo abo min sh 'ma-yo. V 'cha-yim tovim olay-nu v 'al kol yisro-ayl v 'im 'r omayn.

Oseh sholom bim 'romov hu ya-aseh sholom olaynu, v'al kol yisro-ayl, v'im ru omayn.

(Exalted and hallowed be His great Name. Amen.

Throughout the world which He has created according to His Will. May He establish His Kingship, bring forth His redemption and hasten the coming of His Messiah. Amen.

In your lifetime and in your days and in the lifetime of the entire House of Israel, speedily and soon, and say Amen.

Amen. May His great Name be blessed forever and to all eternity, blessed.

May His great Name be blessed forever and to all eternity. Blessed and praised, glorified, exalted and extolled, honored, adored, and lauded be the Name of the Holy One, blessed be He. Amen.

Beyond all the blessings, hymns, praises and consolations that are uttered in the world, and say Amen.

May there be abundant peace from heaven and a good life for us and for all Israel and say Amen.)

As the prayer ended, the hand receded from Jay's shoulder and the body disappeared into the mist gathering as the afternoon light waned. A small group had gathered around Jay and the stranger as they had uttered the ancient prayer in unison, in one voice of the wandering Jew still seeking a land to call his own.

Lt. Colonel Haas wanted Jay to have another conversation with Mayor Klass, this time with an order for the citizens of the "enlightened" town of Weimar.

"Corporal Dakelman, I want you to tell that SOB that he is to get every woman and man of this godforsaken shithole up at dawn tomorrow. They are going to march up the hill to that 'pig farm' and bury the dead with their bare hands. Anyone who refuses to comply with this order will be taken prisoner immediately," Haas instructed Jay.

As Jay delivered the order to Mayor Klass, the man literally shrunk before Jay's eyes. "Nein, bitte, bitte. We did not know. How could we know?" Klass whined.

"How could you not know?" Jay spat out at the mayor, whose short term was to be up in four more days.

That night as Jay lay sleepless in his bedroll, he thought bitterly, "They called it a pig farm! A pig farm!" The insinuation was impossible to miss; pigs, deemed as unkosher by the Old Testament, were forbidden to the Jewish people, and to infer that they were the pigs out for slaughter was just one more of the Germans' secret code, like "the final solution," "relocation," and "cleansing section," to hide from the world their plans to eradicate those of the Jewish faith from the planet forever.

The next morning the troops were up early, most of the men forgoing food but guzzling coffee to wake themselves out of the nightmare that they presently faced. Another day in Buchenwald was not something any of them wanted to repeat, but until relief arrived so that they could move on to Nurnberg, they had to revisit the horror.

As they rode up the hill in their trucks, a long line of men and women, most of whom were dressed in shapeless, shabby coats, carrying shovels and pickaxes, dragged their feet in the direction of Buchenwald. It was eerily silent, for there was little to say.

The American soldiers led the way to swathes of land and pointed. "Dig!" they commanded, and the citizens of Weimar dug. Over and over, the soldiers heard the protests, "We didn't know! We didn't know!" However, even if the people hadn't known, they should have asked. "Where have my neighbors, the Schwarzes gone? Where are the Rosenbergs? The Kleins? Disappeared in the middle of the night?" To turn their heads the other way and not ask these questions enabled the SS to do their worst, taking the silence of the citizens of Germany as unspoken approval of destroying all undesirables in the land.

The medics wanted to look at the infirmary on the property. As they walked, George told the others that he had heard that the prisoners of Buchenwald who were strong enough, were sent to work in a local factory that manufactured rockets. The plant was the state-owned Mittelwerk GmbH, responsible for producing the V-2 rocket, located in the tunnels of once-active salt mines burrowed into the Harz mountains. The prisoners were starved, beaten, and forced to drink water that leaked from the rusty pipes in the decaying factory. Fear of sabotage gave the guards cause to engage in the most extreme sadistic beatings of the slave laborers. Thousands had died in the clutches of the Third Reich.[4]

"Can it get any worse?" Slabicki responded.

That was when the foursome entered the Pathology Block; the beds were empty. There were no inmates being tended to here.

Suddenly, Jay and his buddies heard George moan, "Oh my God! No!" He was standing in the back of the room, staring at a wooden wall with something tacked onto it. The other three rushed back to see what George had found.

"It's skin. Skin ripped off the bodies here. It's being dried and stretched on this board."

The medics gaped at the large piece of skin, shaped clearly like a man's back.

"Slabicki, you thought it couldn't get worse?" Rosario asked.

"Why would they do this?" George asked.

"Let's get out of here," Jay said, heading quickly for the door.

The men were to learn later that Ilse Koch, wife of Buchenwald's camp commander, Karl Otto Koch, had a penchant for lampshades made of human flesh. Tattooed flesh made particularly lovely designs when lit by a dim bulb. Referred to by the prisoners of the camp as "the witch of Buchenwald," Ilse's behavior eventually led to her unpleasant demise. Aside from her cruelty toward the prisoners, she was notoriously promiscuous with the camp's guards, and she also liked money so much that she engaged in financial business that was totally unscrupulous, even by Nazi standards. Ilse ended up in a Weimar prison from 1943-1945 for her theft but was released after serving two years. However, after the war, she was tried for war crimes and sentenced to life in prison, where in 1967, she committed suicide.[5]

Just a few days after liberating Buchenwald, the 86th came upon another camp, Nordhausen. Conditions were the same as what the men had experienced when they arrived in Buchenwald. With the discovery of the second camp, news began to spread that these were not the only such death factories in Germany, and in fact, not just Deutschland, but Poland, Holland, and

Czechoslovakia. Prior to the discovery of hundreds of satellite camps, word began to spread among the troops that the death toll was beyond thousands; it was in the millions.

Six million were Jews. Six million others were political prisoners, homosexuals, Catholics, the mentally ill and "defectives," dwarves, gypsies, Communists, and anyone else who did not fit into the Reich's picture of the perfect Aryan specimen.

Jay found it impossible not to recall the days he spent in Buchenwald and Nordhausen as the years passed. What he had witnessed in those places of hell could never be expunged from memory. What he had seen could never be forgotten or forgiven.

This is what Jay wrote to Thelma following the experiences of liberating Buchenwald and Nordhausen.

April 20, 1945

. . . In the past few weeks, I have been in quite a few places and have seen a great many things. All the stories you have read about this country cannot make you visualize how true it is until you see that it is true. It is pathetic and there is no retribution on the earth or off, or in life or death that can ever be given to the responsible parties. However, this country is not escaping from war---they got away with it last war, but this time it is something altogether different. You should see some of them weep and wail. It was alright when they thought they were the Master Race, but now the shoe is on the other foot!! Of course, when I get to see you and talk to you, I'll have a lot more to tell you, that is if you want to even start listening to me.

Well, Thel, I'm afraid it is getting late, and I owe my mom a long letter. So, I'll have to say good nite to you for now---take care of yourself--Be good and let me hear from you soon. Regards to all.

Love,

Jay[6]

But, of course, when Jay got home from the war, he could never talk to Thelma about the images of what he had witnessed in Buchenwald. To do so would be to taint her imagination forever, and he could not bring himself to do that . . . especially since her own Austrian grandmother had died by a bullet courtesy of Hitler's SS.

Buchenwald
Photo taken by Jay Dakelman

It is the unconquerable soul of man and not the nature of the weapon he uses which insures victory.
General George S. Patton

CHAPTER 10

V-E DAY

As the 86th passed through Koln (Cologne), Jay took many photographs of the city in ruins. He remembered how often Koln had been talked about by his German teachers; what a magnificent city it had been. Now, all that stood above the smoking ruins was the exquisite towers of the cathedral, which miraculously had survived the massive bombings.

On May 2nd, the 86th departed from Eisleben, having been reassigned to the Third US Army. Down the autobahn they sped, passing through all kinds of weather, including a massive snowstorm. The unit stayed overnight in Nuremberg, where Jay couldn't resist taking a red and white flag with the hideous black swastika, like twisted snakes in the center, from the open window of a destroyed building. He couldn't logically say why he took it, but he understood that it had a historic significance that might be important one day. It had been stitched carefully by the hand of a German woman. The stitches were tiny and neatly done. Jay stuffed the flag into his duffle bag.[1]

All of the soldiers in B Company were pulling souvenirs from the ruins of the towns through which they passed. Most even confiscated relics from dead soldiers; Jay took a long saber and Nazi officer's ring from a stinking body as well as a heavy helmet, which also bore the Nazi insignia on the front. His most valuable find was a jeweled dagger that he eventually hid in his wooden chest to show off to his family when he got home. These were his "spoils of war."

The other men grabbed items like victrolas, cameras, and boots made of fine leather. Mike Slabicki paraded around in a Nazi officer's snazzy cap, which Jay caught in a photo. Slabicki plopped the black cap with its fanciful braid insignia onto Jay's head, grabbed the camera, and snapped a picture of Jay, who still sported a dark mustache.

But more important to Jay than the loot that he squirreled away in his trunk were the hundreds of photographs that he continued to take as the 86th raced through Germany, heading to the Austrian border.

The next day the battalion was on the road again, headed for Waisenkirchen, where they were met and guided to bivouac areas, which were in fields near the town. For the next three days, H & S company was engaged in staff and service functions, while A and B companies worked on equipment upkeep. Everyone's mood was beginning to lift as rumors were circulating that the end of the war was imminent, especially after the suicide of Adolf Hitler and his bride of one day, Eva Braun.[2]

The irony of Hitler's death following that of Roosevelt's by only 18 days was bitter for the fighting men of the United States. Surely, these two larger than life Commanders-in-Chief would not be meeting in the afterlife. Surely Roosevelt was headed towards heavenly gates while Satan was waiting below to shake the hand of the most prolific mass murderer in human history.

The battalion moved to Vilshofen on the Danube River, where they were billeted in a schoolhouse. All of their heavy vehicles were parked at a nearby athletic field. In the early hours of May 4th, instructions were received from the 1126th Engineer C Group the battalion would assume maintenance of the Passau, Austria, heavy pontoon bridge.[3]

At 3:30 a.m. on May 9, the 86th departed for Scharding on the German-Austrian border, where they immediately began construction of a heavy pontoon bridge. Despite all their experience, the job was tough due to the strength of the river current. As they worked on this bridge, they received the news.[4]

It was over. The Germans had surrendered.

Jay lay on his cot as the sun was rising. Every breath that he took felt new like he had just been thrust from the womb. No more bombs! No more foxholes! No more burning in the pit of the stomach, wondering if he would ever get home. Now, the question that was foremost in his mind was, "When are we going home?" However, he knew that the 86th was needed to work on bridges to finish up their responsibilities and establish the peacekeeping force in Europe. But wouldn't it be nice to be home in time to see a couple of Yankee games this fall? Or be home in time for football season. Yeah.

Now that a future loomed on the horizon, for what was he fit? Did he want to deconstruct his experiences in war and get a Master's Degree? He had a hankering to attend New York University and study with J.B. Nash, the guru of modern physical education and philosophy of recreation. Would he be able to concentrate enough to study?

Or should he look for a teaching and coaching position and throw himself into working with young men who would be untarnished and naive to what could happen in the real world? He just didn't know.

But, of course, everything hinged on when they would be going home.

And now there was something else to worry about. Rumors were flying that the 86th was going to be granted a brief furlough at home, after which they were going to be deployed again, this time in the South Pacific, where the war showed no signs of being over.

June 6, 1945

Rheinhausen, Germany

Dear Thelma:

After not receiving mail for nigh onto six weeks, yesterday our ship came in and we got lots of mail. I did more than good, as I received 47 letters, including three from you, a letter from May 7 and two V mails from May 6 and May 17. To say I was happy hearing from you would be putting it mildly. What a problem it will be to answer all of my mail. I am thinking of hiring a private secretary, one who can type better than me, to help with my correspondence. These German typewriters are really a problem to get used to, I can tell you that.

I think I told you that on V-E day we worked from 3:30 AM. until late at night working on a bridge. It was nothing like we expected when the war was over. We were way down in the south of Germany in the province of Bavaria but then the First Army called for us to come back and we knew the First Army was going back to the States, so we supposed we were heading for the States too and our morale went sky high. We traveled 500 miles in two days and came through such places as Frankfurt, Nuremberg, Cologne and other big cities or should I say remnants of big cities, for that is all that they are, I'm pleased to say.

Anyway, we landed in this place called Rheinhausen, which is across the Rhine River from Duisburg where we are maintaining a Bailey Bridge across the Rhine River. Rumor has it that we are awaiting orders for shipment back to the States; I am a pessimist and have my doubts. But Thelma, if such rumors are correct then I will see you this summer and will take you up on that offer to make my stay at home as short or as long as it may be an enjoyable one.

Although my folks don't go down the shore for the summer, and I used to go to the Poconos to work in a camp, I still like to go to Bradley Beach. So girlie, you had better get me your summer address quickly so that I will know where I can locate you when I come walking home this summer, I hope. You ask me what I think I would like to do if I get a furlough this summer. Well, most of all I want to have a good time, I want to go dancing and go to shows and go out with some girls and have a good time. I want to go out with some good-looking American girl I can talk to and who understands an American. I want to go swimming and I want the companionship of someone who will help me forget this past year. I want to forget the Army and I want to stay away from too many G.I.'s. I want a good time and I have been saving plenty of dough to blow the works.

Perhaps you wonder why I feel that way. Well, I am afraid I will come home only for a furlough and then head out to the South Pacific for more combat. I know what the past two years have been and I expect at least two years out there in combat and I dread going out there. So, you see, in a short furlough, I will have to make up for not only the past two years but also the two years that I face in the future. You see, this point system kind of leaves me in the lurch. I have only 29 points for service and 19 points for overseas. I was no hero and got no purple hearts as I was very lucky, so I got no points for that. I participated in 5 campaigns, so I have 5 battle stars (Battles of Normandy, Northern France, Ardennes, Rhineland, and Central Europe).

I was not married and did not have any kids to get any points on, so I lost out there. All in all, my total is a mere 73 which adds up to South Pacific; here I come. Unashamedly I will feel I have had more than my share of luck and two more years of combat will be tempting fate a little too much. Combat is all a matter of how lucky you are, and I have been an extremely lucky person. Anyway, that is why I want to do what I told you when I get home for my short leave which I might get.

Let me tell you that you flatter me and inflate my ego too much. Didn't Dotty tell you how conceited I am and only a little flattery will go right to my head. So, you want to be careful what you tell me about myself. But really, I don't care if you compare notes with Dotty Klockner. I was only kidding you before. I really like Dotty and think the world of her. She is a good kid and helped me out plenty when I was going to school. Someday, I hope to repay her for all her kindness towards me. I also like her mother and dad very much. On the few times that I was up to their house they really made me feel right at home. You know when I was going to school, I was living away from home and that made things, although advantageous in some respects it also made it very disadvantageous in other respects and the little kindness they showed me helped me immeasurably.

I hope that by this time you have received the perfume. I hope you like it. I tried to get some of the famous Chanel, but I just couldn't do it. However, I can truthfully tell you that the perfume that I sent you is one of the better French perfumes. You know I know a lot of perfumes as I used to help my dad in the store and learned a bit about it. I hope that it arrived safely; tell me whether you got it and if you gave the lanyard to Dotty. As I told you I made it out of German Parachute trooper wire. It isn't how good the thing is, but it is out of souvenir material, and I made it myself. Let me know what, how, when, and where you were when you received the package.

You wanted to know if I typed by using one hand or if I used all of my fingers. Well, I use the touch method and use both hands. I can't tell you that it is a little hard to get used to the German keyboard as there are a few different things on it: e.g., (a's with umlauts) etc. I am not that good of a typist, but I do well enough to get along and make my correspondence a little easier.

Recently, I have read a few books: Strange Fruit by Lillian Smith, Wild as the River by Louis Bromfield, Razor's Edge by Somerset Maugham: Lively Lady by Kenneth Roberts: Green Years by A.J. Conin: and a few others. We haven't had a motion picture in quite a while, and I sure wish they would get around to it. We have been playing a little softball but nothing much to speak of; the recreation and education program is nothing like the army had promised it would be when the European War would come to a successful conclusion. But then the Army talks a good deal about the morale of the troops but oftentimes they do very little to help it improve.

I have a great many more pictures that I have taken and some very interesting ones at that. I was debating with myself whether I should bring you some or send you some, and after a lengthy argument with myself, I have concluded to bring them to you. However, even this outbreak of optimism is too much so do not stop from writing to me. Anyway, I don't think you would like a picture of me in your wallet. Anyway, I have a mustache and by the time you see me, I will probably have shaved it off; that is if I lose my nerve, I may keep it on just to show some people. I don't intend to be dictated to.

I am sure that they showed you people back home some of the German atrocities; I don't know if they carried the punch of seeing it in pictures. I saw the places at Nordhausen and Buchenwald and they are things that I will never forget in all my life. I hear what you say about the people back home, never forgetting it; it is true. Please don't forget it is the most inhuman thing you could believe, and I will tell you more about it when I see you.

Well, I guess I have raved on enough and so I will close now with all my best regards to everyone at home. Take care of things and I will be seeing you soon, perhaps even sooner than you think and I hope sooner than I think. Do not stop writing and you better start to use my new APO address which is 408. So long now and be good and if not be careful.

Love,

Jay

Each day, the men watched large columns of army trucks transporting former concentration camp victims to railroad stations with the hopes of returning to their homes. However, these displaced persons were not going to find much worth going back to as whole villages had been wiped out in Austria, Poland,

Czechoslovakia, Hungary, anywhere there had been large populations of Jews. And, even if their towns were intact, their homes had been confiscated and were not available to them anymore. The Jews were not welcomed back to their native lands by their former neighbors. In Poland many of those looking for lost family members were murdered by citizens who harbored hatred and resentment toward the staggering victims of the Holocaust.

Many trucks carried German POWs, taking them to various enclosures and sometimes even carrying them all the way home. Once in their hometowns, they were discharged from the Wehrmacht legally. Throngs of refugees who had been forced from their homes during air raids and advancing armies were traveling in all directions. Some rode bicycles loaded with personal belongings, while others rode in reconditioned German vehicles. People were moving all over the countryside, wearing the blank expressions of the deceived and defeated.[5]

The civilians whose homes were in the surrounding villages were trying to reconstruct living quarters from the bombed-out ruins that had once been their domiciles. Women, children, and the elderly toiled to eke out enough food to survive. There was almost nothing available in the markets, and when there was a little bread or sauerkraut to be had, the lines were huge.

As the 86th passed through the towns of Neuss, Rheinhausen, and other nearby villages, the German people tried to befriend the Americans. In many cases, they thronged around billets of GIs with film, watches, and other valuable items, hoping to exchange them for a few cigarettes, some bits of chocolate, or anything edible.

General Eisenhower had laid down specific regulations forbidding the American troops to fraternize with the Germans, which the Germans had great difficulty in understanding. After all, the war was over; they were now at peace. Anything that had happened during the war had not been their fault; they were only following orders. If they had not followed orders, they would have been shot. They didn't know why their neighbors had been disappearing. They hadn't seen anything. They hadn't heard anything. They were not evil, just misled.

June 15, 1945

Dear Thelma,

Well, last Sunday night, I was back in Rheinhausen, Germany, listening to the radio when the First Sergeant walked in and said, "Pack up, fellows we leave tomorrow at 4:30 a.m. We all almost went nuts---We yelled, screamed, and carried on---Brooklyn, here we come. We cried---we are on our way home.

The next morning, we were ready at 4:30, for none of us slept. We loaded our trucks and took off. Well, instead of heading westward toward Antwerp or Le Havre, we headed back Eastward from which we had just come. First to Cologne to cross the Rhine, then on the autobahn to Frankfurt and then east to Nuremberg---then to Munich through Munich to a town about 40 miles from Munich called Wasserberg among the Bavarian Alps. We are stuck here, and we can't fathom the reason why---We're First Army troops and were attached first to the 15 Army and now to the 3rd Army.

Our situation is lousy. We are up in these darn mountains in the sticks, miles from civilization. We are about 80 miles from Innsbruck and about 70 miles from Berchtesgaden. Our home is an old, deserted saw-mill. The food is miserable---it was mostly K rations but yesterday we had C rations. Today we were supposed to have chicken, so they sent us 17 chickens for 129 men---consider how much we had. We were fed better in combat.

There are no shows for us---there is nothing for us to do. It is driving most of the men nuts. Now that the war is over, the Generals are returning home to receive the plaudits of the people---but poor G.I. Joe who slept in the foxhole and was shot at, can't even get a furlough. I know I had my last furlough in July 1943. Tell me, don't you think a person deserves at least 7 days away from all this? But really, I should not complain because there are others worse off than me. All I can say is that now the war is over here, and we don't have to sacrifice lives; there is no need to do anything for us. I have lost faith in all propaganda fed to me and say tell it to the Indians.

This province and country of Bavaria is very picturesque and beautiful. However, in my present state of mind I cannot appreciate it that much.

I suppose by this time you are either down at Bradley or getting ready to go there. How are things there---I still have hopes of seeing you and going out with you this summer but I'm not as sure about it now as I was a month ago and each day, my confidence drops another degree. But I keep hoping and praying for a miracle. Pray for me----pray for me!!

Well, I'm afraid I have over-extended myself and no doubt you are tired of hearing me cry the blues so I will close. Please give my regards to all the folks. I still hope to see you soon.

Lovingly,

Jay

On June 1st, Company B was given orders to dismantle and remove the treadway bridge that they were maintaining. However, the job became complicated when the men did not have the proper equipment to disassemble the bridge, which was one that they had never used before. The company secured about 50 German POWs to perform the manual labor. Within two days, the bridge was dismantled and piled onto the riverbanks. The pieces were loaded onto pontoon trailers and hauled to a nearby railhead where it was being loaded onto freight cars.[6]

Lt. Blackburn, the commander of A company, led A Company back to Rheims, France, where they attended a six-day school, learning about the M-4 bridge, a new heavy bridge being used by the US Army. German liquor was rationed out to troops in this area. Each soldier received a bottle of fine cognac.

Also, for the first time in 15 days, mail had caught up to the unit, which boosted everyone's morale. Since they had been moving so much over the last weeks, it had taken a lot of time for the APOs to find them.

Several days later, both A and B companies went to Kripp, Germany to load the now empty trailers from B company. Once again, the German POWs were used to complete the job and prepare the vehicles for the tedious journey back to the Third US Army area near Munich.

While enroute to Munich, the men passed through Nuremberg. At this moment Colonel Haas wrote, "During this day of travel, we passed through the great Nazi city of Nuremberg, the city where Nazism was born, and by the scars that were left by the allied bombings, it must surely have died there. . . Early in the afternoon as the convoy passed through Munich, many a memory drifted back to the days of hearing

Hitler making his speeches to the world. All now left of the great city were heaps of rubble left by the thousands of bombings."[7]

The 86th reached the vicinity of Wasserburg the next day where H & S company and the medical detachment were billeted in a farmhouse and adjoining buildings. Jay took delight in photographing the farm, including a pretty, blond milkmaid. A company slept in an old sawmill, and B company stayed in neighboring civilian homes and the railway station.

While in Wasserburg, the troops once again performed maintenance on their vehicles and worked on the upkeep of a local bridge. 80 POWs were withdrawn from a local stockade and put to work, cleaning and painting each piece of equipment, with personnel from each of the two companies supervising the work. Battalion headquarters, H & S company and the medical detachment were also doing staff and service functions and maintenance and repair.

Passes were doled out to the battalion personnel for visits to the Bavarian Alps and Hitler's hideout at Berchtesgaden. With a group from each of the three companies going sightseeing each day, the trip and tour generally took about twelve hours.

Jay was particularly exuberant about their tour of Garmisch Partenkirchen, as it had been the site of the 1936 Winter Olympics. Just seeing the stadium and fields surrounding it put Jay in touch with his athletic roots. But Jay had another mission in mind, other than taking in the breathtaking beauty of the Bavarian Alps, ski runs, and the Olympic Stadium. He was bound and determined to visit the factory of the renowned Adi Dassler and meet the man who fashioned the shoes that the great Jesse Owens had worn in the 1936 Summer Olympics.

While at Panzer Jay had learned about the Dassler brothers, who had established a small shoe company in their mother's wash kitchen in a small Bavarian town. He and a small band of other guys were interested in seeing the factory, which was now recognized as the premier maker of soccer and track spikes in the world. They got directions to Herzogenaurach, where the factory was based, and once there, in his best German, Jay asked if he and his friends could meet Mr. Dassler.

An extremely handsome man, Adi Dassler came from the back of the factory where his office was located and greeted the young Americans.

"I admire your shoes greatly," Corporal Dakelman said to the shoemaker.

"Danke Schön," Dassler replied.

"When I go back to the States, I plan to be a football coach," Jay explained. "Perhaps one day, my whole team will be able to wear your shoes." Jay was careful not to admit that his future squads would be playing American football as opposed to European futbol, more commonly known in the States as soccer.

Dassler pulled out several pairs of cleats for the men to see. Jay offered to buy two pairs, one white with three red stripes across, one white with three blue stripes.

"Nein, nein," Dassler said, pushing the shoes towards Jay. "You take these. A gift. Maybe someday your team will wear the shoes of Adi Dassler."

And, indeed, not only would Jay's teams wear the shoes of Adi Dassler, but a great deal of other athletic gear, all bearing the famous Adidas logo.

Hitler is finished—but the seeds spread by his disordered mind have firm root in too many fanatical brains. It is easier to remove tyrants and destroy concentration camps than it is to kill the ideas which gave them birth and strength.
Harry S. Truman

CHAPTER 11

HOME

Although the war in Europe had been over for months, Jay's dreams of going home permanently were fading quickly. In a letter written to Thelma on August 9, 1945, he states:

In mid-September, word came that the bridge school was finally closing and the remaining men of the 86th were beginning to head toward Rheims, France for the beginning of their long dreamed of journey across the Atlantic. The soldiers were loaded onto boxcars in Rosenheim, Germany. The many photos that Jay took of the joyful, young men, many of them still wearing their combat helmets, show them squatting in the doors of the boxcars, trying to get fresh air.[1]

The first stop of the train was in the city of Munich, and next they paused in Ulm, which like so many other towns in Germany, was a vast wasteland of rubble. Through Strasbourg, the continuing portraits of destruction loomed; Jay snapped photo after photo to show those at home what real war looked like.

With thousands of men traveling to Rheims, food was scarce, which made Jay all the more grateful for the Hershey bars that his mom had sent from his dad's pharmacy. He shared them with his friends, Yorman and Thomas, and wondered where some of the great pals he had made back in those halcyon days in the Cotswolds of England were on this day. Had it really been two years since he had left New Jersey? Had it been 15 months since he had last been on British soil?

Finally, a huge sign loomed in the distance. It read, "Camp Cleveland, Welcome to Rheims." The men grabbed their bags and jumped down from the trucks that they had boarded on the final leg of this part of the journey. They were assigned to barracks and quickly headed for "the Brass Rail" for a decent meal, pointing at the painted murals in the PX of sexy women and military achievements of the war. A realistic painting of General Eisenhower with the background behind him of the American flag greeted the men when they entered the PX to buy a few personal items since their supplies were so depleted. They were on American soil at last (sort of).[2]

19 September 1945

Dear Thelma,

There is no sense waiting and waiting because that takes too long, so I'll tell you now: I am still only on my way home. We left Rosenheim last Friday and rode for three days in boxcars. All we had to eat was cold C rations but I stacked up some candy, so we did o.k.

The ride wouldn't have been as bad, but we kept getting sidetracked. When we arrived here at Rheims, you can imagine our dirt. I thought I would get a nice hot shower but all I got was a cold one.

Since arriving here, we have been working continuously. There have been all types of records to get in shape: service records for 20s form 201, immunization records, physical inspections, teeth inspections---today we gave shots and I had to help shoot the influenza shot---only 1,000 men. It is really a hectic race---we turn in clothes, get new clothes, get clothes taken away, issue other junk. If there is a hard way of doing anything, the army will find it.

At the present time, I am at the A.A.C. (Assembly Area Command) in or rather 18 kilometers from Rheims, France. There are several huge camps here---Camp Cleveland, Brooklyn, Philly, Pittsburgh, N.Y., Chicago and others. I am being processed here at Camp Cleveland. I have no idea when we will leave here but rumor has it---we will leave here Sept. 28 for Camp Lucky Strike in Le Havre. This is the camp where you wait for your boat. So, honey, if all goes well, I hope to be home by the latest, the last week in October, if nothing goes wrong!

That ought to be plenty of time for us to take in a few plays and a few of the big football games---some dances and some dinners and some, yeah---and some. Anyway, that is if you don't object to having a good time with me---why do you know, Oct. 11 will be exactly two years since I left the States, so I have a lot to make up for.

Here is something---I have 78 points at the present time, 80 points are needed for discharge---however, I'm sure of a 30-day furlough and I expect by the time my furlough is up, the points will be lowered to 75 and I'll get my discharge. I can have a wild time or a good time in that month.

Say I picked up a bottle of Passion de Zaflay perfume for you and it is the most exotic I have ever whiffed. I don't know whether to carry it or send it. I think perhaps I'll send it and hope it beats me home so you can have it.

I am very impatient, sweating out these days. I can't wait to get my feet on U.S. soil soon. But I know that can't be far off. Well, it is late, and I'll close now---my regards to all and I'll see you soon.

Love,

Jay

P.S.B.B.D.C.Y.C.A.M.

6 October 1945

Marseilles, France

Dear Thelma,

It is about 4 p.m. this fine Saturday afternoon and I managed to sneak into the Red Cross and get a table, so I thought I had better dash off a few lines to you!!

There is not much new here; the latest rumor is that me with 75 and over in points may be permitted to leave on the next shipment. Naturally, I am sweating it out and hope that it is true---but of course, one can never put stock in what you hear from the Army---they'll do you every time if they can---so what? Anyway, I'm still hoping against hope---I guess.

In case I really am coming, I think you have a good idea, we'll walk in and surprise Dot. You could call her and tell her you're coming over to see her and then we'll walk in there. Gosh, she'll be surprised---but no uniforms because if I get discharged and can buy some new clothes, I want to get out of this stuff as soon as possible. But now maybe I'm counting my chickens again---anyway, I'm near the ocean---they can't take that away from me unless they send me back to Deutschland.

I had high hopes of catching most of the football season and I still have hopes of getting the big games in November---if I'm lucky. My kid sister goes to Penn, and she writes her boyfriend is mgr. of the team so if luck holds and the dice turn up seven maybe we'll make a Penn game. Otherwise, we may have to settle for a pro game in New York or maybe Princeton. But we'll see when the time comes around---o.k.?

Yesterday, I went into Marseilles on a pass. All narrow streets except in the middle of town are quite modern and have beautiful shops. They have beautiful shops for dresses and hats but the prices---!! It cost an arm and a leg for something. I went into a shop for a manicure---yup---(you know I never had a fingernail when I left home, used to bite them down to the cuticles, ask Dotty. Now I'm getting manicures).

Anyway, these Frenchies really know hairstyles. They wear their hair miles up into the air. Wish I could draw or explain it---anyway they know their stuff. However---we do not care for the French---to see them, you'd think they won the war, and we were wearing their clothes and using their equipment. Then I ran into a few American WACs parading around. The WACs have a terrible reputation here and every G.I. distrusts them and their behavior and so the good must pay for the lewdness of some. We all think a big mistake has been made and our government should get them home quickly.

The black-market flourishes here---American money brings $2 for 1-100 francs for $1, Cigarettes from 14 to 20 dollars, soap

$1.00 a cake, socks $2 to $3---and all kinds of prices. I had a pair of civilian shoes I carried from home and had for a while (about 3 ½ yrs. old). Well, I sold them for 500 francs or $10, but I lost it and $50 more in a crap game.

We have only francs and throw money around like water because it means so little here. I just cannot wait to get home. I am tired and disgusted with all of this.

Incidentally, your letter made good time---it was postmarked September 24 and arrived here Oct. 4--- so maybe you should keep writing to me for a while---anyhow, being as I don't know when I'll be coming.

You say they put on shows trying to get men to enlist---well, I'll tell you a secret---I was never drafted---yup I'm an enlisted man (but for a reason, of course). However, the army is doing everything possible to discourage anyone from reenlisting in the way they do things. Everyone here is disgusted and down.

There is no sense in going through any ordeal waiting for me. In the first place, it doesn't pay, and in the second place you're liable and probably will be terribly disappointed---you know that, don't you? Anyway, I'll consider it---I mean calling you before walking in---in any event I intend to surprise you!!

You know I used to play a lot of badminton and tennis too while at Panzer and got to be good---however, it is now quite some time. My efforts have been limited to a ping pong table in which quite egotistically, I can say I'm damned good. Anyway, we'll get together on some things. About the only thing I don't like to do is to swim ---but I like to dine (and go out for dinner).

I am also looking forward to seeing your enlarged photo doing a shoulder stand---it must be quite the thing!

You added in your letter, and I quote, "You know, I'm far from a goddess." ---anyway, I don't know about that unless you've been using someone else's pictures---Anyway, I usually strike out. But you can't have any idea as to what I'm really like in person. Maybe I should tell you my bad points instead of egotizing myself---e.g., my very uncontrollable temper and a few other minor items---anyway, we'll see.

Well, I guess I'll get around to closing as it is almost time for that slop they call chow. Boy, I'm looking forward to some good meals and soon, too.

Well, give my regards to Len when you write and my best to your mother and father! And to everyone else at home---I'll see you soon, take care, and be good.

Love and kisses,

Jay

B.B.D.C.Y.K.A.M.

While Camp Cleveland wasn't exactly a luxury hotel, there were several amenities that helped the men to relax. There were daily softball and baseball games, rather primitive tennis courts, and a huge movie tent called "The Hippodrome" with nightly shows.

The men were permitted to go into the city of Rheims, which provided a nice distraction for the fellows who kept crossing days off the calendar waiting for the final leg of the journey to Le Havre.

October came and finally, Jay climbed aboard a truck headed for Marseilles, where once again, the wait continued at Camp

Calais. On tours of the pretty city of Marseilles, Jay resumed his hobby of photographing pharmacies to show his father.

Marseilles, France

12 October 1945

My dearest Thelma:

Let me see if I can bring you up to date on my very unpleasant and uninteresting autobiography. Last time I wrote, I told you all of us under 80 points would be included in going home.

Well, the Major from my outfit went to bat for us and all of us under 80 (we all had 75-80) stayed with the 179th to go home. Boy, we were happy and excited and thankful. Then came our break.

We were assigned to a ship---the Santa Maria---no, not Columbus' ship but some beat-up old tug but we didn't care because we were headed home and going in anything, even Columbus's Santa Maria. The ship was supposed to land on the 12 (today) and we were to leave soon after. But can you imagine, the boat never left New York.

There are 45,000 homesick G.I.s in this camp who are practically stranded because of the strike at home. It is impossible to express my and all the other fellows' feelings. We feel that we are being let down. It did not take trouble to get us here and the government broke strikes quickly then. Why in 72 hours, I was processed and on a boat sailing for Europe when I had to come, but it's taking all kinds of difficulty to get us back.

We all feel like sailing in and we could handle those strikers---we killed plenty of Germans. What's the difference between a little more blood on our hands and the people back home---evidently, they've all forgotten those poor guys who went through everything---it's a wonder our dead from Normandy to the Elbe don't turn in their graves.

Perhaps I am speaking too strongly but some of the things we are told, read, and see, aren't pretty.

I was talking to a sailor in Marseilles the other day who had just docked from N.Y. He told me the same thing that shocked me. He said the rumor at home because fellows with 75s and above were not home yet was that they had V.D. Of all the lies and false stinking propaganda, that tops it.

We didn't quit in the foxholes, and we didn't go on strike when we had to build a bridge---but now, when we should get a break, our own people fail us. Why only yesterday 19 ships were canceled from sailing here. Now I ask, is that fair? Is it?

So, you see the situation---I cannot say when I will get home; it may be in 3 weeks or maybe by New Year's. I sort of think it will be about Thanksgiving time, but I hope it will be sooner. Anyway, perhaps I'll make it for my birthday---November 29. I sure hope to make it so we can take in some football this year. How about it?

I got mixed up in a crap game last night and lost all my money. I dropped about $300---not bad, huh? I just couldn't make a hand --- just unlucky. Oh well, I'll borrow some dough and perhaps I'll make a lucky hit! Anyway, I got a couple of back month's pay coming so we'll do it. O.K., baby?

Last night I went to see the show, "Salome, Where She Danced." It wasn't too bad, and it passed the time. I also saw "God Is my Co-Pilot." Pretty good, too. They have huge outdoor movies here. We must go after supper and get there at 5:15 in order to see the show. The show starts at dark---7:15.

Well, I will close now, give my regards to everyone at home---

Love and Kisses

Jay

PS I have a lot of paper kisses to collect from you.

B.B.D.C.Y.K.A.M.

The following is the final letter that Jay sent to Thelma because, after a quick sojourn to the French Riviera and the stunning paradise of Monte Carlo, the men made it to Le Havre. Jay, with his trusty camera around his neck, snapped photos of the men lining up to board the S.S. Sea Robin, which certainly did not have the elegance of the converted luxury liner, the Queen Elizabeth had when she had brought them across the Atlantic on route to war.

Marseilles, France

16 October 1945

Dearest Thelma,

Today, I received your letter of September 20---the one you told me about going to wade through some ice cream with me. I don't think I should eat too much; I weigh too much now. I think I hit around 180 and I was only 169 when I graduated from Panzer. Well, the news is fair---we are on the alert and tonight, we turned in our French money for American dough.

I didn't have much to turn in, but I have two months' pay coming to me when I get home. So, I won't be broke. Well, to continue, we are restricted to the area and are supposed to get on the boat on the 18 (Thursday and we are supposed to sail on the 19).

Please notice I said supposed because, Thelma, we can never tell when things will change in the army---to say I'm sweating it out is mild. Yes, I am looking forward to hearing you sing---it better be good!! But then, being you, it should be. Well, why should I hold out B.B.D.C.KY.K.A.M. means "Bye-Bye Darling Consider Yourself Kissed and Missed" I wanted to hold out but couldn't do it, so that's it---how do you like it? The boat I'm coming on is supposed to be the "Sea Robin" ---Well, I have so much to say I better close---we have a lot to do when I get back. My regards to all the folks.

Lovingly,

Jay

The voyage home on the small ship, The Sea Robin, was swift. The weather had gotten raw as winter was closing in now. Still, the men aboard her enjoyed walking on the decks, breathing in the salty air, and having nothing to do except contemplate their futures. Jay took photos of his friends, Juny Thomas and Tony Busetti as they hung out on board, watching the porpoises escort the S.S. Robin through the Strait of Gibraltar.

On this journey, Jay was not sleeping five bunks high near the ceiling as he had on the Queen Elizabeth at the beginning of the war. His cot was lumpy, but a joy compared to years of sleeping in leaky tents on the cold ground. He spent many hours just luxuriating in the novels that he had scrounged up to take with him on the voyage home. He tried to imagine what it would be like to see his mother, father, and sister again. How would they react when they lay eyes on him for the first time in over two years?

On the afternoon of October 25, 1945, the men raced to the deck to witness the moment for which they had been praying for years. Jay, ever mindful of documenting critical moments, captured his first pictures of American soil as the ship rolled past the New York shoreline. Every inch of the deck was loaded with men, all eager to get a glimpse of home.

At the first sight of the great, green woman guarding the Hudson harbor, a cheer began to ripple through the crowd of war-worn men as their weariness faded, and hope began to stir in their breasts. It had been an eternity since she had bid them farewell.

As the S.S. Sea Robin silently slid past the Statue of Liberty, hats flew into the air, men grabbed each other in fierce hugs, and tears fell unabashedly from eyes that had not seen such a beautiful site in years. The Statue that promised justice and liberty to all, the thing for which they had risked their lives, stood steadfastly to greet them at the end of their perilous journey.

There was no doubt in Jay's mind as to what he needed to do as soon as the ship docked into her berth in New York Harbor. As the tugs neared the S.S. Sea Robin to escort her into her berth, he was determined to execute his plan even though he would be breaking the rules. Although the men had been warned not to leave the ship, there was no way that he was going to spend this night waiting for what he had been dreaming of doing for so long. So as darkness fell, Jay, along with several other soldiers, crept off the ship while those on guard duty looked the other way.

Jay, who had shaved his mustache off on the voyage home, tugged at his jacket and headed for the bus station, which he knew well, having traveled to the city so often for the jazz concerts and Yankee games that he loved. He bought a ticket and boarded the bus headed for Newark, which was about a twenty-minute ride. He got off on South Orange Avenue and walked briskly, asking directions just once for the street that he sought.

He stood in front of the tall, three-family house, 97 Columbia Avenue, his soldier's cap clasped in his hands and nervously rang the doorbell. He could see the lights on in the parlor of the Klockner house, which was right across the street, and hoped that Dotty and Jimmy might be there at this very moment.

The door opened, and a beautiful, petite woman with a jaunty, chiffon scarf tied around her auburn curls appeared. She stared at him wordlessly for a moment, her mouth forming a perfect O, expressing both shock and elation.

"Jay!" she screamed and threw her arms around his neck.

They were perfectly matched in height and stature.

"I'm home, Thelma," he said. "I'm home."

Fin Part I

Jay's parents, Louie and Ida Dakelman ca. 1921

Jay, a dapper little man at the age of 3 in 1924. (Photo taken by L. Dakelman)

Jay's Bar Mitzvah portrait, 1934. His paternal grandmother, Becki died the week before the ceremony, so the festivities had to be canceled and only the ritual took place.

Carol Dakelman, Jay's sister in 1946, a student at the University of Pennsylvania. (Photo taken by L. Dakelman)

1942 - Jay as the center for the Panzer football team.

Jay played catcher for the Panzer baseball team, but loved to bat, 1942.

Dr. Margaret C. Brown, the fearsome president of Panzer College, 1942. Students would quake when they received the message, "See me. MCB"

The Medical Detachment of the 86th Pontoon Battalion, First Army Corps of Engineers. (Jay is bottom right. Other members of the Medical Detachment were John Costello, George Kopp, George Medakovich, Mike Rosario, Simon Sacks, and Stanley Slabicki).

In the tent, 1944, Jay and his buddies.

Jay amid a gaggle of French girls, July 1944.

Coming off the battlefield at Remagen, 1944. (Photo taken by Jay Dakelman)

The 86th building pontoon bridges at the famous site of the Bridge at Remagen. (Photo taken by Jay Dakelman)

Building bridges to cross the Rhine at Remagen. (Photo taken by Jay Dakelman)

Jay standing by a captured Nazi tank in the Ardennes Forest during the Battle of the Bulge.

Jay loved to ride his motorcycle over the countryside rather than sit in the cramped Army trucks.

Engaged to be married, Thelma and Jay at Bear Mountain, 1947.

The bride cuts the cake; August 17, 1947. Thelma becomes Mrs. Jay
Dakelman.

PART 2

VICTORY

Whether sixty or sixteen, there is in every human being's heart the lure of wonder, the unfailing child-like appetite of what's next and the joy of the game of living.
J.B. Nash

CHAPTER 12

SUMMER CAMP WITH J.B. NASH

Like most veterans returning from Europe after the war, Jay was confused about what he wanted to do with the rest of his life. Finding a teaching job in the middle of the year was not likely to happen and with so many young men flooding the job market with qualified candidates, searching for stable work, like teaching, was frustrating. Jay worried, too, that his mind was not ready for the rigors of conducting his own classroom so even if he procured a post, would he be up to the task?

"Doc," as most of his customers referred to Louie Dakelman, Jay's pharmacist father, put Jay to work in his old position as a soda jerk in the store when he returned home so that he would have a purpose in getting up each day. Doc was thrilled to have his still boyish-looking son within sight again and frequently peeked up from his heavy spectacles perched on his bulbous nose just to make sure that Jay was really there. The constant, nagging fear that had plagued Doc constantly for the last three years finally was waning.

Although Jay often seemed distant and exceedingly quiet, Doc knew that his son was smart and would figure out the right path for his future given a little time. He understood, too, that Ida, his wife, still harbored the hope that Jay would opt for medical school, especially having had so much experience in the field during the war. However, triaging and operating on human beings was the farthest thing from Jay's mind as he pondered his options. He had seen enough gore to last him a lifetime. The battles he yearned for now were on the playing field for points, not corpses.

He conferred with his buddy, John Altounian, about the possibility of going to graduate school at NYU. The renowned educator, Jay B. Nash, was currently a professor there and the opportunity to study with Nash was too good for either of the young soldiers to pass up, especially with the G.I. bill picking up the tab.

John and Jay were accepted to the fast-tracked program and made their way to Lake Sebago in Sloatsburg, New York in the summer of 1946. As the guru of the philosophy of recreation, Nash's program of studies required his students to immerse themselves in the joys of communing with nature by living in tents and "roughing it" while they went to classes, served as counselors for the youngsters who attended the camp, and soaked in the aura of the greatest theorist of physical education in the 20th century. Although camping was the last thing that Johnny or Jay ever wanted to do after their experiences in Europe, the opportunity to study with Nash proved irresistible, even if it meant sleeping in leaky tents again.

Jay Bryan Nash (1886-1965), a determined scholar and educator, had joined the other early leaders in the effort to have physical education, health education, and recreational education recognized as legitimate fields of study. He loved being outdoors, was a born teacher and prolific author who espoused the importance of caring for the body and mind as essential to one's well-being.[1]

Dr. Nash had graduated from Oberlin College in 1911. He studied at the University of California and Columbia University and received his Doctor of Philosophy from NYU. Springfield College conferred upon him the honorary degree of Master of Science.

From 1919-1926 Nash served as a teacher, a superintendent of recreation, Oakland, California and director of Physical Education for the state of California for two years. He then became an associate professor at NYU, rising to a full professorship in 1928, and ultimately became chairman of the department.

The trouble with studying with someone like Nash, who had boundless energy and a mind that churned ideas constantly, was that the war-worn students who attended camp in the summer of '46, had trouble keeping up the demanding pace of the work that Nash assigned to them.

However difficult the challenge, Jay and Johnny recognized the value of studying with Nash. "Students around the world came to respect and love this man who took such a keen personal interest in each of them," Nash's obituary stated.

"Such a person gains the respect and confidence of his associates and fellows. He was entrusted with many tasks—local, national, and international—most of which were completed with distinction. And so, many honors were conferred upon him in recognition of his marked contributions."[2]

In the meantime, Jay's relationship with Thelma had been developing steadily. After Jay had returned home, they saw each other almost every weekend. If Jay couldn't borrow his father's car to make the drive to Newark, the red-headed girl hopped on the train to New Brunswick and would often stay overnight at the Dakelman home on North Third Avenue in Highland Park. Since Jay's sister, Carol, was still a student at the University of Pennsylvania, Thelma would stay in Carol's room on her weekends with the Dakelmans.

Although Thelma knew that Jay liked her a lot, she remained insecure about his intentions because he refrained from speaking about a permanent commitment, and she wasn't getting any younger. Their friends, Dotty and Jimmy, were getting married in May, and several of her other friends from work and the Hizomer Choir in which Thelma sang, were engaged. To make her even more anxious about their relationship, at the end of a lovely weekend with Jay and his parents, Jay never spoke of plans for the next weekend. She sat by the phone all week, willing him to call, which sometimes happened as late as Friday evening for a date on Saturday. He was driving her more than a little crazy with his apparent lack of insight to her desire for a permanent commitment.

When Thelma found out that Jay was spending the entire summer at Lake Sebago, she was deeply disappointed that they would be separated for a large part of the good weather months again. What if he found a shapely, cute, co-ed while at camp? Was she wasting her time with this guy?

She discussed her options with down-to-earth Dotty shortly before Dot's wedding to Jim.

"Oh, hang in there, Thelma," Dotty encouraged her. "Jay's just nervous about how he's going to be able to support a family right now. Give him a little more time."

Dotty's words were helpful, but that nagging, little clock in the back of Thel's curly head kept going, "Tick, tick, tick." The thing was, she adored Jay, and she knew that he cared about her since they did spend so much time together.

Fortunately, her parents remained silent on the matter except for the fact that Pa remarked that Jay was so quiet on his visits to Columbia Avenue that he hardly knew the young man was there. Thelma mused that Pa was slightly insulted, thinking that Jay wasn't trying to get to know the family, but Thelma knew that there were dark places in Jay's mind that sometimes he could just not escape. Although he never did go into detail about what he had witnessed overseas as he had promised in his letters that he would, just the distant expression in his deep brown eyes told her all that she needed to know.

Jay's first letter from the NYU camp to Thelma arrived in early July. He wrote, *"There are tennis courts and yesterday, after I arrived, I went swimming in the lake, which is large and very beautiful."*

He complained about the rigorous schedule that Nash had designed for the students. *"We get up here at 5:50 a.m. and run a mile at 6:15, which is good because I want to keep from gaining weight. We have classes from 8:00-10:00 and 1:00-2:00 every day, but we don't have classes on Saturday and Sunday so if there is a way into the city I will come."*

Dr. Nash counseled his eager students on jobs that were available since he had a great pipeline all over the country. John visited a school system in Hartford, Connecticut, but he was not impressed with the situation there. For one thing, his interview had been scheduled for 8:30 a.m. and the superintendent had not seen him until 12:30. The longer that John sat in the office waiting, the angrier he got. Former soldiers despised wasting time since they felt that so much of their lives had been thrown away already.

Jay informed Thelma in his next letter, *"I had a call about a job, so I wrote to see about it. I am not crazy about the location as it is in Memphis, Tennessee at a state college. If they want me to go all the way out there to No Man's Land, they'll have to pay me something worthwhile."*

He continued to write about his job search, *"I wrote a letter for another job today in Pitcairn, Pa. which is just outside of Pittsburg. They want a football and basketball assistant coach and a baseball coach. The salary is $2700. So, I applied; what can I lose? Tomorrow morning, John and I are having an interview with Dr. Nash about jobs, too. He says opportunities are coming in. So maybe I will be working this fall after all.*

"You know, if I get my M.A. and get a job for the fall, why then, baby, I'll be on the road and nothing will stop me, but if I don't, I'll just step down and quit. So, we'll have to see what's what!!"

Thelma felt a flush of excitement course through her as she read the last paragraph of that letter. It seemed that Dotty's advice had been on the right track. If Jay did land a job that offered him a permanent income, hopefully a marriage proposal would follow. Even if the salary wasn't terrific, she had a secretarial job and between their two incomes, they should be able to manage nicely.

The matter of the job took a back seat for most of July, unfortunately, as the workload for the Master's candidates increased exponentially. Jay wrote of his frustrations to Thelma and described the topic of his Master's Thesis:

N.Y.U. Camp
July 10, 1946
Dear Thel,

I am behind in writing to you, but I am so far behind in my damn work that I just don't know what's up. Every day, instead of it clearing up, it gets more confusing. I'll have so much to type by the end of the six weeks, a term thesis which is almost like a master thesis in triplicate; in fact, it is my Master's thesis and honey listen to the topic, try to figure it out, or if you see Jimmy and Dotty ask them if they can understand it,

My topic or title is—

'What are the Physiological Effects of Training on Producing Organic Power and Greater Efficiency in the Distance Run.' If you see Jim, ask him if he knows of any material on this subject and if he could send any up, I'd sure appreciate it. Johnny Altounian is writing on the 'Physiological Effects of Fatigue and Poor Posture as it Relates to the Neuromuscular, Circulatory and Respiratory Mechanisms.' Almost as bad as mine. All in the remaining four weeks, too.

It seemed obvious to the students in the accelerated summer class that the specific titles assigned to them for their theses were designed to further Nash along in research that he was conducting to aid him in writing his next textbook. This notion irritated the hell out of Jay. He would have been much more interested in doing research on the physiological impacts on an athlete in playing football or something to do with specific recreational activities that could be incorporated into a physical education classroom or community recreation facility. However, Jay understood Nash's game plan, and the tradeoff for completing a Master's Program in an accelerated program was to help the venerated professor further his own career.

Thelma did her best to assist Jay in the final weeks of camp. She conferred with Jimmy Dow and sent Jay a book that Jimmy thought would be helpful in Jay's research on his obscure thesis topic. She confirmed in their brief phone conversations that the subject matter was not one of his choice, but one of Dr. Nash's selections, as research that he needed to further his own theories.

Jay wrote, *"Thank you and Jimmy for taking an interest in me and for sending me the book by McCurdy and Larson. However, I own the book and have it here with me. Then, too, this fellow Larson is my professor and I have him for the course and as you might expect there are hundreds of books by McCurdy and Larson floating around this place. I don't think that there are any other books that you could obtain for me at the Newark Library. They probably have many books on the subject I'm dealing with, but you'd never in a million years be able to locate them so there is no sense in knocking yourself out and trying. Anyway, I'll make out o.k. without it. Thank you for your interest but I can make it o.k."*

With the time racing by and the thesis deadline looming, Jay was beginning to see some easing in his workload as he neared the completion of his coursework and thesis. His next letter included the encouraging news, *"I am trying to clean up most of my work so that I can make it home this weekend. Suppose I come home on Friday and stop off in Newark, and go home later in the evening? But then maybe that isn't a good idea, what do you think?*

"Glad to hear that your mother and father are up in Saratoga. I guess your father is enjoying the rest and your mother is probably enjoying being away. Too bad about your girlfriend Gladys not coming to stay with you, but then perhaps you are better off without her, what do you think? Say you had better watch out so that you don't get too sunburned, or you'll be in no condition for wrestling."

Then, just as NYU Camp was nearing its final days, the miracle call that Jay had been praying for came. The principal of Highland Park High School, Alger Y. Maynard, contacted Dr. Nash and asked if he could speak to Jay Dakelman. Dr. Nash took down Dr. Maynard's phone number and told him that Jay would call as soon as his afternoon class was over at 2:00.

When Dr. Nash put the phone number into Jay's hand later that day, he patted Jay on the shoulder and said, "This is the principal in the town your folks are living in now, right?"

"Yes, sir," Jay replied, his heart skipping wildly.

"Well, go to my office and give him a call. And, Jay, I hope that it is good news for you. You deserve a shot."

Dr. Maynard explained to Jay that he wanted him to come into the office at Highland Park High School for a job interview the following week. "It's getting close to the beginning of school," Dr. Maynard explained, "and we have a recent opening that we need to fill."

Jay agreed to the interview and took a moment to call his mother and tell her the good news. She was equally excited and held her breath until Jay arrived home with his dirty duffle bag and living in tents behind him for the rest of his life. He also contemplated what a job offer would mean in terms of his relationship with Thelma. Was he ready to get married? He wasn't sure, but he also did not want to take a chance on losing her.

Well, for now, he would have to take it one day at a time.

If the world were perfect, it wouldn't be.
Yogi Berra

CHAPTER 13

HIGHLAND PARK HIGH SCHOOL

Jay gazed up at the majestic white dome of Highland Park High School, a grin stretching across his youthful face. He felt that the interview with Dr. Maynard and Physical Education teacher and coach Austin (Bus) Lepine had gone well and hoped that a phone call offering him the job would come quickly.

Dr. Maynard's secretary had ushered Jay into the inner sanctum in the early afternoon in late August. Dr. Maynard, a studious-looking man who wore wire-rim spectacles, offered a stiff smile as he reached out to shake Jay's hand.

"It's nice to meet you, Jay," he began. "I've heard some good things about you from Dr. Nash, and from Chet Redshaw down at New Brunswick High School." Redshaw had been Jay's high school football coach, and although things had not always gone smoothly between them, by the time Jay graduated, Redshaw and he had come to an understanding.

Seated near Dr. Maynard's desk was a giant of a man, thin but raw-boned. He wore gray sweats and had a silver whistle on a lanyard around his neck. Two very prominent front teeth gave his mouth an appearance not unlike a rabbit's. Dr. Maynard introduced Jay to the coach, saying, "This is Bus Lepine, the basketball legend from Rutgers University. I'm sure you were aware of the great basketball team of 1936 down at the University. Bus was a huge reason for the success of that squad. He is our Head Football, Basketball, and Baseball Coach at Highland Park High School."[1]

Having attended New Brunswick High School a few years after Bus, Jay had certainly been aware of the tall man's prowess at their alma mater. After all, Bus had been an All-State Basketball star in his senior year. In fact, his senior picture had a place of honor in the school's trophy case.

Bus raised a hand in greeting as Dr. Maynard began the formal part of the interview. He asked Jay about his summer studies with Dr. Nash on the theories regarding the importance of sports and recreation in the modern world.

Jay regaled Dr. Maynard and Mr. Lepine with stories about his recent studies and keen interest in the importance of recreational activities for everyone from the youngest to the elderly as well as his own participation in sports, particularly the incident in which he lost his front teeth shortly before student teaching was to begin.

"I understand that you have a strong interest in history," Dr. Maynard said. "Can you tell me about that?"

Jay explained that although European history was fascinating, his passion was for American history, particularly military exploits. An avid reader, it was not uncommon for Jay to stay up most of the night reading if a book had a hold on him. He particularly loved historical novels.

"Of course, this past summer I did not have much time to do any pleasure reading," Jay said.

"Well, if you come and work for us, your pleasure reading may be curtailed for quite some time. Let me tell you about the position that we have available. Unfortunately, it is not at the high school. You would be rotating between our three elementary schools, Lafayette, Hamilton, and Irving Schools, teaching Physical Education to the youngsters starting on the fourth-grade level. We would need you as a part-time Guidance Counselor the other two days of the week. Of course, the job would entail coaching three sports seasons as well."

Bus jumped into the conversation. "I need a good football assistant and a junior varsity basketball coach."

"What about the spring?" Jay asked. "I love baseball. I played catcher in high school and college, and I am a huge Yankee fan."

"Forget baseball here, son," Bus languished in his chair. "I'm the baseball coach. You would have to coach track."

Jay blanched. Track? What the heck did he know about track and field? Very little, except for what he had learned doing his Master's Thesis on distance running. Although it was disappointing to find out that the baseball position was not within reach and that he would be roaming all over Highland Park, a job was still a job, and he would learn to make the best of it.

During the interview Jay and Bus tried to measure each other up, considering that their lives would be intertwined closely if Jay came to work at HPHS as both men hoped. Although they hadn't had an opportunity to speak much, and they made as odd a couple as Mutt and Jeff, they were developing an unspoken rapport already that just felt right. They were linked by their strong roots in the New Brunswick community and high school alma mater. They were destined to learn that they had similar views on work ethic and "winning isn't everything . . . it's the only thing."

Dr. Maynard concluded the interview by shaking Jay's hand again and assuring him that the young candidate would hear from him within the next day or two.

Jay didn't have to wait very long for Dr. Maynard's call, which came the next morning. "Welcome aboard, Jay," the principal said. "I have a feeling that you will have a long and successful career here with the wise, old Owls of HPHS.

"Listen, Bus is eager for you to get started coaching football with him. The team is already in its double sessions, getting ready for the season. Can you come by the school later today and sign your contract?"

Jay's face flushed with excitement, but he managed to ask the question that he had avoided until the offer was made. "May I ask what the salary is?"

"Sure, we are offering $1500 for the first year," Dr. Maynard announced as though it was a king's ransom. Jay gulped. It was far from what a former soldier, who already had a Master's Degree in his content area, coaching three seasons, would have expected to make, but with the school year so close to starting and no other potential offers in sight, Jay agreed to the terms.

"I will be over after lunch," Jay said. "I'm helping my dad out this morning in the store. I guess I'm going to have to give him notice anyway," he laughed. "Please tell Bus that I will check in with him later."

The next phone call that Jay made was to Thelma. "I just wanted to make sure that you're coming down to Highland Park for the weekend," he said.

"Yes, I am," she replied, feeling butterflies flutter in her stomach. "How did things go with the interview?"

"Good, great, in fact. I got the job, and I will start coaching tomorrow."

Thelma's eyes misted momentarily with relief. She realized that Jay needed desperately to begin his career. After all, he had worked so hard on his Master's and teaching and coaching would take his mind off of the past events of which he was still unable to speak. The job meant, also, that he now might be ready to make the permanent commitment that she was hoping would come.

The next day Jay reported to Bus's "office," which was a tiny cubicle under the school's stage. The large room with bleachers that pulled out from one wall was the gym, with its freshly lacquered wooden floor. The closet in which Bus's desk sat was also small, and since the ceiling was so low, Bus had to stoop to fit his 6'3 frame into the space.

"Hey, Jay," he said. "I'm really looking forward to working with you. Sit down and let's talk for a couple of minutes before we go out and introduce you to the boys."

The two men chatted about their personal lives; Bus was married to a tall, athletic blond named Marge, also a New Brunswick girl. They had an eleven-year-old daughter, Gail, who would be in the sixth grade this year in the junior high classes. Jay told Bus about his girl, Thelma, and they agreed that it would be nice for their ladies to meet one evening in the near future.

"I'm the third football coach at HPHS," Bus informed Jay. "The first was Al Buschhorn. His team didn't do too well, so Paul Hancock came in and took over the reins for the next four years. The team record was still terrible until his last year when they were 6-1. Then I got the job in 1943 and we have been doing very well. However, we play a tough schedule and it's going to be a challenge this year, especially since we were 8-1 last year. Unfortunately, we lost a lot of seniors, and this is going to be a rebuilding season. We open with North Plainfield the third weekend of September."

Bus indicated that it was time for them to go out to the field and introduce Jay to the other assistant coaches, Dick Steadman and Bill Malthaner, as well as the 34 members of the 1946 Highland Park Owls football team.

The next few weeks sped by, with the opening day coming in the third week of September. Jay was getting used to his schedule of starting his day teaching Phys. Ed to the sixth graders, which he found that he was enjoying immensely. Gail Lepine, Bus and Margie's daughter, an eager young lady, was in his class at Lafayette School, which gave him another link to the Lepine family.

Preparing lessons for his students every evening was a task that the young teacher enjoyed thoroughly, even though he had to do it late at night since football practice and meetings often went until almost 7:00.

The latter part of the school day was completed in the Guidance Office at the high school. Jay found that he had a knack for helping the bright students of HPHS find the right college to suit their needs and dreams moving forward. In those early days, college applications and fees were nowhere near as complicated as they became later in his career.

Since Jay's family were members of Avas Achim Synagogue, the Orthodox congregation in New Brunswick, Jay decided to invite Thelma to join the Dakelmans for the celebration of the Jewish New Year 5707. Thelma's family was not very observant, so Pa did not object to her going away for the holidays. She took the train to New Brunswick on Wednesday afternoon, September 25 and a taxi up to the house on North Third Avenue since everyone was working when she arrived.

Ida was just getting home from the pharmacy where she did Lou's bookkeeping and helped Thelma with her overnight case.

"Happy New Year!" Ida greeted Thelma gaily. "It really is going to be a very happy one this year, Jay's first Rosh Hashanah at home in four years."

Thelma nodded and began to help Ida prepare the festive meal that would start off the joyful holiday. She was cutting apples up for the pre-dinner tradition of eating the fall fruit dipped in honey to symbolize the hopes that the new year would be a sweet one.

Jay breezed in, hyped up because the first game of the season was only days away. He and the other coaches had been drilling the team repeatedly on their skills to guarantee a win in their first outing. He went to his room, changed from his grubby sweats, washed up, and returned to the table just as Louie was sitting down, exhausted from a long day of standing on his feet. Although still in his forties, he felt like an old man because his feet never stopped hurting. He had even taken to wearing orthopedic shoes to help his aching feet.

Ida was a good cook, bringing out the traditional favorites for the season: chicken soup, chopped liver (one of Jay's favorites), and a savory brisket cooked in tomatoes and onion. Before eating, Louie carved the shiny braid of challah, and the family chanted the blessing over bread to signify thanks to God for his bounty and the joy of being together.

After the dishes had been washed and put away, Jay invited Thelma to take a walk with him since it was a beautiful night. Stars were twinkling above, and the air was crisp. Thelma wrapped a shawl around her narrow shoulders and together they walked toward Raritan Avenue, the center of town with its shops, bakeries, and numerous beauty parlors. The ladies of Highland Park were always concerned about looking their best, so salons flourished in the tiny borough.

Their stroll ended in the garage as it often did since there were few places for a moment of privacy when the family was home.

Jay motioned for Thelma to sit next to him on an old bench, which she did, and they enjoyed a few moments of kissing and being together on such a happy occasion.

"So, Thel," Jay began, looking at his stubby fingers a bit shyly. "I've been home for almost a year now, and I think it's going well between us. Right?"

Thelma's heart quickened a little. Was this finally it? What she had been praying for since Jay had first visited her on Columbia Avenue.

"Yes," she nodded, auburn curls bobbing.

"And now I've got the job . . . but it's not a lot of money . . . but, well," he stammered, "what do you say we get engaged?"

Thelma's green eyes filled with tears of joy (and relief). She nodded and waited a moment to see if her new fiancé would present her with a sparkling, little diamond ring to seal the deal.

He cleared his throat in embarrassment, knowing what she was expecting to see. "Here's the thing," he said hesitantly. "I would love to get you a nice ring, but we are going to really need a car. So, I am going to ask you if we can hold out on getting an engagement ring and use the money to buy a car instead?"

"Okay," she agreed enthusiastically, wanting her future spouse to see how cooperative and unselfish she was being. She could see his relief in her attitude by the relaxing of his taut shoulders.

"Do you have any idea of when we will tie the knot?" she asked.

"I was thinking maybe next summer, just before football season begins."

And this was how life married to Jay Howard Dakelman was going to begin for Thelma Jacoby Dakelman. Every decision made in their life together to be determined by an athletic schedule for one sport or another. But that was okay. She had her man, and together they went inside to share the happy news with Jay's parents.

Thelma could hardly wait until tomorrow when Jay's sister, Carol, would arrive from Philadelphia by train so that she could tell Carol that she was finally about to gain a sister. Although Thelma was several years older than Carol, the two young women had hit it off and were developing a bond that would last them a lifetime. In fact, she had decided already to ask the diminutive Carol to serve as Thelma's maid of honor.

The Owls were off to a great start, winning their first two games in the '46 season. Then disaster struck. One by one, HP fell to their opponents: Somerville, Bound Brook, Rahway, Princeton, Metuchen, Springfield, and Sayreville. Five of these seven games were shut outs, with the offense scoring a total of 21 points for the entire year. Jay was livid as well as frustrated.

Just two seasons before, the Owls had been undefeated for the first time in the school's history. They had captured the Group II Central Jersey Championship, putting the first trophy of its kind in the trophy case located in front of the school's auditorium.

So, how did this disaster happen? Jay knew the answer to this question. Bus lacked the vision in football that he had in baseball and basketball. Having never played the game, he didn't feel it in his bones the way that Jay did. Jay realized, also, that he had to find a way to get Bus to see things as acutely as he did and let Jay run the offense. It was critical for the future success of the Owl football teams.

On the home front, plans for the wedding were speeding along. Sam and Fannie Jacoby had secured the Kruger Auditorium in Newark, for Sunday, August 17, 1947. Thelma's talented and handsome brother, Milton, who was a lawyer by day, would entertain the guests with his outstanding and popular band. His wife's family, the Silpies, owned Kruger's Mansion and they were delighted to be hosting the large, prestigious wedding at their venue. Thelma and Jay looked forward to the big day with great enthusiasm, although Jay was already fretting about money, something that he did as much as he worried about each upcoming sports season.

Since the war had been over for only a little more than a year, a honeymoon to Europe did not make sense, so Thelma and Jay found a cruise to Newfoundland, dropping port in historic Nova Scotia. It would give them a rare bit of private time for the "wrestling" that they so enjoyed.

For the most part Jay kept his worries inside, not discussing them with other friends or family members. He was like the Spartan boy who had picked up a fox on the route to school and rather than let it go and be seen by his teacher and classmates, let it eat his insides until he fell from his desk. Stoic and silent, Jay rarely let on about the worries and memories that haunted him every day of his life.

Instead, he hid his problems with his enthusiasm for teaching and coaching. He loved his job, loved Highland Park High School, and enjoyed being a member of the highly regarded professional staff. And for now, being home and safe was enough for him.

Jay in his first office at Highland Park High School

Photo taken by Thelma Dakelman
Jay, August 1947, on his honeymoon with Thelma in
Newfoundland

The majority of society is ignorant and brainwashed from the influences of technology which affect every day of leisure and recreation.
Jay B. Nash

CHAPTER 14

THE IMPORTANCE OF RECREATION IN SMALL TOWN AMERICA

7:30 A.M. On an early July morning, JoJo Policastro opened his brown eyes and bounced out of bed. It was already hot and stuffy in his room, but JoJo didn't care. He threw on a tee shirt and shorts and raced to the kitchen where his husky-throated Mom had placed a cereal bowl and spoon on the table. JoJo chose Wheaties so that he could stare at the picture of Joe DiMaggio on the front of the box. Wheaties! Breakfast of Champions! JoJo shook out a healthy portion into the bowl and doused it with fresh milk from the Forsgate Farm in nearby Jamesburg.

Marie, short and rounding into pleasant plumpness, put a brown bag onto the table and said, "Don't forget your lunch, JoJo. I don't want you to starve. There's an extra peanut butter and jelly sandwich in there for Teddy in case he forgets his." A thermos full of cold milk made a metallic clank as she plunked it on the table as well. She plucked two apples from the Frigidaire and slipped them into the bag for good measure. JoJo was wolfing down his cereal, eagerly checking the clock. 7:45. Oh boy. Only a few minutes until his best friend, Teddy Kubiak, was meeting him outside for the quick bike ride to Highland Park High School, site of one of the three recreation camps sponsored by the township each summer.

This was the first day of the summer program that JoJo and Teddy adored. The whole summer lay before them, and, as usual, they had great plans for it.

JoJo's father, Joe Policastro, Senior, had long gone to his job as part owner of White Sales, the trucking company that he and his brother, Anthony, had established together. JoJo was very proud of his father, a proper businessman who donned a crisp, white shirt, starched and pressed to stiff perfection, a black suit and soft Italian leather black shoes, buffed to a glossy shine. Joe Senior had a booming voice, often filled with raucous laughter when he was with his three beautiful children, lovely Valerie, lively JoJo, and little Richie.

JoJo finished his cereal, leapt to the sink and gave his beloved mother a quick kiss on the cheek. "See ya later, Mom," JoJo said, grabbing his brown bag lunch and baseball glove. No doubt there would be an impromptu game on the dry field near the site of the camp after lunch today and JoJo needed to be prepared.

Teddy was waiting outside, and the boys hopped onto their bikes and soared the few blocks to the high school. "Hey Teddy," yelled JoJo, "bet you can't make it to the high school without having to brake." With that, JoJo raised both arms in the air and lifted his feet off his bike pedals.[1]

By the time the two boys soared to the back lot of the high school, Mr. Dakelman was already undoing the padlock on the shed where the camp supplies and athletic equipment were kept. The two wide doors swung open, revealing to the campers who had gathered around the shed, a plethora of new arts and crafts materials, gleaming boards for caroms and checkers, and sports equipment to keep every youngster busy all day.

There were two other recreation sites in town for the summer camps; one was on Kersey Street, not far from JoJo's house and the other was in Donaldson Park on the South side of town. However, since Coach Dakelman was in charge at the high school site, it was mostly boys who clamored around to start setting up the caroms and checker boards on upside-down garbage cans. The caroms game was a perennial favorite, and groups of children rotated all day long, waiting for their chance to poke at the caroms with wooden sticks.

Mr. Dakelman took out the horseshoe spikes and set them up a little bit away from the lone tree on the campsite, under which several arts and crafts tables were arranged for those who were interested in the craft of the week. Pretty soon, the metallic clang of horseshoes hitting the spikes added to the din of children's happy voices, free at last from the bondage of homework, teachers, and school.

As a former Eagle scout and participant in many recreational activities during his Master's Program at NYU, Jay was surprisingly deft at craftwork such as basket weaving and lanyard braiding despite his stubby fingers. The campers always marveled at his own lanyard, woven in the Highland Park High School colors, maroon and gray, using a combination of complicated stitches. When the children begged Mr. D. to "make me one," he smiled and said, "No, but I'll teach you how to make one for yourself." Then he would ask, "What color lanyard do you want?"

The children could select two colors and Mr. D. would put the necessary hook in place and get the youngsters started on their weaving of the snake stitch, the easiest stitch to make. When they had mastered the snake, he would demonstrate the barrel and the box stitches and before they knew it, the campers would sport their house keys on their own lanyards. After making one for themselves, they set about crafting one for their fathers, followed by weaving a colorful potholder on a small loom to take home to their moms.

JoJo and Teddy joined a group of kids who were scanning the bulletin board with the calendar of events scheduled for July.

"Wow! Look, a Yankee game in two weeks!" Teddy pointed out to JoJo.

"I can't wait. Let's get permission slips from Mr. D. and bring them back tomorrow. I don't want to miss out on this one. Look, it's the Yanks against the Red Sox!"

Jay smiled, watching nine-year-old JoJo Policastro and his best friend, Teddy Kubiak. He already had an eye on JoJo's throwing arm. For a youngster, he was accurate and could lob a pass much further than most boys his age. Teddy had a passion for baseball that was unusually deep; Jay had a good feeling about the future of both these young athletes.

Highland Park, with its active main street, Raritan Avenue, was a "Mayberry" of the North. From Cooper's Five & Ten to Sally's Steakhouse to Joe Fierro's barber shop to the Jack and

Joan children's store to the aromatic A & P, twelve consecutive blocks catered to the needs of the residents of the borough.

From its earliest days in the late 19th century, Highland Park took care of its children, providing healthy and enriching programs for them to enjoy all year round, not just during the school year.

As Physical Education programs grew nationwide, including courses on recreation, a teacher of Health and Physical Education was likely to be involved in creating and fostering programs to improve the lives of children during the summer as well as throughout the school year. Many other teachers enjoyed working with their young learners during the summer months as well, fostering programs in reading, writing, sciences, and the arts. The idea was to keep the children's skills from becoming stale before school re-opened in September.

Established by a township ordinance in 1947, Highland Park offered elementary school children the opportunity to enjoy supervised play during the summer months. Bus Lepine oversaw the activities as he and Jay put their heads together to create a program that became the model for other towns in the area.

The cover photo of *Highland Park in the 20th Century* shows the children from the neighborhood of Irving School, one of the town's three elementary schools, receiving awards at a "circus" party. The children were invited to bring an array of stuffed animals and prizes were given for the best horses, elephants, giraffes, bears, donkeys, lions, and seals.[2] Taken in 1948, among the adults in the picture are Austin "Bus" Lepine, supervisor of recreation; Mary Fortna, playground supervisor and elementary school teacher in town; police captain Fred Scheidig; and Mayor Alvah H. Cole.[3]

At Lafayette School Alice Boyce, a dedicated primary teacher, spent the summer weeks reading to the children who came to play in a supervised environment. A sprinkler was set up on the school playground for the kids to cavort in during the heat and humidity of a Jersey summer.[4]

According to Leon Kroll (Class of 1955), the daughter of Hymie Katz, an affluent business owner in Highland Park and borough tax assessor, loved hearing Mrs. Boyce read to the children who attended the Lafayette site. On days when Mr. Katz would pick up his little girl, he would treat her and the other children still in attendance at the day camp to ice cream pops from the Good Humor truck that circulated the neighborhood.[5]

In 1945 Katz sponsored the first Hyman Katz Day, where 300 township children frolicked in Donaldson Park, competing in games and contests for prizes, for which Katz paid. When Jay joined the recreation staff in 1947, Katz would provide him with a generous check each summer to purchase toys and games from Meyer's Toy Store in New Brunswick as prizes for the day's competitions. As one of the first "corporate sponsors" in the area, Katz would provide 30 gallons of ice cream and milk for the day as well.

The children howled with laughter while competing in potato sack races, ball tosses into wooden baskets, bobbing for apples, and even a fancy parasol contest.[6] Having worked with J.B. Nash in the study of recreation activities, Jay was innovative in creating games that even the most awkward kid could win. The object of Katz day was to level the playing field for all the children so that they could feel successful and satisfied. Even if they didn't win a coveted prize, they had a fun day under the blazing July sun.

Although Halloween was still months away, a costume competition was held on Katz Day. "On July 29, 1954, Katz's Kostume Party awarded prizes for Kutest, Kuaintest, and Korniest costumes," reports the book *Highland Park in the 20th Century.*[7] Therefore, one didn't necessarily have to be athletic to take home a prize on Katz Day.

Hymie Katz Day was one of the high lights of the summer for the children in town, and Mr. Katz beamed with joy each year as he watched the festivities.

Overseeing the high school summer program gave Jay several opportunities that helped the athletic program at HPHS. First, Jay could keep his eyes on the youth who showed promise in certain sports. One of the talents that made Coach Dakelman so successful was his ability to assess a student and know in what position and sport he would excel. A kid with an exceptional arm might be destined for glory as a quarterback (like JoJo Policastro) or a shortstop (like Teddy Kubiak.) If a boy sprouted up during the summer, suddenly sporting limbs like a daddy longlegs, a high jumper might be born.

In looking for pole vaulters, Jay always espoused, "I look for the kid who is a little bit 'crazy' because you must be crazy to pole vault."[8] He was fond of youth who were independent thinkers and curious about the world in which they lived. However, Jay also demanded discipline and playing by the rules. If a student deviated from that recipe, he wouldn't remain on a Dakelman team for long.

Jay enjoyed the dusty days on the playground behind the high school. He was often spotted carrying his latest playbook under his arm in case he was struck by an idea during the scorching summer days. Working in the summer was essential since his annual salary was pittance. However, in the beginning of his career, the summer job barely bought groceries. But the advantages to the schedule, the proximity to home, and the chance to watch the development of his athletes was too good to pass up.

Each year, Bus and Jay planned exciting trips for the kids who attended the program. There were two Yankee games a season, which were extremely popular. In the early days of the camps, the Mets hadn't come into being, but the Dodgers and Giants hadn't yet left the metropolitan area. The cost of bleacher seats and bus rentals were minimal so most kids could afford to go and still have money for a hot dog and soda at the famed Yankee Stadium.

The Bronx Zoo, Cowboy City, and Palisades Park were some of the other destinations that the youngsters got to visit. Probably the most popular trips ever planned were the two trips each summer of 1964 and 1965 to the New York World's Fair. The World's Fair, located in Flushing, New York, was a long hour and a half ride from Highland Park, but the buses departed at 8:30, bringing the kids to the gates of the Fair by 10:00 a.m.

Counselors and volunteer parents accompanied the children on the memorable field trips. Bus and Jay didn't always get to attend, but they did manage to make the trips to Yankee Stadium each year.

In the 1950s and 1960s, there was not an abundance of swim clubs for families to enjoy in Middlesex County. However, the YMCA in New Brunswick, about two miles from the program sites in Highland Park, had a nice-sized indoor pool. Each week, the children could take the transportation that was provided to the Y and enjoy the highly chlorinated pool "downtown." The kids arrived at camp wearing their bathing suits under their shorts and shirts and dove into the pool quickly upon arrival at the site in New Brunswick.

After a refreshing hour's swim, the students stood in line at the candy counter to purchase penny licorice strings and lollipops for the ride back to Highland Park. The splashing and laughter that occurred in the pool made wonderful memories for the children who felt so lucky to have the opportunity to swim, even if just for a brief time.

As time went on, Bus moved into school administration and no longer had his summers free. Jay took over supervising the three campsites: one at beautiful Donaldson Park, just down the street from his home on South Third Avenue, one at Kersey Street in the vicinity of Irving School, and the high school. His daughter, Beth, took over managing the high school site and ordering all of the materials needed for the expanding arts and crafts programs, as well as the board games that the kids loved to play. Gradually, girls began to come to the high school site. Beth grew fond of a six-year-old girl named Suzie, who wore a shy smile and had light brown hair that fell to her waist.

The recreation department also sponsored the town's Little League Baseball program, which was highly successful and gave Bus Lepine the opportunity to gauge the talent that would be coming his way eventually.

In the 1950s and 60s, parents supported their children in Little League in many productive ways. For example, on the evening of August 19, 1953 the active mothers of the Little Leaguers played a game against their sons, which ended in a 12-12 tie.[9] The mother of Teddy Kubiak, Marge Kubiak, played that night and was fortunate enough to see her son play in major league baseball some years later when Teddy became an Oakland A.

The kids who took advantage of the free programs looked forward each summer to having a great time and making memories to last a lifetime. Bus and Jay played a key role in keeping the program afloat for decades, something for which the Moms and Dads and Highland Park children were eternally grateful.

And equally important, the boys who would one day wear the maroon and gray uniforms of the Highland Park Owls, were given the opportunity to get to know the great men who would one day mold their futures.

Athletic competition develops some of the noblest qualities and talents in people. They must learn the secret of their own bodies, their strengths and weaknesses, their struggles and breaking points. They must develop the capacity to concentrate and the habit of self-discipline through long hours of exercise and fatigue as they learn to take account of their own strength. They must also learn how to preserve energy for the final moment when victory will depend upon a burst of speed or a last push of strength.
Pope John Paul II

CHAPTER 15

JoJo

The acrid stench of death was burning his nostrils. Ashes were swirling around him, clinging to his uniform which dripped with cold sweat. The thick air chained his limbs to the dank earth, bringing him closer to the hand-hewn channels filled with skeletal bodies. The taste of morbidity lay on his tongue as tears streamed down his face. There was no air here. He couldn't breathe. He couldn't escape. He couldn't get air into his lungs. He was dying with them, the victims of the Holocaust. They tore at his clothes, dragging him closer and closer to their naked torsos, boney fingers, and cracked skulls.

Jay sat bolt upright. According to the pink RCA clock radio on his night table, it was 2:40 a.m. The nightmare had returned, and he knew that he would not get back to sleep. He turned on his bedside lamp and groggily opened the latest Irwin Shaw novel that he was reading.

He was disturbed again; he knew it. Bus had confided to Jay about a rotten rumor that was circulating the tiny borough of Highland Park. Now that Bus had retired from coaching football, Jay was supposed to be the heir apparent. However, supposedly, members of the Board of Education whispered amongst themselves that they would never approve of a Jewish man leading the football team of Highland Park. Over their dead bodies.

"How could this be happening here?" Jay wallowed in his pain and grief. He had given so much of himself to this job, this town, these kids whom he loved beyond all measure. How could he, who had sacrificed three years of his young life to fight for freedom on the European front, be denied the job of his dreams due to his faith? This was an impossible situation and one that was fraught with humiliation.

In the morning, Jay called his good friend, Joe Policastro Sr., one of the owners of White Sales, a large trucking company in New Brunswick. Jay had known Joe's son, JoJo, the quarterback of the Owls football team and gifted athlete since he was a little boy on the summer playground at the high school. JoJo stood out as one of Jay's greatest joys in coaching. Not only was he fast, but he also had an arm that could possibly land him in the pros if he went to the right college, and even better, he was showing great aptitude for the strategies of the game. What was even more important was that when he coached JoJo, the young man absorbed every word and used Jay's advice to his advantage. The kid was smart!

Jay imparted the rumor to Joe Sr. that he had been told, not only by Bus but by a few other people who would be in the know as well. When Joe Sr. heard the story, his Mediterranean blood bubbled with anger.

"Jay," he said in his deep baritone, "we are not going to allow those men to prevent you from doing the job that you were destined to do."

Immediately, the boulder of doubt tumbled off Jay's chest and he began to breathe again.

"Leave it to me," Joe assured Jay. "I will take care of this."[1]

And take care of it, he did. Joe Sr. called the father of every football player on the team and asked them to come to the next Board of Education meeting to speak on Jay's behalf, which most of them did.

The sparkling new cafeteria where the Board of Education meetings were held was buzzing with the voices of angry parents who had come to express support for Coach Dakelman.

Joe Sr. was the first to grab the floor. "I am here tonight, along with many parents of the young men on the Highland Park High School football team, to speak on behalf of Jay Dakelman. Our young fellows have been working with Coach Dakelman since before they got to high school. They revere him and have trust in his ability to continue a tradition of winning.

"We are here tonight because we have heard speculation that this Board," Joe Sr. pointed to the Board president, "was planning to look elsewhere to bring in a coach to replace Mr. Lepine. Well, there's no need to look elsewhere; Coach Dakelman has been waiting to take the helm of this team since 1946, when he first came to our school."[2]

Several other agitated parents rose to voice their opinions that Coach Dakelman had earned the job by spending extra time with the boys daily to help them learn their plays and fine-tune their skills. After hearing the testimonials of Jay's dedication and genius as a playmaker, strategist, and "surrogate father for some of the boys on the team," the Board of Education had no choice but to approve him for the position of Head Coach.

Therefore, Jay took the helm as Head Coach for the football season of 1959.

"When Jay took over as Head Coach of the team, we all felt like we had been liberated," JoJo (Class of 1960) recalled. "It wasn't that Bus was a bad coach; he was just different. He coached from a position of pessimism. He would say things to us the night before a game like 'if we can hold them so they won't go over the goal line, we stand a chance to win this game.'

"With Jay, it was different. He was always optimistic, and he made us believe that we could and would win. And we did."[3]

In the 1958 season, Highland Park had been off to a great start. However, as the Owls were about to take the field against the tough farm boys of North Hunterdon, JoJo sensed that Coach Lepine was particularly skeptical about this game. "These guys are big and fast, and they are probably going to run all over us," he growled in the locker room before taking the field. "If you listen to what the other coaches and I tell you to do today, maybe we'll have a shot at beating them and make it through the year without losing a game."

As Bus was delivering his usual "doom and gloom" talk before the game, Coach Dakelman caught JoJo's eye. Coach D. gave him a surreptitious wink and pointed to his chest, signaling to JoJo, "Just pay attention to what I tell you to do, and it will be okay."

JoJo breathed a sigh of relief. Ah, there it was again, that encouraging smile that allowed JoJo to believe in his abilities to go out and win the tough game, no matter how much Coach Lepine eyeballed you.

The Owls hustled out to the football "stadium," which consisted of a few sets of bleachers on the sides of a cow pasture. North Hunterdon was in the hilly western section of New Jersey, not far from the border of Pennsylvania. Looking at the monstrous farm boys who played for the school, JoJo gulped and fought a stomach cramp for a moment.

Once he got his hands on the ball, however, he felt more secure, and the game turned into a strong defensive battle. The fact that Highland Park had been undefeated this year so far was due largely to JoJo's ability to get the job done in a pinch. However, despite the heavy hits and physicality with which this game had been played, the score was still 0-0. With just a few seconds left on the clock, Coach Lepine beckoned JoJo to the sideline for the play with which the coach hoped to nail the game.

"Here's what we're going to do, Joe. I want you to call a quarterback sneak," Lepine directed.

"Gee, I don't know, Coach, what if I drop the ball?" JoJo asked, his quivering voice giving way to the butterflies whomping in his stomach.

Bus growled back, "You'd better not drop the ball."

Years later, thinking about that play, Joe Policastro moaned, "Of course, this turned out to be a self-fulfilling prophecy. I fumbled at the five-yard line and the game ended in a 0-0 tie, blemishing our perfect season. Well, Bus couldn't let it go. Bus never cursed; the worst thing he would ever say was 'Applesauce,' which is, of course, what he said about our season at the fall sports banquet. Jay was never like that. He built you up, never looked to embarrass you.

"Jay was salty with his language," Joe continued, "but he was a master motivator because he could always find that thing in a kid that made him want to do better. After Bus's negative pep talks, kids would strive to concede to Bus, 'I'll show him, I can do better . . .' but with Jay, kids wanted to achieve because Jay made them believe that they could."

As the season of 1959 began, Jay adopted his first "woe is me" persona for gridiron theatrics. Although the prior year, HP had been undefeated with its 8-0-1 record, only four lettermen were returning. Fortunately, the backfield was in good shape with JoJo as quarterback and the fleet-footed Donnie Bell as halfback.

"Jay had a system that really worked," JoJo recollected. "We practiced hard on Monday through Thursday. On Friday, we didn't practice because Jay believed that if we didn't know the plays by then, we weren't going to. But on Friday nights, we were expected to be at the high school for a team meeting, which was very important. And God help you if the coaches found out that you didn't go straight home after a team meeting.

"Saturdays were game days, and on Sundays, the coaches got together in the morning to review the game film and look at films from the opponents of the upcoming week if they were able to get a hold of them. Everyone knew the routine and the discipline of the system worked well."

The season of 1959 opened with Highland Park crushing the Tigers of South Plainfield, 39-0, which extended HP's winning streak to ten straight victories. The Owl line was proving to be immovable, allowing South Plainfield to gain zero yardage in the entire game. JoJo completed two touchdown passes in this game, one to Eugene Fais and another to fullback Rich Tretsky. Donnie Bell was the leading ground gainer on that bright fall afternoon, catching several passes, dazzling the crowd on defense, and scoring a touchdown. The icing on the cake was when Jack Vanacore, playing on defense, intercepted a pass and ran forty yards for a touchdown.

Exuberant over their first win, the Owls jumped up and down and cheered as they entered the locker room to celebrate their first taste of victory. It was very sweet indeed.

The following week the Owls faced Clark Township, but the game didn't get off to the smoothest start. The Clark defense turned out to be tougher than expected. Dropped passes and fumbles marred the first half and when the team retired to the locker room for halftime, the score was tied at 0-0.

Joe looked at Donnie Bell and said, "I do not want this to end up like the North Hunterdon game last year."

"Me neither," Donnie agreed.

Coach Dakelman overheard the boys talking and asked them what they thought needed to be adjusted. He listened intently to the players and then addressed the entire team and gave some insights on what they had to do to change the trajectory of the game.

The second half went better. On the opening kickoff, Bell grabbed the ball and ran 52 yards, which took the Owls inside Clark territory. George Willan scored several plays later from the five-yard line, and HP was on the board. Unfortunately, Jack

Vanacore, the kicker missed the extra point, but at least the Owls had the lead.

Later, in the third period, a 45-yard drive culminated with JoJo pulling off a quarterback sneak and Vanacore making the extra point. The game ended in a 13-0 win.

Having defeated Clark, Jay was nervous that the team would be too cocky to play their best against the one team they really needed to beat this year — the team that had marred their perfect season the year before —North Hunterdon.

Although the team was pumped up when they took the field on Saturday afternoon, the game remained scoreless until the waning minutes of the second quarter when the Owls engineered a 45-yard march to the goal line. Rich Tretsky dove over for the score and Jack Vanacore made the first of four extra points that he scored that day. The key play of the drive was a 35-yard pass from JoJo to Donnie Bell.

Then with stunning rapidity, the Owls scored three times in the third quarter to guarantee the victory. A few minutes into the second half, JoJo threw the ball to Bell who dashed down the sidelines to score. Although Highland Park scored 27 points to win the game, the farm boys of North Hunterdon did manage to score two touchdowns, so this game was not the shut-out that the Owls had wanted to take.

Piscataway, a large township that bordered Highland Park, was the next opponent on the Owl's schedule. JoJo gave an inspired performance against the gold and black Chiefs, passing, running, and directing the team to a 27-6 victory. Joe threw scoring passes of 25 and 5 yards to Jim Borden and Jack Vanacore, respectively in the first half and then scored himself on a 54-yard dash in the fourth quarter. The only touchdown that the Chiefs scored on the day was the result of three consecutive fifteen-yard penalties against Highland Park.

When the refs threw the flag for a third time, Jay ripped off his hat and smashed it to the ground. Then he went chest to chest with the man in stripes, screaming himself hoarse.

The crowd roared. They got a charge out of seeing Coach D. lose his cool when the refs were out of line. But the truth was, Jay never lost his cool with a ref. In fact, every lunge towards the officials was calculated and occurred when Jay felt that the pendulum needed swinging to the Owl's side. Of course, the fans and the team didn't understand this. Jay was, truly, a master psychologist, and because of his carefully timed histrionics, he usually succeeded in turning the tide for his squad.

Steinert, located in the Trenton area, was a much larger school than HPHS, which was unnerving for the Owls. However, they won the fifth game of the season, 41-0, with five players scoring six touchdowns. Donnie Bell was the leading scorer with two touchdowns. On the first play from scrimmage, he circled the end for 52 yards and exuberantly held up the football as he crossed the goal line. Kicker Jack Vanacore scored the next touchdown from the 14-yard line, and Gene Fais grabbed a 38-yard pass from JoJo to put another six points on the scoreboard.

The stands at Sayreville High School were always spirited when their team took the field. However, Highland Park quickly quelled the cheering with JoJo passing for two touchdowns, one to Rich Tretsky, the other to Jim Borden, and then he took the ball across the goal line on a quarterback sneak. Donnie Bell had an outstanding game, scoring once on a 70-yard off-tackle sprint and again on an 80-yard pass interception. Jack Vanacore converted two of six extra-point attempts. The Owls took home a 38-0 victory.

Bernards High School proved to be another high-scoring shut-out with HP winning 34-0. JoJo scored one touchdown himself, threw for two more, and set up a fourth. The first score of the game came after Donnie Bell intercepted a pass and ran it back forty yards. Donnie and Rich Tretsky brought the ball down to the one from where JoJo sneaked over for six points. Early in the second quarter, Donnie caught a 31-yard pass, which produced the second score. George Willan carried the ball four consecutive times for a total of 31 yards for the third score. It was another sweet victory.

The eighth game of the season was against Frenchtown. However, it seemed for a while that the winning streak of more than two seasons was about to come crashing down. Behind 14-7 for most of the game, JoJo was able to score on a ten-yard keeper play, climaxing a 52-yard drive with six important points. Jack Vanacore's boot tied the game at 14-14 and it looked like the teams might end in a tie.

JoJo could hear Coach D's voice muttering from behind him, "A tie game is like kissing your sister."

No! Not a tie. Two passes, one to Jack Vanacore and the other to Eugene Fais and the Owls came away with a down-to-the-wire finish. (It was a good thing too, because JoJo did not particularly want to kiss his sister, Valerie).

Now the team of 1959 faced one last opponent . . . the dastardly Bulldogs of Metuchen. Everyone knew that Coach D. especially despised Metuchen. He wouldn't even drive through the town, often taking circuitous routes home to avoid having to set foot in the neighboring borough.

Before the team took the field for practice on Monday, the boys were asked to assemble on the bleachers in the gym. The coaches needed to address them. Jay and his assistants stood in a line in front of the empty gym with grim expressions on their faces; hands crossed in front of them, heads tilted down. Jay took a step forward and the boys could tell that something serious was afoot.

In his hands, he held up a condolence card. He showed it to the young men in front of him and announced grimly, "I need to read this to you."

The room was silent.

"To the Highland Park River Rats, Deepest condolences from the Bulldogs of Metuchen for getting your asses kicked on Thanksgiving Day. Do you hear us howl? We are coming for you. You are dead birds."

Pandemonium broke out when Coach Dakelman finished reading the card. Donnie Bell stood up and snatched the card from Coach's hands and looked at the return address on the envelope in which the card had come.

"Jeez! Look at this. It's stamped from Metuchen. These jokers really sent this card."

Every practice that short week, the coaches brought out the card and showed it to the team again, raising their ire to a feverish level. At the traditional pep rally the night before the game, Coach D. showed the condolence card to the entire school body who had come to cheer on the team and roast the Bulldogs in a bonfire behind the school building.

On Thanksgiving morning, JoJo rose earlier than ever, knots in his stomach. There was so much riding on this game. The undefeated season. Keeping the coveted Goal Post Trophy for another year as tradition between the two schools had dictated since 1936. The State Championship. His parents' pride in him. Coach Dakelman's first year as Head Coach with an undefeated season that would begin his legacy.

From the opening kick-off, however, the game seemed charmed. Metuchen fumbled the ball and Jim Borden recovered it. Three plays later, Donnie Bell plunged over from the one and Jack Vanacore converted the extra point. The second drive for HP covered 56 yards and ended with a pass from JoJo to Borden.

In the second quarter, Donnie slipped through the Bulldog line and squirmed 35 yards for a touchdown, giving HP a 20-12 half-time lead. Even though HP had the lead at half-time, it was clear that Coach D. was not happy. He gave a rousing speech, using as much of his "colorful language" as he could muster. He let his team know that he wanted them to win this contest in a blaze of glory that would forever punctuate the 1959 season as one of true championships.

The team rallied for the final gasp of the year. At the beginning of the third quarter, Donnie intercepted the ball and returned it 33 yards for a touchdown. As the drive ground on, JoJo, who was used to calling the plays more than 50% of the time, looked to the sidelines and mouthed to Coach D., "What should we do now?"

Coach shrugged his shoulders and gave a half smile. "I got you this far," he called back. "You figure it out."

Seven plays later, JoJo connected on a 34-yard pass to Borden to make the score 33-12 and put the game out of reach. The remarkable Highland Park defense had held the Bulldogs to

98 yards of offense while Highland Park had gained 339 yards on the day.

As the final seconds ticked off the clock, the Highland Park fans were screaming in awe of an undefeated season. The football team now had a 19-game winning streak. As the clock hit 00:00, a wave of young men surged toward their beloved coach and lifted him as high as they could in the air. The smile on Coach Dakelman's face was the biggest of his life. This moment was forever.

After all, "Winning isn't everything. It's the only thing."

The following evening, the Policastro family hosted one of the biggest parties in the history of Highland Park. Not a lavish home, but certainly a comfortable one; a banquet was set up in the finished basement of the house. On the center of a large table sat a roasted pig with a baked apple in its mouth. Platters of pasta and salad, rolls and butter surrounded the main attraction. Everyone filled their plates and cheered exuberantly as each player came into the room.

The piece de resistance, however, was the incredible cake crafted by the Berkley Bakery. Set up as a football field with the final score of the game in the center, a team of miniature football players in maroon faced a team of blue for a kickoff. The goalposts stood at either end of the cake, resplendent in maroon and gray ribbon. It was just the most delicious football field anyone had ever seen.

As the evening wound down, Jay went to thank Joe Sr. for all his incredible support to him and to the team. The men shook hands and then grabbed each other in a hug.

JoJo happened to walk in as the two men he loved most in the world embraced in the sweetness of success, victory, and watching a boy grow into a man.

JoJo looked at Coach Dakelman with tears in his eyes. Soon, he would be leaving Highland Park for some college, undetermined as yet. However, the story of JoJo and Jay was not ending here; in fact, it was only just beginning.

And it wasn't until years later that JoJo found out that it was Jay who had bought, signed, and sent the condolence card from the Bulldogs of Metuchen.

I'm a very competitive person. I just refused to compromise with excellence and never let up on what I demanded from the kids, and I never expected less from the kids than I was willing to give myself. If you don't do it yourself, then you can't expect it from others.
Jay H. Dakelman

CHAPTER 16

THANKSGIVING 1964:

HOW TO ACCOMPLISH AN

UNDEFEATED SEASON

A question asked frequently of Jay was, "Which of the games that you coached was the most outstanding?" he would usually answer, "The Thanksgiving game against Metuchen in 1964."

Jay's sixth season as Head Coach started off similarly to the five preceding years. Coach Dakelman was moaning about his defensive line and various other deficits that he worried about on the team.

Arnold Markowitz, a sportswriter for *The Star Ledger,* observed an early fall practice and commented, "It was past suppertime, but Jay Dakelman wasn't having any yesterday. The

Highland Park football coach wanted a certain reverse play run right.

'I don't care if it takes until 11:00 o'clock,' he yelled to his players. 'You're going to do it right.'

"So, they kept doing it. But a defensive lineman named Sano kept getting into the backfield to foul up the play."[1]

After trying to impress upon Sano where he was supposed to be, Jay then turned his attention to the guard who kept letting Sano get by him. Every detail of the play was caught and attacked when it was wrong.

Then Jay turned his attention to Jeff Watkin, an end, who kept running into trouble. Dakelman demonstrated to Watkin how to put his man down by hooking his knee.[2]

Even though Watkin had caught ten passes already in the season of 1964, Jay was livid that he couldn't get the block right. Again and again, Jay yelled, "Run it again, run it again!"[3]

Markowitz wrote, "The way he was storming about, you'd think this was the junior high taxi squad. Not an unbeaten varsity. But this is a part of the Dakelman technique. It is a technique that will give him a 49-4-1 record in six seasons if Highland Park can beat Metuchen on Thanksgiving Day."[4]

Jay gave a lot of credit to his coaching staff for the success of the season so far. For example, Don Arrigo, the new line coach who had just graduated from Westchester State College in Pennsylvania, had instituted two techniques that Jay attributed to Highland Park's winning record.

One of the techniques had to do with an unusual way of running the fullback draw in which Gary Beno, the fullback, would charge the line then hesitate. Quarterback Rich Policastro, the talented younger brother of JoJo, would then run behind Beno. While the defense would be chasing Policastro, Beno would fly down the field for 15 or 20 yards, not realizing that Poli had given the ball to Gary. The trick of this play was that Policastro slipped Beno the ball in an unconventional method from behind. Although it is easy to fumble the ball this way, the two players could do it smoothly and gain the needed yardage.[5]

Jay recalled having seen fellows from Westchester State demonstrate this play at a convention the previous year, and when Arrigo joined the HP staff, Jay told him that he wanted to start using this new play that was bound to confuse their opponents.

"For years, we haven't been able to run a punt back for a touchdown," Dakelman complained as he explained the second new technique that Arrigo introduced. "This year, we have had two and we got big yardage gains on several others. With Joe Pancza and Nate Stevenson deep to catch the kick, the line holds fast for a moment instead of charging the kicker. Then it peels back a single file in a direction predetermined by guard Sam Tumolo. Then it forms a wall in front of the ball carrier and moves back upward."[6]

Trick plays were one of the gimmicks that Coach Dakelman kept in his arsenal to keep the other teams on their toes. Joey Pancza, one of the halfbacks on the '64 team, laughed, "Coach Dakelman liked to put in one trick play every week," he reported. "That way, when the scouts from our opponents reported to their head coaches about that new play, the opposition for the next week would waste time preparing for a play that we were not going to be using again instead of concentrating on plays that we used regularly."[7]

Jay also liked to praise Jim Rogers, his assistant who ran the defense. "We use five or six different defenses in a game," Jay confided to Arnold Markowitz of *The Star Ledger*.[8]

One evening a few days before Thanksgiving, Jay interrupted his daughter, Beth, while she was doing her homework. The look on his face told her that something was terribly wrong.

"I have to go over to the Policastro's house," he said.

"Why?" Beth asked.

"Mr. Policastro had a heart attack and died," came the solemn reply. Jay had been the first person that the family had called in this traumatic moment. At the time, JoJo was a student at Holy Cross University, and Richie was the current quarterback for Highland Park and as big an asset to the team as his older brother had been.

The most shocking aspect of Mr. Policastro's death was that he had been only 41 years old at the time of his passing, and because most of the team knew and loved Mr. P. for his generosity and team spirit, they grieved with Richie and his family. However, despite Mr. Policastro's passing, there was still an important game to be played on the upcoming Thursday.

On a crisp Thanksgiving morning, Thursday, November 26, 1964, spectators, including alumni, parents, teachers, and students streamed into Memorial Stadium in New Brunswick for the traditional Turkey Day Classic between the Owls of Highland Park and the Bulldogs of Metuchen. Spirits were high, especially since the previous year, the game, although played at the request of Former First Lady Jacqueline Kennedy, had been solemn, with the band playing only a halftime hymn in memory of the recently fallen John F. Kennedy. Highland Park had won that game, but the usual excitement had been dulled by the shock that Americans still felt less than a week after the assassination of the vibrant, popular President.

Jay often remarked that Metuchen could have an 0-8 season, but if they beat Highland Park and took home the Goal Post Trophy for the year, it was as if they had won the Super Bowl. And although they had nothing on the line except that, as well as breaking Highland Park's string of undefeated games, the Bulldogs came out barking like madmen.

In the first quarter, the Owls got as far as the Metuchen 39, but a Policastro punt was blocked due to a poor hike from the center. Unfortunately, Metuchen recovered the ball on the HP 29-yard line, but then got a five-yard penalty. On the next play, Joey Pancza intercepted the ball on the Owls 15, but the Owls were charged with clipping and the ball was set back half the distance to the goal.

After the Owls gained only nine yards and made it to the 17, their punt went out of bounds on the Metuchen 39. Quickly, Metuchen picked up a first down to the 27 on two running plays and a pass from Meyers. After a three-yard pick-up on a running play, Gary Harris went through the middle to the 9 but fumbled. Sandy Mironov of the Owls grabbed the ball and the first quarter ended in a 0-0 draw.[9]

The momentum began to swing toward Metuchen in the second quarter. Jerry Meyers, the Metuchen quarterback, hit George Muha with a 33-yard scoring pass early in the quarter for a score. The Bulldogs scored the extra point and led the game 7-0.

The Owls didn't waste any time scoring after the next kick-off. Jeff Watkin grabbed the ball on the kickoff from the Owl's own ten-yard line. He ran it to the 27 yard line. Pancza picked up five yards and then Nate Stephenson added 11 on an end run to put the ball on the Highland Park 43. On the next play, Policastro faded back and hit Pancza on the right sidelines with a pass and the latter raced 35 yards to score. The play covered 57 yards. However, kicker and backup quarterback Jack Simcsak missed the extra point, so the Owls were still behind, 7-6 when the half ended.

At halftime, Joe Pancza went up to Coach Dakelman and complained about the Metuchen guys holding him and the ref not calling it. "They just keep grabbing me," Pancza protested.[10]

"Uh huh," Coach replied, making a mental note to start getting on the refs about it.

Metuchen got the ball when the second half began and moved it down to the HP 43. However, the Owls took over on downs. Aided by a 15-yard penalty, HP then moved the ball to the Metuchen 11. Pancza ran to the two, and then the Owls were penalized five yards. On the next play, Pancza was hit for a five-yard loss, putting HP all the way back to the 11. Joey was furious, stomping his feet, face red with rage for getting called for a penalty when the Bulldogs were still getting away with holding him. Even though Coach Dakelman was exhibiting his infamous antics, throwing down his cap and screaming at the officials, the referees remained blind to the fouls against Pancza.

Frustrated, the Owls tried a fake field goal with Simcsak throwing the ball to Pancza instead, but Joey was knocked out of bounds at the 2 and Highland Park had lost its scoring opportunity.

Metuchen wound up on its own 3 after three plays and a Bulldog punt went out of bounds on the 46. Fueled by their anger after not scoring on the previous set of downs, Highland Park needed only three plays for their second score of the match. Policastro hit Pancza with a pass near the right sideline on the 12 and Joe raced to the goal line as fast as he could. However, for the second time that day, Simcsak, who was usually flawless in his PATs, muffed the kick again and the score was 12-7, still too close for breathing room.[11]

Metuchen took the ball over on its 20 following the kickoff after the touchdown. McCombs burst through the middle of the Highland Park line but was pulled down by the safety after racing 27 yards to the 47. Meyers then passed to McCombs, who broke into the clear and reached the 1-yard line before being stopped. On the next play, McCombs dove over the line and scored Metuchen's necessary second t.d. Muha kicked the extra point, catapulting Metuchen into the lead.

Highland Park started a drive from its own 20 at the close of the third period and reached the Metuchen 6 where it was held for downs. The big play in this drive was a 20-yard run to the Metuchen 23 by Rich Policastro. The Bulldogs were penalized again, putting the ball on the Metuchen 13. Everyone in the stands thought, "This is it. This is where Highland Park will grab the lead." However, HP was not able to score, and Metuchen took back the ball.

The next time Highland Park got the pigskin back, they marched down to the 15-yard line again. Then Joey Pancza caught a Policastro pass, scoring a third touchdown for the Owls. However, the refs threw a flag and called back the score, citing an illegal man downfield.[12]

Having had the wind knocked out of them, Metuchen was able to hold HP and had a chance to take the ball in the other direction again. After two successful runs, the Owls dug in, with the clock tick, tick, ticking down to the final four minutes. Fans were biting their nails through their woolen mittens, holding their breath to see what miracle Jay was going to spring to win the game.

Rich Policastro tried a pass to Pancza, which didn't work. Joey looked at the sidelines where his buddy Glen Meltzer, the Owls standout end, was sidelined with a broken wrist, which he had suffered the previous day. Joe couldn't help but smile when it popped into his head that it was often Glen with whom Coach Dakelman sent in the plays. The only problem with using Glen for those missions was that usually from the bench to the huddle, Glen forgot which play Jay had called.

In fact, in one game earlier this season, Coach D. had written the play on a slip of paper for Glen so that he wouldn't forget it. Excited, Glen held the slip of paper and said, "Play 52."

Just then, a referee became suspicious and ambled over to the Owls as they were finishing their discussion of the play. Seeing the ref heading toward them, Glen stuck the slip of paper into his mouth and swallowed it just as the official queried, "Okay boys, what's going on here?"

The offense looked up innocently at the referee and said in unison, "Nothing. . ."[13]

Now, here they were, down to the wire. This team had worked too hard, cared too much to give up now. And then Poli said, "I'm going to pitch a little screen to Gary, and you're going to go, man, go."

The play started. Gary took off, Richie hit him perfectly with the short pass, and then Beno took off down the field. Big man Craig McGrath, who later played for Army, made a critical block that took out two players about six yards in front of the line of scrimmage, which cleared Gary's path to make it across the goal line with seconds left in the game.

The perfect season was saved in that miraculous moment.

As the young men lined up for the final kick-off of the game, Richie looked at Jack Fertig, a sophomore who was going to boot the ball back to the Bulldogs one more time. Since Richie was still reeling from the sudden death of his dad, it had been insanely difficult for the gap-toothed young man to concentrate completely on football.

"Man, I thought we were going to lose this one," Richie said, shaking his head.

Fighting back tears, Fertig said gently, "You didn't honestly think that your father would let us lose today, did you?"

Richie gave a serene smile and silently thanked Joe Policastro Senior for always being there when the boy needed his dad.

Highland Park's performance in this last game of the season had been as sparkling as a glass of champagne. Jeff Watkin had established a school record with his 11th pass interception, the 17th of his scholastic career. Rich Policastro had completed 10 out of 14 passes for 234 yards and his three touchdown passes, adding up to 26 for the season, which enabled him to break the record set by his brother, Joe, in 1959. Richie had gained over 1000 yards passing during the season. Gary Beno led the tackling with 17 on the day.

As was tradition, once the Highland Park team and band buses crossed over the Raritan River Bridge, the buses stopped to let the kids out for the celebratory march down Raritan Avenue, the main street of the town.

Jack Simcsak, furious with himself for nearly costing the team the game by missing two PATs, threw his mouthpiece into the Raritan River as the team disembarked the bus. But soon, the exuberance of his teammates in the big win overcame his anger and he joined in the revelry as the band played:

Cheer, cheer for Highland Park High.

Keep up the spirits, don't let them die.

As our boys march down the field,

There is no team to which we will yield.

Cheer for the red and cheer for the gray!

March onto victory, show them the way,

As our boys go marching on,

We'll cheer them to victory.

A vital team characteristic is the ability to overcome adversity.
Any team acquires experience and endurance as it learns to
fight back. This, in turn, builds the kind of character which
seldom crumbles at a time of crisis or testing.
Tom Landry
(Coach of the Dallas Cowboys, 1960-1989)

CHAPTER 17

1976: THE DREAM TEAM

Felix Lee was the running back that every coach dreamed of having. At 230 pounds, in both his Sophomore and Junior years, Lee had rushed for over 1000 yards. As his Senior year approached, he was bigger and stronger than ever so the challenge to gain more yardage than previous years was going to be a spectacular one.

At the New Jersey State Outdoor Track and Field Meet of Champions the previous June, Lee resembled a locomotive, barreling down the track in the finals of the 100-meter dash. He rocked slightly from side to side as he outran the rest of the field so fiercely that it looked like he had to get out of his own way as he zoomed down the track.

College coaches from all over the country had been calling about Felix Lee for the last two years, but now the recruiting had gotten serious. Lee was a decent student, a well-mannered and soft-spoken young man, who lived in the weight room on most days after school. He wore his hair in a full Afro, and his startling green eyes sparkled every time he pressed the button on his boom box to replay the O'Jays singing "For the Love of Money" as he pumped iron.

Felix Lee was one in a million.

Not only was Felix a shining star on the football team, but he was also surrounded by a galaxy of outstanding and committed athletes who were already sweating through the week of double sessions that began once the NJSIAA opened the season officially for practice on August 31st.

Jay eagerly anticipated a great season with Junior Bob Nawy as quarterback, an able athlete, Georgie Brunson, Felix's best friend, at wingback, the agile Riese brothers, Mitchell and Steve, also at wingback, and Alan Figg at fullback. None of these athletes came near Lee, who played tailback in size, but they were smart and fast, allowing for a lot of optional plays to be designed.

"Oh yes," thought Jay, "this is going to be a fun year."

1976 brought another new aspect to the season that was going to make it an exciting year. Through Jay's efforts, he had managed to solicit seven other schools to join Highland Park in the creation of a new conference designed to accommodate the smaller schools in the Central Jersey area. Since the disbandment of the Garden State Conference in 1971, Highland Park had been an independent school, which had made scheduling for the football season a nightmare. Although Highland Park was a small school, its stellar reputation as a football powerhouse caused other schools of its size to shy away from scheduling a match against them.

At that time, the Middlesex County Conference consisted of 13 schools, including Carteret, Cedar Ridge, Colonia, East Brunswick, Edison, John F. Kennedy, Madison Central, Perth Amboy, Sayreville, John P. Stevens in Edison, and Woodbridge.

South River and New Brunswick had decided to leave the MCC and join Highland Park in the new conference. The other schools that were moving to the Bicentennial Conference were North Brunswick, St. Peter's, St. Pius, St. Thomas Aquinas, and South Brunswick.

In a conversation with Mark Plescia, a correspondent for the *Home News*, Jay expressed his joy at the creation of the new conference. "Today, it is a necessity to be affiliated with a conference. If you're not in a conference, then you are left out."[1] He also noted that a league format facilitates scheduling and creates healthy rivalries with added fan interest. Jay continued, "Each game becomes important in league standings, and the kids get more recognition being on a conference team."[2]

A few critics of the new league alleged that the Bicentennial Conference was composed of weaker teams that couldn't cut it against the larger schools. Jay countered that attack by arguing, "This conference will be a strong, competitive conference and will have several outstanding teams that could compete in any league."[3]

Yes, this was going to be the sweetest year of his eighteen as Head Football Coach. He could just feel it.

Then, disaster struck. Early one morning before practice, Felix and some of his teammates were horsing around in the gym, as young men will do. Suddenly, as Jay was writing some notes in his office, Jay heard Paul Pappas yell, "Hey Coach Dakelman, Coach, come out here quick. Felix is hurt."

Jay sprang from his wobbly desk chair, ran out the back door of the gym and saw Felix lying prone on the asphalt parking lot. Felix, moaning in pain, explained that he and Paul had been jumping off the back steps of the school and he just went down. Felix managed to get up and hobble away, trying to shake off the pain.

The next day Felix had Murph, the gifted Athletic Trainer that Highland Park High School had inherited when Murph retired from his job at Rutgers University, check out his leg. Murph examined Lee's knee and shook his head sadly. As Jay stood by, he knew that he had seen enough injuries in his time to know exactly what this was: a torn ACL, which would mean a season-ending surgery, and a very "iffy" future for the highly sought-after fullback.

By lunchtime Jay knew the verdict, and it wasn't a good one. Felix would never don his high school uniform again. In fact, surgery was scheduled already for the following week when the torn cartilage would be removed from the talented young man's damaged knee.

Jay took his seat at the end of the kitchen table and put his head in his hands as he fought back tears. All the time and effort that this fabulous athlete had put into becoming the best back in Middlesex County history had been crushed in the blink of an eye. Done. Over. An undefeated season? Ha! That was a laugh.

As Thelma laid a tuna fish sandwich in front of her distraught husband, Beth did her best to cheer up her father's flagging spirit.

"Come on, Dad," she said, "you know that you'll come up with something. You still have a great team there."

He looked up at her and grimaced. "You don't understand," he growled. "You can't make chicken soup out of chicken shit."

If he hadn't looked so dejected, Beth would have laughed at Jay's sullen response. First, he was a miracle worker; everyone who loved high school football knew that. Second of all, it was Jay's nature to take on an air of despondency when an injury occurred, or some other disaster threatened to disrupt the success of an impending season. And certainly, he did not mean what he said about the team without Felix Lee. Although losing Felix was a tragedy, not just for the Owls but for the future of an exceedingly talented, young man. In her heart Beth knew that it would be all right, but at that moment, nothing was going to console Jay.

Trying to explain how a 17-year-old boy deals with the devastation of such an injury is nearly impossible, but Felix Lee confided that when he went into the hospital for surgery, "Coach Dakelman was so loving and kind to me."[4] Jay had become, for Felix, as he had for so many of his athletes, a substitute father, filling in for men who were missing in the lives of their sons.

Hearing Felix talk about the development of his relationship with Coach D. is a beautiful story. "In the spring of my 8th-grade year, I was hanging around the track and Coach invited me to practice with the high school team."[5] From then on, Felix became aware that Coach Dakelman was keeping a watchful eye on him.

Felix had little exposure to the idea of attending college or playing football at a major university powerhouse. "One day, Coach called me into his office and had me sit down. He started talking, and whenever he talked, I just listened."

"He went on about the attention that I would be getting from college scouts and the pressure that it was going to cause me. He went on and on and I just sat there and listened. When he finished and I walked out of the office, I remember thinking, 'I have no idea of what Coach was talking about.' That's how inexperienced I was."[6]

Despite Felix's injury and subsequent surgery, the college scouts did not stop coming to Highland Park to meet the outstanding athlete and continued to invite him to their big schools on college visits. Jay was heartened that the attention hadn't waned despite Felix's setback.

The first game between the new Bicentennial opponents, St. Thomas Aquinas of Edison and Highland Park was played on Saturday, September 25, 1976. As the team prepared to take the home field, Highland Park High School graduate Barry Levine, an outstanding sportswriter for the *Home News*, talked to Jay.

"It isn't bad enough that we lost Felix to the knee injury last week," Jay groaned, "on Monday I found out that senior Frank Jiminez, a two year-year starter as 'Monster Back' is academically ineligible. Due to these two losses, we had to revamp our offensive and defensive units this week, and we only had three days of practice to do it."[7]

Once the game got started, it was obvious that the defense was having difficulty in containing the Trojan's shifty Junior tailback, Mark Santangelo, who ran for 108 yards in six carries. For a while, the HP Owls revamped secondary looked vulnerable against the pass, but it did manage to stop St. Thomas three times inside its 22-yard line during the first half.[8]

The first time that the Owls got possession of the ball, Bill Brunson began and ended the drive, scoring Highland Park's first touchdown on a 22-yard run. The extra point was kicked by Bob Stavrides.

Late in the first half, Bob Nawy, the Owl's quarterback, threw the ball 60 yards to Mitchell Riese and HP scored its second touchdown of the game, but the extra point was blocked, making the halftime score 13-0.[9]

Taking advantage of one of the five Highland Park turnovers, St. Thomas finally broke through the Owls' defense and marched 80 yards in three plays for their only score of the game. In fact, after their one touchdown, the Trojans never penetrated deeper than the Owls' 43-yard line for the remainder of the contest.[10]

Jay's comments after the game were carefully worded to give praise where it was due but to point out where work needed to be done. "Considering it was the first time that Alan Figg and Billy Brunson played together in the backfield, they did an adequate job. Figg was quick off the ball. So was Brunson, but he must learn to read holes and follow blockers."

Dakelman also explained that after Lee's injury, he decided to revamp the offensive philosophy of the game. "We went away from a basic 'I' attack to a 'Wing T' offense. We lost a lot of our inside running attack when Felix got injured."[11]

Of the performance of the new backfield, Jay stated, "Bobby (Nawy) threw the ball well and (Bob) Stavrides made some excellent catches . . . The Rieses, Steve and Mitchell, were a big help, returning kicks, catching passes, and punting. Also, Ken Carkhuff made an excellent block so Mitch could run for the TD after he caught the pass."[12]

Praise went to Ray Harrison and Paul Waller. "They were excellent, just excellent. Harrison plays touch all the time and leads our defensive line while Waller, a linebacker, gives us the leadership that we need. Also, Mike Ryan made some good plays at the end."[13]

All in all, Coach Dakelman was happy with the team's first triumph of the year, concluding, "We weren't sharp, but we had so many changes and adjustments to make that it really wasn't too bad for the first game."[14]

On October 2, Highland Park faced its second Bicentennial opponent, North Brunswick. Highland Park jumped to a 7-0 lead with 5:08 remaining in the first quarter when Nawy combined with senior wingback Mitchell Riese on a 33-yard scoring pass. Bob Stavrides then booted the first of four successful extra points in the game.[15]

The Parkites added another score on the opening play of the second quarter when Nawy clicked with Stavrides, a wide receiver, for 66 yards. Stavrides had managed to get behind the Raiders' secondary, catching the ball near the North Brunswick 30, racing the remaining yards untouched.[16]

The Owls increased their halftime lead to 21-0 with 2:25 remaining when Junior Steve Riese scampered seven yards around the left end into the corner of the end zone.[17]

Harrison, an offensive tackle, made an excellent effort on the play, blocking one defender and shielding another to assist Riese into the end zone.[18]

Highland Park made its final score on the first play of the 4th quarter when Steve Riese caught a 40-yard pass from Nawy.[19]

Jay gushed about the win, "Our kids were great, just great. The kids really worked hard in practice all week and invested their time rather than spent it.

"Nawy threw the ball exceptionally well, especially when he went long for the three touchdowns . . . Defensively, our kids played a superb game. We got a great pass rush from our front five ends, Joe Campbell and Mike Ryan, tackles Adam Mosston and Raymond Harrison and middle guard Sal Raspa. The secondary of Ken Carkhuff, George Brunson, Bob Stavrides. Mel Dixon and Steve Riese both showed marked improvement over last week.

"Also, linebackers Paul Waller and Vinnie Hudson did an excellent job."[20]

Coach Dakelman showed the level of his expertise by commenting on changes made to the offense during this week's practice. "We're using an offense similar to the one used by George Conti at Metuchen High School 15 years ago." Then Jay added, "We're starting to come together as a team now . . . I just hope it continues."[21]

Despite continued adversity, Highland Park kept rolling as the Owls met their third opponent of the year, the Monroe Falcons. Coach Hughie Walsh, a legendary instructor who had left his post at South River to be the first Head Coach at the new Monroe High School, admitted at the end of the game, "There was a six-minute stretch from the third to the fourth quarter where they just blew us out."[22]

Until that point in the game, it had been a tough contest between the two teams. One play before the end of the first period, the Falcons lost the third of what would be six fumbles in the game. The recovery by Adam Mosston of HP led to a 37-yard scoring drive capped by a 10-yard sweep by Junior Steve Riese.

On the next series the Falcons came back with a Glenn Pfeuffer score. However, that was all the scoring that Monroe would do in the game, which Highland Park won, 30-8.[23]

Reflecting over this latest win, Coach Dakelman mused, "We played the first half poorly. In the second half, we came out with our chins up. We came to play. In the second half, we were more aggressive; we covered the corners better. And Paul Waller and Ray Harrison were just outstanding on defense."[24]

Coach Dakelman had praise for the offense as well, especially for the running of Steve Riese." We lost Felix Lee, now George Brunson is hurt. Steve Riese is doing just a great job. We're a young team with a lot of sophomores and juniors. We only had one senior in the backfield all day. But that whole offensive team was charged up. We've come along as a team."[25]

Coach Walsh agreed with his counterpart, saying, "They probably were the better team. They just wore us out. We played hard but Highland Park always has a good team."[26]

The fourth game of the '76 season was against Jay's high school alma mater, New Brunswick. Played on October 9, Highland Park's staunch defense limited the Zebras to 116 yards in the game, giving them another victory, 19-0. Although Highland Park had competed in many sports against New Brunswick over the years, this was their first gridiron match, and bragging rights for the teams from the "banks of the old Raritan" caused a lot of friction between the competitors as the game unfolded.

Highland Park went into the locker room at halftime with a 6-0 lead, which they were lucky to have. Late in the first half, New Brunswick, on their own 23-yard line, had a second and seven. They swept to the right, but the pitch was bobbled, and the fumble was recovered by defensive tackle Raymond Harrison, who ran it in for the Owl's touchdown.

In the initial drive of the second half, Highland Park moved 62 yards in eleven plays. Quarterback Bob Nawy, who had completed one of seven passes in the first half, was successful in all six of his pass attempts on this drive. The last toss was to Bob Stavrides, who scored the touchdown.[27]

On New Brunswick's next series of downs, the Zebras attempted the same sweep. . . and got the same result. Highland Park's middle guard, Mike Krisza, pounced on the loose ball on the New Brunswick 12-yard line. The Zebras contained the Owls but were unable to move, forcing them to punt from their 17.

With 1:05 remaining in the third period, Steve Riese scored another touchdown from a sprint-out pass from the five-yard line. This was the culmination of an 11-play drive.[28]

With eight minutes left in the game, Zebra Coach Bob Miller inserted safety Derwin Booker at quarterback, who moved New Brunswick 43 yards to the Highland Park 17. However, Stavrides nabbed the ball in the air, raising the ire of the frustrated New Brunswick squad. A squabble had broken out earlier in the fourth quarter, which the officials had quelled. However, with 2:34 left to play in the game, another fight broke out between the rival teams. The referee grabbed the game ball and wisely signaled that the game was over.

Despite the dubious ending of the game, Jay was elated. He spoke to the press, raving about his defense. "We have only allowed two touchdowns in four games," he said. "Raymond Harrison (tackle), Paul Waller (inside linebacker), and Mike Ryan (end) played exceptional games for us. Mike Krisza, who we inserted as a middle guard at the start of the second half, helped us control their big fullback from running up the middle on us."[29]

Jay praised corner linebacker Ken Carkhuff for helping the Owls to control New Brunswick's fierce fullback from running up the middle as well.

With New Brunswick's hard-hitting defense designed to stop the Owl's outside running attack, Highland Park ran effectively inside with fullback Alan Figg moving well on dive plays. "Figg played much better in the second half, but he is capable of playing even better," Jay mused, thinking about how to motivate Figg to do more.[30]

Of course, there was praise for the offense as well. Coach D. pointed out that Nawy completed nine of 18 passes with Riese and Stavrides catching four each.

Always conscious of how the opponents on the losing side felt after a game, Jay praised the athletes of his alma mater. "New Brunswick did an excellent defensive job against us … They stopped us on the outside very well . . . They have very good personnel on defense."

The dejected New Brunswick coach, Bob Miller, whose team was now 0-4-1, lauded the hard play of his kids despite the bitter loss. "I was extremely pleased with New Brunswick. We did very well and I thought that we contained them until they found a defensive weakness in the flat area. Our defensive ends, Jim Holeli and James Lockhart, and inside linebacker Joshua Galbreath played outstanding games."[31]

A week later, Highland Park faced South Brunswick, the only other undefeated team left in Middlesex County. Acting on his promise of the previous week, Coach D. employed Figg to the best of the young man's ability. "Figg finally ran the way we thought he could," remarked Jay after the contest." "But our second half ground attack can be attributed to the outstanding play of our whole offensive line."[32]

The game was tight, 7-6 in favor of the Owls, at the beginning of the 4th quarter. Swiftly, in the span of 1:44, Highland Park burst forward, scoring two rapid touchdowns to take a 19-6 lead.

Quarterback Bob Nawy, who completed 13 out of 19 passes on the day for a gain of 149 yards, took the ball in for the first of the twin t.d.'s on a quarterback keeper, following a 30-yard drive.

Seconds later, South Brunswick's q.b Rich Nasdeo threw the ball directly in the line of sight of Bob Stavrides, who returned the pigskin for 33 yards, falling at the 5-yard line. Two plays later, Steve Riese raced five yards into the end zone on a quick pitch. It wouldn't have happened if Raymond Harrison hadn't made a block, creating a hole for Reise to drive through.

Not willing to surrender, and with plenty of time left on the board, South Brunswick's talented return man, Ben Grover, grabbed the ball on the kick-off and sprinted 77 yards to the Owl's 7-yard line. One play later, halfback Greg Richardson, slicing off tackle, rammed across the goal line for the much-needed score.

Nasdeo then flipped a pass to Herb Pemberton for a two-point conversion, narrowing the Highland Park lead to 19-14 with 8.43 remaining in the game.

The battle continued until the bitter end. With less than a minute to play in the game, Alan Figg scored from the ten-yard line as the culmination of a four-play drive that covered 24-yards.[33]

George Bossow, in his first year as head coach of South Brunswick praised his team by saying, "We didn't give up through the game. When we were down 19-6, we could have folded, but we battled back. Highland Park has a good team, and you have to be good to beat them. But I feel that we still have a good team even though we lost."[34] Once again, Jay lauded the defensive play of Joe Campbell, Mike Ryan, Adam Mosston, linebackers Vinnie Hudson, Paul Waller, and monster back Kenny Carkhuff.

The opponent to be faced on Halloween worried Jay during the days that followed. St. Peter's, a weaker link in the Bicentennial Conference, was having a rough year, and Coach D. had learned over the years that sometimes the underdog became the most fearsome opponent. The players read the newspaper articles each week and were aware of their next rival's weaknesses, often allowing for sloppy play. To make matters worse, several players became ill during the week and missed practice. All in all, Jay could feel that the team was flat.

Protecting their best start since the team in 1967, Jay pondered how to rev the kids up for the St. Peter's game. Just as he had predicted, St. Peter's dominated in the first quarter of play, with a 7-0 lead.

Fortunately, in the second quarter, the Owls realized that if they were going to win this contest, they had to settle down and play well against a worthy opponent.

The turnaround started when Joe Campbell recovered a Cardinal fumble at the HP 31. Gaining 69 yards in the next few plays, Alan Figg became a hero, recovering an HP fumble in the end zone for the first Owl touchdown of the day. A two-point conversion was scored when Nawy passed the ball to Steve Riese, giving Highland Park a one-point lead.[35]

St. Peter's went through one set of downs before having to punt to Highland Park after the Owl's touchdown. Just five minutes after their first score of the day, Nawy tossed the ball to Bob Stavrides, who took it in for another HP touchdown.

In their next possession, Riese grabbed a screen pass from Nawy and darted 44 yards to his goal-line destination. The knot in Jay's chest began to ease a bit as he felt the boys find their juice again. "I don't like to lose," he said to himself, "and neither do they."

After the game, which Highland Park ended up winning 40-15, St. Peter's Coach Cary Hamrah, in his first year, bemoaned the loss. "If we would have scored on that second series when we lost the ball, we might have had a chance to win. We caught Highland Park flat and that gave us a psychological edge."[36]

As he waited for the weekly phone call from the local radio station, WCTC for their 5:00 football wrap-up program called "Football USA," Jay rested in his favorite, battered armchair in the paneled den of the Dakelman home. "Winning is a compulsive thing," he thought. "But every week, protecting that undefeated record becomes harder as the wolves become hungrier to take you down."

In later years, Jay came to refer to that hunger as "eye of the tiger."

In discussing why professional teams rarely repeated back-to-back Super Bowl wins, Jay used the lyric from the second *Rocky* movie to explain it. "When you win consistently, your opponents get hungrier and hungrier to take you down. Those who want it the most win. That's why you don't see back-to-back Super Bowl Champs. Eye of the Tiger."

How does one continue to convince a group of 15, 16, and 17 scrawny kids that they are of championship ilk? The next few weeks were going to present extremely challenging games, starting with the November 7 contest between the Rams of South River and the Owls. Although the Thanksgiving Day game and the annual battle for the Goal Post Trophy had established Metuchen and HP as traditional rivals, often, the games against South River provided the thrills that led to a more bitter rivalry. Highland Park had a long string of wins over Metuchen in the last two decades, but the fights against the Rams were becoming legendary as the power shifted back and forth between the two towns every year.

Coming into the South River game this year, the Ram's record was 3-2, while HP was still undefeated. But a 3-2 South River team was a force that was going to have to be faced with an unwavering belief that a perfect season was within reach.

The November 7 game pitted two outstanding quarterbacks against each other, Bob Nawy of HP and Keith Hudak of South River. Hudak, who was only a sophomore, had thrown 13 touchdown passes in the previous five games while averaging 25 passes a game. Although young, he presented as a formidable opponent against Nawy.

The first half of the game went scoreless, largely due to the two excellent defensive teams that were pitted against each other and several missed scoring opportunities by both squads.

However, that changed as the second half began. The Owls took the opening kickoff in the third period and marched 69 yards down the field to score the game's first touchdown. A nine-yard pass from Nawy to Steve Riese climaxed the drive with 7:14 left in the period. Stavrides kicked the extra point, giving the Owls a 7-0 edge.[37]

Coach Dakelman and Bill Csatari, the Ram's coach, agreed that the next series of downs defined the game's outcome. The Rams took the kickoff and moved quickly from their 23-yard line to the Highland Park 19 where they had a first and five situation.[38]

Attempting to pass, Hudak rolled right and fired deep, but the Owls' safety, Melvin Dixon intercepted the ball on the HP 2-yard line and returned it four yards.

Three plays later, Riese took a quick pitch from Nawy and swept left end aided by blocks from Dixon, Harrison, and Alan Figg. He broke down the sideline, cut across the field near the South River 35 to score on an 87-yard jaunt to account for the last score of the game.

Once again, Jay lauded his defensive players. "This has just been a real team effort all season. We had bad breaks early in the season, losing three key seniors, but we've got guys like Mitchell Riese, who are playing hurt and giving us 100 percent of our reserves who worked so hard in practice."[39]

Jay explained the Highland Park strategy that had prevailed during the week of practice. "We were determined to take away their passing attack. We knew that their backs would pick up yardage, but we didn't think that they could beat us on the ground. We felt that Waller was good enough at middle linebacker to hold up the middle for us and that Harrison was quick enough to put real pressure on their quarterback. The defense really worked for us," he added.[40]

With the drubbing of South River, Highland Park clinched the inaugural championship of the Bicentennial Conference. However, there were still several tough games ahead before the Owls could relish their championship. Highland Park fans were also beginning to talk about HP's winning streak, which had been extended now to twelve consecutive games over the last two seasons.

On Saturday, November 13 Highland Park faced its meekest opponent, St. Pius, a tiny parochial school in Piscataway. The first half of the game was relatively close, with the St. Pius club only one touchdown behind, 13-6.

However, following the second-half kickoff, the Owls drove 59 yards in 8 plays, finished off by a Nawy screen pass to Stavrides. Jay had now dubbed the offense "The Junior Connection," which consisted of Bob Nawy at quarterback and receivers Bob Stavrides and Steve Riese, and exulted in this stunning drive so soon into the second half.[41]

When the Bruins got the ball on the next set of downs, middle linebacker Paul Waller intercepted and set up the next touchdown for Nawy to Riese on a seven-yard pass. The final score of the St. Pius' game was 33-6.[42]

Coach Dakelman had expressed his disapproval of the New Jersey football playoff system for years, as had many other area coaches, such as Frank Capraro of Woodbridge and his brother, Vince Capraro of Edison. The first round of the playoffs was held on the Saturday before Thanksgiving. That meant that the qualifying teams had to play two tough games within five days, which penalized the strongest competitors.

Frank Capraro bemoaned the system to sportswriter Irv Bank of the *Home News*, stating, "It's been a long season. We had

Stevens, Colonia, and Carteret earlier and now must play Madison to get into the playoffs. Then, if we do play on the 20th, we must come back just five days later and play Edison with the possibility of still another game on December 4."[43]

Coach D. concurred with Capraro's assessment. "It's a shame only the eight games count and not nine. This way a team must play in the playoffs and then come back just five days later. The fall and winter seasons shouldn't have to conflict. I've been saying that all along. We may have to postpone our opening wrestling match on December 20 because 10 of our 12 wrestlers are on the football team. You can't expect them to play a football game on December 4 and be ready to wrestle six days later."[44]

Jay's proposed solution was to either move the start of the winter season back to mid-December or eliminate the Thanksgiving Day games and start the football season earlier. His suggestions seemed to be falling on deaf ears at the NJSIAA, New Jersey's governing body of high school athletics.

Despite the concerns of the seasoned coaches, Highland Park hosted Green Brook on Saturday, November 21st for the first round of the Central Jersey Group I Championships.

Before taking the home field for the semi-final round, Coach D. had his boys huddle around him and sent out the following message," It's all about field possession today," he almost whispered. "Get good field position from the very first kick-off."

The first half of the game see-sawed two tough defenses against one another, disallowing any scoring. Both offenses felt frustrated as nothing seemed to be working for them.

All of that changed in the beginning of the second half. Mitchell Riese took the kickoff on the 29-yard line, broke up the middle, then slanted left and raced 71 yards for the first touchdown of the game. The Highland Park fans went wild as the Owls grabbed the momentum and never stopped from that point on.[45]

Green Brook could not move the ball on its first possession of the half, and Highland Park took over on its own 27 again. Six plays later, Steve Riese broke off the left tackle and scored a 21-yard touchdown.

Still in the third period, Robert McKinney drove the ball across the goal line following a 13-yard run by Alan Figg, which had kept the drive alive. Figg also scored the final touchdown in the 4th quarter, completing a 51-yard drive. Figg, a junior, was the leading ball carrier on the day with 128 yards in 16 carries. In all, HP had rushed for 288 yards to Green Brook's 63.

Green Brook eked out a score late in the fourth quarter to avoid a shutout, but Highland Park had won the right to face a very tough Keansburg in the Championship game.

With only a few days to practice, Highland Park faced its toughest opponent, the one team that would be out for Owl tail feathers on Thanksgiving Day. Every year Jay would comment, "When Metuchen has a losing season, if they beat Highland Park, they think they have won the state championship."

There was a traditional ditty sung all week at HPHS before the Turkey Day classic. "What's the good word? Beat Metuchen! What's the good word? Beat Metuchen! What's the good word? Beat Metuchen High."

Aside from the pride in winning the game and bringing the Goal Post Trophy home for another year, there was a unique feeling to this inter-town rivalry. Highland Park and Metuchen were mirror images in demographics, charming Main Streets, and student achievements. Metuchen, nicknamed "the Brainy Borough," has been home to a few people of renown, including poet John Ciardi and, much later, Governor James Florio, State Senator Barbara Buono, Basketball Star Marqus Blakely, and David Copperfield, the magician.

Highland Park was home to a myriad of professors from the prestigious Rutgers University, which was why the student body of the high school consisted of so many bright, talented, and curious young people. The Highland Park - Metuchen contest was never so much brawn as it was smarts against brains . . . the HP-Metuchen match-up was a rivalry of smart kids who understood the nuances of the game.

For these reasons and to protect an undefeated season, Jay was especially tense as Thanksgiving Day neared. For years, the Thanksgiving Day Classic had been played in Memorial Stadium in New Brunswick since the anticipated crowd, composed of proud parents and alumni, was too large to be played at either HP or Metuchen High Schools. New Brunswick played its Thanksgiving rival, South River, at Rutgers Stadium each year, which made Memorial Stadium available at 10:30 on Thanksgiving morning.

As could be expected, the game turned out to be a nailbiter for the 4200 fans who crammed into the old, concrete stadium. Unfortunately, Steve Riese sustained an injury in the Green Brook game and had to be replaced by Junior tailback, Bob MacKinney. Injuries had plagued the Owls from the beginning of this remarkable season, and Jay pondered if this would be the one that broke them.

Highland Park's offense was hampered throughout the game by turnovers. Of its 10 possessions, five were terminated by turnovers, three interceptions and two fumbles.[46]

Metuchen struck first when sophomore linebacker Frank Bruno intercepted a pass and ran for a 45-yard score. The crowd went wild, stamping its feet and hooting at the Owls in a jeering manner.

However, right after the Metuchen score, HP drove 70 yards in 12 plays. With 1:09 left in the half, Alan Figg bolted across the goal line, having carried the ball seven times during the drive. As the first half ended, the score was tied, 6-6 as each team had missed its extra point.[47] Unless Jay could turn things around during his halftime speech, the undefeated season might just slip away before the final championship game.

The only other touchdown of the day occurred as the second half opened. HP marched 62 yards down the field in 16 plays, letting Figg take the ball in again. A two-point conversion made the score 14-6, which ended up being the final tally.[48]

After the game Metuchen Coach Frank Springer reflected, "I knew Highland Park was a good football team, but they were much better and tougher up front than I thought they were when I saw them last Saturday against Green Brook."[49]

Springer continued, "I'm proud of our kids. I came here trying to turn around a football program and we won five out of nine games. However, I won't consider this program turned around until we beat these Owls."[50]

Once again, it was the HP defense that had won the day, holding Metuchen to four first downs and a net offense of 890 yards, only 11 in the second half. Jay commented, "This was our best defensive effort of the season. The kids have done the job all year but were especially outstanding against Metuchen."[51]

Finally, it was crunch time. Aiming for his 12th sectional title since he became Head Coach in 1959, HP's achievements in the 1976 season had been astounding. The Owls had rolled up 244 points against their opponents, who combined had scored 60. Steve Riese had scored 13 touchdowns and Bob Stavrides had six touchdowns and 18 PATs. Alan Figg had crossed the goal line six times during the year. Bob Nawy led Middlesex County in touchdown passes with 13, six of which had been nabbed by Riese and six of which Stavrides had caught.

In a conversation with his former team manager, Barry Levine, now a *Home News* sports reporter, Jay reminisced over the exciting past 12 weeks, starting with Felix Lee's devastating injury, the loss of George Brunson, and now the impact that Steve Riese's knee injury could have on the championship game.

"Our kids are really nonchalant and have taken everything in stride," he said. "We don't have demonstrative kids . . . They generally act with quiet determination."[52]

But the opposite could be said about the coaching staff, which was concerned about Keansburg, always a tough team. This year, Keansburg was returning to the Sectional gridiron, having lost the championship to South Hunterdon the year before. Although they weren't undefeated this season, they had won eight out of ten games, losing only to Red Bank and Freehold. Jay knew that of all the teams that HP had faced this year, Keansburg was the strongest.

Jay switched his comments to discussing the defense once again with Levine. "Our offensive line, center Jack Tunison, guards Lee Greenberg and Paul Waller, tackles Brian Lakin,

Adam Mosston, and Raymond Harrison, and ends Melvin Dixon and Bob Stavrides just haven't received the recognition that they deserve for all their fine blocking this year, but they have been so, so solid. They have been firing off the ball and making those necessary holes."[53]

Jay, never a good sleeper, had spent several sleepless nights since Thanksgiving, planning how to reconstruct the offense without Steve Riese, who was the third-leading scorer in Middlesex County. Not only was the fleet footed Riese an offensive standout, he also started in the defensive backfield, punted, and returned kicks.

Bob MacKinney, who had done a fine job in the Metuchen game, filling in for Steve, was going to have to rise to the occasion once again against Keansburg. His season stats were solid, having carried 37 times for 186 yards. "Bobby reads blockers well and is more of an inside running threat than Steve, but Riese has more outside speed and is a little better receiver," he thought.

The good news looking forward to the big game was that Georgie Brunson was going to have an opportunity to return for his final game. Although he wasn't going to have his full speed up to par, it would be wonderful to see the kid don his shoulder pads and helmet for one last go as an Owl.

"I'm going to play Mitch Riese a little more," Jay continued his self-talk. "Mitchell can always get us yards. He's a sneaky runner and a sure handed receiver. He's blocked better than we ever thought he would and has just done an excellent job."

Jay fretted about Keanburg's powerful quarterback, Ron Hayes, who had thrown for more than 1,100 yards during the season. Their running back, Joe Jimenez, had star quality. The defense was going to have to be perfect on game day to bring home Jay's 12th sectional championship since 1959.

Coach Dakelman with Alan Figg, Steve Riese, and Bob Nawy of the Dream Team

Perfection is not attainable, but if we chase perfection, we can catch excellence.
Vince Lombardi

CHAPTER 18

WHAT IS THE MEANING OF VICTORY?

A few days before the Keansburg game, a letter written to Jay on lined notebook paper arrived at the high school. It read:

Mr. Dakelman,

I would just like to give you my congratulations on a terrific season and to wish you the best of luck. I don't think I can make it to the championship game, but you know that my spirit will be there.

I am proud to say that I went to H.P.H.S., and I played football for you, and to say that you really taught me a lot. Not only about football but about life in general, and a lot of the advice that you and Mr. Policastro gave me really comes in handy, and I will never forget either of you for it.

So, tell all the guys I said, "Good luck" and "Kick Ass," and if they don't bring that Championship to HP, I'm going to kick each one of their asses personally.

Good luck and thanks for everything,

Mal

P.S. I'd like to see a shutout![1]

This enthusiastic letter, written by former player David Malatesta, buoyed Jay's jitters as he realized that he had hundreds of former athletes who were watching and rooting for their alma mater as the team approached the championship final.

The "Mr. Policastro" to whom David referred in his letter was JoJo, Jay's former All-State quarterback, who had gone to Holy Cross University, dashing dreams that one day he would be an NFL quarterback. JoJo had other aspirations when he began college; he wanted to be a lawyer.

"Holy Cross was hard," Joe Policastro averred in remembering his days in Boston. "They made you take 18 credits a semester, with courses like Philosophy and Religion. I majored in Political Science, which meant that I had to take 18 credits a semester."[2] Coupled with football practice and a pretty sweetheart named Mary, JoJo had little free time.

"I was supposed to become an attorney and had even been accepted to law school up in Boston, but when my father died, I realized that I couldn't study law. My mother needed me to look after her interest in my father's business, White Sales, which he co-owned with his brother. When my father passed, we inherited only 41% of the company, so for me to make sure that my Uncle Tony didn't cheat my mother, I went to work there . . . and I hated it," JoJo explained.[3]

Whenever he could spare a minute from the company, JoJo returned to the one place in the world where he truly felt at home,

Jay's office. He complained bitterly to his old coach about how miserable he was in business, and Jay listened compassionately.

Finally tired of hearing his protege complain about being so unhappy, Jay made a proposal to the young man, who still held so much promise and enthusiasm for sport and life.

"I have an idea how to fix your problem," Jay began. "We can't find anyone certified to teach Driver's Education. How would you feel about taking a course at Montclair State College to get certified to teach it here? If we can get Dr. MacKenzie to agree to that plan, you can become a teacher and coach football, basketball, and baseball here at Highland Park."[4]

To JoJo, this plan presented a great solution to his dilemma. The Superintendent, Dr. MacKenzie, readily agreed to Jay's proposal, and within weeks, JoJo went from being a businessman to a teacher and coach with the man who had become a second father to him.

JoJo achieved a Master's Degree in teaching at Kean University, including courses that enabled him to become an administrator if he chose to do so down the line. He came to realize during the early days of teaching that he loved working with young people, teaching them how to drive safely. But the best part of the job was coaching. He came to see things now from the point of view of his mentor, Jay Dakelman, and every day added a new trick to his growing arsenal of teaching tools.

Although the two men were different in temperament, the bond between Jay and Joe, as the younger man came to be known as an adult, grew exponentially over the years. They confided in each other, Jay imparting information about his youth, his years in the armed forces, his relationships with family, friends, and colleagues that he shared with no one else. They spent more time together than Jay spent with anyone else in his life, and their love and admiration for one another provided the support and trust that they found with no one else in the world.

It was a surprisingly mild day for a December football game. The Owls had the home-field advantage because of their flawless record in the 1976 season. The sizable crowd on both sides of the stadium sipped on hot chocolate and watched an uneventful first half. A completely defensive battle: when the young men came out to play the second half, it was difficult to feel which way the momentum of this championship play between Keansburg, who had lost the title last year to South Hunterdon, and Highland Park, protecting an undefeated season, was going to go.

Midway through the third quarter, Keansburg broke the deadlock, moving 60 yards in 14 plays with a six-yard pass from quarterback Ron Hayes to tight end Joe Mahr for a touchdown.[5] The key plays during the drive were a nine yard, third-down pass from Hayes to halfback Mike Paulicki, giving Keansburg a first down on the Highland Park 46. Then, faced with a fourth and one situation on the HP 13, Hayes flipped a five yard, square-out pass to Mahr for a first down on the HP 8. Two plays later, Mahr caught a pass from Hayes near the five-yard line, broke to his left, avoided one tackler, and scored. Pete Trapasso then booted the first of two successful extra points.[6]

The touchdown pass was only the fourth of the season that Highland Park had allowed by its strong defense.[7]

The Owls were flat. The offense did not click during the entire game. In the second half, they managed only one first down, and had a net offense of minus 10 yards on offense. The closest they came to scoring was on their first possession of the half when the Parkites reached the Keansburg 47 on a seven yard pass from Nawy to wide receiver Bob Stavrides, but then relinquished possession following a punt.[8]

Late in the fourth quarter, Keansburg iced the game when tackle Tom Mell recovered an Owl fumble on the HP 17 with 4:22 left on the clock. Eight plays later, Joe Jimenez, a hard running 5' 6, 165-pound senior halfback, slanted off right guard from the one-yard line to score. The touchdown came with 25 seconds remaining in the game. Trapasso booted the extra point through the goalposts, ending the championship contest in a 14-0 shutout against the Owls.

The stunned fans of HP sat in the stands for a few moments, dejected and disbelieving as the undefeated season and Central Jersey Championship slipped away. They consoled themselves by saying that most of the key players would be back next year and that they would bring the trophy home in December of 1977.

Surrounded by reporters, Jay assessed the devastating loss. "I guess the injuries finally caught up with us. Kenny Carkhuff, a junior linebacker, missed the game because of a leg injury and Steve Riese only played a little because of a knee injury. Every time we played, we had at least one regular out of the lineup. It's a tribute to our kids that they were able to take up the slack . . ."[9]

Eager to retreat to the locker room to meet with the young men who had brought so much heart and joy to their parents, school, coaches, and beloved hometown, to console them and tell them how much he believed in them, Jay addressed the reporters, "Keansburg was a good team today and just beat us. I can't complain. I'm very proud of our kids."

Nawy, Harrison, the Riese boys, Georgie, Waller, Stavrides, Figg, and always, always Felix, were like sons to him. There was so much more that he wanted to teach them about life, about

225

winning and losing, about what was important in the scope of the wonders that faced them ahead. And, of course, start revving them up to come roaring back next year to win that elusive 13th championship.

When Jay walked through the back door of the school, into the locker room, his footsteps echoed in the eerie silence as the defeated kids were trying to deal with their bitter loss. A few had tears in their eyes, feeling that they had let him down when it really counted. He had the power to change their attitude at this moment and he was going to do that. Part of being a great coach was modeling how to rise above losing, which truthfully, Jay hated to do.

He began to speak in his raspy, after-game voice. "When this season began," he started, "I didn't know where we were headed. I don't think that I expected to get as far as we did. I have never coached such a disciplined, committed, and respectful team as you have been."

He pointed to one of the motivational posters that hung on the locker room walls, which read, *"Winning isn't everything; it's the only thing."*

"Victory is important in life," he chose his words carefully. "Be a winner in the classroom, concentrate on your studies, listen to what your parents and teachers tell you. That is how you win big in life. Understand that defeat is only a small price for being there, on the field, where you played today. Your coaches and I couldn't be prouder of the efforts that all of you put in this year. I will never, ever forget this season and all that you gave. . ."

He paused and added, "And now it is time to start planning for next year."

With his words of approval, the team began to whoop and cheer. It had been a championship season. After all, they had clinched the inaugural title for the Bicentennial Conference . . . and the accolades were only beginning to come in.

Bob Nawy, Bob Stavrides, Steve Riese, Raymond Harrison, and Paul Waller were named to the Bicentennial Conference "All Team." In the Middlesex County Football Coaches Association selections, Harrison, Stavrides, Waller, and Nawy made the All-Team honors.[10]

Always a modest individual, Jay's contributions to education were always about the students first, which is why the accolades that he began collecting for the season of '76 started to mount; he was caught off-guard and humbled. First, he shared Coach of the Year honors with Jim Gilrain, Head Coach of Carteret High School, from the Middlesex County Coaches Association.

Two of the most important newspapers in New Jersey dubbed Jay Coach of the Year. The first was *The Daily News* of New York City and the second was *Star Ledger* of Newark.

Lloyde S. Glicken, the feature sportswriter from the *Star Ledger,* published a defining article about Jay in the paper. It read:

There are very few men in the business of coaching football in New Jersey to whom the other men go in quest of knowledge. One of them is Jay Dakelman of Highland Park. When he talks football, either formally at a coaching clinic or informally at a cross-the-table session, the coaches listen —and learn. Dakelman proved his strategic ability this past season. Before the campaign began, his top back, a 230-pound runner named Felix Lee, suffered a severe knee injury. The season was only two games old, when another big runner, George Brunson was hurt and left for the year. So, Jay Dakelman took a team that was designed for the run and turned it into a through-the-air alignment. And through the air, it went to 10 straight victories before the charge was halted by Keansburg in the Central Jersey Group I final.

In every one of these 11 games, a player who started the week before was out of the line-up because of a series of injuries that might have given a lesser coach pause. Dakelman overcame problems, produced an outstanding record and became a solid choice as the *Star-Ledger* High School Football Coach-of-the-Year. He finished the season with a cumulative record of 122-31-2. He was denied a Sectional championship. But his earlier teams had won 12 of them. The field considered for the honor was strong. Erwin Sloan performed brilliantly at Clifford Scott, falling just short of a State Championship. Chappy Moore took a Notre Dame team that hadn't won two previous seasons to the championship round. Frank Bottone won 11 straight with New Providence. Doug Wilkins guided Mountain Lakes through a perfect year.

Charles LaBarca was the one who ended Highland Park's bid for perfection with a fine Keansburg team. Jerry Moore guided Somerville to a state crown. And, of course, Tony Verducci's Seton Hall team was the best in the state.

Dakelman, however, bested them all, adding to an already imposing reputation. His winning percentage in football is a shade under .800. But that comes as no surprise to those who know the quiet-voiced gentleman. He spent 21 years coaching track and field, won five state and 16 sectional championships, and compiled a winning percentage in dual competition that comes to the self-same .800.

He started his football career as a center at New Brunswick High in 1936. "I was an average center," he reports quietly. Then, he played four varsity years at Panzer. What does he recall of those pre-World War II days?

"I was the manager of the super basketball team that won 43 straight."

Then came the war and service in the European theater as a combat medic in five major campaigns, things like Normandy Beach, the Battle of the Bulge, the Malmedy Massacre.

After discharge, graduate work in physical education at NYU followed. In September of 1946, he joined the Highland Park Staff as assistant basketball coach and head track coach.

In 1959, he took over as head football coach and promptly produced a 9-0 record. There have been, in his career, 3 perfect seasons and one where an all-winning season was marked by a single tie.

"We had to go to a passing offense this season because we lost Lee and Brunson," he explained. "We won with Bob Nawy at quarterback and Bob Stavrides at end.

"But, before the year was over, we lost our leading scorer, Steve Riese, who was hurt in gym class. For the championship game, we lost linebacker Ken Carkhuff. But that wasn't the reason we lost; Keansburg just outplayed us."

That also is typical of Middlesex County's dean of football coaches. He never alibis for losses. And he gives the kids the credit for success.

On the side, he helps the NJSIAA run a good part of its championship track program.

And he answers questions about football posed by his fellow workers in the coaching business.[11]

Jay was the honoree at two special dinners that celebrated his Coach of the Year awards. On Thursday, January 27 at the Robert Treat Hotel in Newark, Jay received a stunning ring from the *Star Ledger*. Diamonds surrounded a sapphire stone, set in silver with the legend "Coach of the Year" inscribed around the center gem. Sponsored by the Annual Boys' Clubs of Newark, the dinner celebrated the prowess of coaches and athletes each year for their achievements in all sports.

More than 1100 people attended this magnificent event, which included many leaders of the metropolitan business area and sports celebrities.

The members of the first string All State *Star Ledger* team also received their rings at the prestigious dinner.

On December 3, 1976, Jay received the following telegram, which really shocked and awed him:

Congratulations, you have been selected as a 1976 *Daily News* Football All-Star Coach. You and your fellow coaches will be honored during the special ceremonies on the playing field at Shea Stadium preceding the Jets-Cincinnati game on Sunday, December 12. Please arrange to meet us at 12 o'clock sharp at the Shea Stadium Press Gate. Bring this mailgram for easy identification. Following the game, you will be our guest at a reception and dinner in the Biltmore Hotel, Madison Avenue and 43rd Street. Please confirm that you will attend by Thursday, December 9, by telephoning 212-949-3556 between 10 a.m. and

4:30 p.m. Monday through Thursday. We look forward to seeing you on December 12. Please note that only All-Star Coaches and the All-Star teams will be guests on this occasion. Bill Travers, *Daily News.*[12]

At this auspicious event, Jay received a second Coach of the Year ring, one that he cherished for the rest of his life. A large ruby stone, embossed with a gold football, set in 14 K. gold glinted from his finger. Jay wore both rings frequently even though he didn't like wearing jewelry much because he found that it often got in the way. However, these two rings reminded him forever of the sacrifices that his committed athletes had made to honor their coach so publicly.

Congratulatory letters poured in from former players, parents, college coaches, and colleagues. Frank Burns, Head Coach of Rutgers Football wrote, "Jay: Read the paper today. Congratulations on 'Coach of the Year. Best of luck. See you soon, Frank."[13]

From former Panzer classmate and the Athletic Director of Piscataway High School, Bob Sterling penned, "There was never any doubt, going as far back as our Panzer days—you were always out front!! Great to have a friend recognized for his ability— congratulations again. Sincerely, Bob."[14]

Each March Jay attended the National Coaching Clinic, held in Atlantic City. Over the years, Coach D. had developed a tight friendship with Gene Felker, the Executive Director of the National Coaching Clinic and a former pro football player. On February 17, Jay received a letter from Gene, informing him that the awards committee of the National Football Clinic had selected him to be the 4th Annual Master Coaching Award recipient for the State of New Jersey. The presentation of the award was going to take place at the convention in Atlantic City on Wednesday, March 23rd, 1977. Jay responded immediately and was elated to have been recognized by this prestigious group.

With all his connections, Gene managed to bring in highly recognized college and professional football coaches to address the attendees of the convention. Souvenir glasses, listing the names of the speakers, were doled out to all of those who came to hear the latest news and learn strategies that would hopefully help their teams become the next champions wherever they played. Jay treasured these glasses, showcasing them prominently in the living room of the house on 3rd Avenue. However, no one was ever allowed to drink out of them lest they break.

Shortly before the festivities were to occur down the Jersey shore, Felker sent an acknowledgement to Jay regarding his acceptance of the award from the National Coaching Clinic. Gene wrote, "Dear Jay, Thanks for your great and humble letter. I realize it takes many important and vital ingredients to develop a successful football program, but most important is proper leadership. You, my friend, are responsible for that single area that brings all other things into place. My congratulations to you on the award; you certainly are deserving of this token of excellence."[15]

A former athlete who ran on Jay's track team reached out to his coach; a young man named Mark Berkowitz. His letter lauded Jay for the success he had achieved in the business world. He wrote:

Dear Mr. Dakelman,

This letter may come as a surprise to you. However, I feel that it is long overdue. I am living in the Baltimore area, and I'm employed as a sales manager for the Drackett Products Company. This management position meant a transfer away from Highland Park and away from all my friends. The purpose of this letter is to thank you. This feeling of gratitude is extended because of your philosophies as a coach and as a man. They have made me a successful person. I have learned from you the meaning of having a good attitude, being self-motivated, and the determination to become #1. Only through hard work has success come and will continue to come my way.

It started in my freshman year as a member of the spring track team. During a varsity meet, I was able to run in a second heat of the quarter mile. This was my first race ever. After I won the race, you came over to shake my hand and congratulate me. I knew then that if I wanted to get ahead in this world, I was going to have to work very hard.

I am sure, Mr. Dakelman, that I am not the only person who has benefitted in life due to your leadership. I still carry with me those locker room sayings, especially "The only difference between good and GREAT is a little EXTRA effort."

I try to instill this into my salesmen. In fact, when I took over this district in Baltimore, it was in last place. I am proud to say now that we are currently in 2nd place out of 18. The #1 position is still within reach, and I have plans to obtain it by the year's end. Thank you again. Sincerely, Mark A. Berkowitz. [16]

So, there it was; the season of 1976 was now one for the record books. It had been an exciting season with unexpected surprises. There had been devastating injuries that had robbed young men of the opportunity to be part of the battle to win the

233

sectional championship. There had been wins that should not have been possible except for the grit and determination of football players who refused to quit, who wanted to make their coaches believe in them as much as they believed in their coaches.

And what of Felix Lee? What was to happen to him in the afterglow of the season that never was for such a talented star as he was? George Chaump, one of Woody Hayes' premier recruiters at Ohio State, breezed into Highland Park to recruit the one fullback that the Buckeyes had their eye on all fall. That young fellow was Felix Lee who would be on his way to Columbus, Ohio in the autumn of 1977.

"He has the size and speed to be a great one . . . We started following his career during his sophomore season at Highland Park . . . He had that unfortunate knee injury prior to the start of his senior season, but we were able to judge him on his performances as a junior and sophomore. We felt that with his size and speed, he could be a great fullback."[17]

Chaump noted that OSU had three strong returning fullbacks for the next season, including Jeff Logan, Paul Campbell, and Chuck Hinton, but Felix was a little bigger and stronger than any of the others. "We listed Lee as one of our 'prime' candidates at the top of our recruiting list . . . other factors were that Lee came from a school like Highland Park which realized what it took to win and that he was well schooled in fundamentals by Coach Jay Dakelman.

"And when he came to visit us last month, our team doctors examined his knee and were totally impressed by the way he has rehabilitated it, so the injury was not a factor."

The soft-spoken Lee was so relieved to have the recruiting pressure lifted from his shoulders on Thursday that after he left the signing meeting with George Chaump and Coach Dakelman in Jay's office, he cartwheeled across the gym. Seeing this, Chaump just shook his head in disbelief and Jay grinned.

Seeing his protege who had been so disappointed about the way things had turned out this year, excited about his future playing for the legendary Woody Hayes, Jay felt the knot in his stomach unwind and, once again, he began to breathe.

The only place success comes before work is in the dictionary.
Vince Lombardi

CHAPTER 19

A LEAGUE OF THEIR OWN

Highland Park High School fielded its first football team in 1937. Coached by Al Buschorn, in the first two years of having a varsity squad, the Owl's record was a dismal 1-10-3, but their opponents had been very tough and established teams.[1]

In 1939 Paul Hancock, who served as the Athletic Director, took the reins as Head Coach and started the Owls on their winning trend. In his four years as Head Coach, HPHS posted a 14-14-2 record, winning the Little Five Conference Championship in 1952.[2]

In 1943, Bus Lepine took over the helm for the Owls and garnered a 5-2 record in his first year with a shocking victory over Metuchen 3-0. Icky Klaus kicked a field goal with 16 seconds left in the game, leaving the Bulldogs stunned. Beating Metuchen under any circumstances was always sweet, but this win was particularly thrilling. Sixty years later, this win remains as one of the defining moments in Highland Park football lore. During Lepine's tenure, from 1943-1958, Highland Park's record was 85-47-9, a winning percentage of .553.

When Jay took over the team from Bus, he was ready to institute his own system and mold the young men to fit into his work ethic. In his 19 years as Head Coach, the teams' record was 138-34-2, an incredible percentage of .802.

Of Jay's prowess at the helm, Charlie Bloom, one of his former players wrote, "Jay was an innovator, using five or six offensive sets and multiple defensive ones, such as the Sayreville Spread. I can remember always having the best equipment, the best scouting reports, and never having detention on a Friday. Football was hard work, but under Jay's guidance, football became an enjoyment."[3]

Jay, who could not abide losing, and especially losing unfairly, never got over the fact that in his first year as Head Coach, 1959, his phenomenal squad had a 9-0 record but was denied the State Championship due to the Colliton System used by the NJSIAA to determine the winner. The Colliton System was an arbitrary system that was based on the strength of a team's opposition as opposed to having a flawless record. Carteret, with a record of 6-2-1 was awarded the title that year, a fact that continued to burn Jay for the rest of his life.

One of the things that constantly banged around in Jay's brain was the issue of how to measure team equity in creating championship games and meets that were fair to all schools. When he first came onto the sporting scene, the New Jersey State Interscholastic Athletic Association, the governing body of athletics in New Jersey, went strictly by the number of male athletes in the 10th, 11th, and 12th grades in each high school to create four large groups for championship competition, which many people thought was the fairest way of dividing up the member schools.

However, as Jay quickly learned, although theoretically, it seemed like a solid foundation on which to base championship competition, other factors changed the balance so that competition was not always equitable. For example, each year Highland Park's football schedule had HP, a Group II school in the 50s and 60s, and a Group I school in later years, playing schools that were more than twice their size. Piscataway, East Brunswick, and Sayreville, for example, were Group IV schools, which meant that they had a greater depth in the number of students who could play for their squads.

When the NJSIAA proposed a new system based on power points, Jay raised his voice against the plan. The proposal called for selecting the top sectional team in each group by numerical rating to compete for state group championships. The next four teams in the ratings would then play for the sectional championship in each group.[4]

Jay ranted to Glicken, "I don't like the proposal. A team can be picked to be among the top four for the group championships, losing in a close game to the eventual champion and having nothing to show for its season. Another team, rated lower in the point system, could win the sectional title.

"I thought championships were supposed to be won on the field. Now, we'll pick the best team in the section on points. That's almost going back to the Colliton System," Jay growled.[5]

A growing dilemma that added to the lack of parity was that many of the small schools in Central Jersey wanted to avoid playing Highland Park. Even though Highland Park High School never had more than 800 students within the four grades that attended the school, they played fearsome football that many weaker teams wanted to avoid.

While on one hand, it was complimentary that smaller schools didn't want to face HP on the turf, on the other hand, it meant that although the Owls were winning nearly every week, they were taking a beating when the larger schools were able to substitute athletes more frequently during games. Injuries to the athletes plagued the Owls throughout Coach D.'s career.

One solution that Jay found palatable was for Highland Park to be part of a conference of schools. In the late 1960s, he was able to muster a group of teams in Central Jersey to form a small league called the Garden State Conference which included Roselle, Roselle Park, Clifford Scott, Metuchen, South River, and Highland Park. However, by 1971 this small conference had disbanded, leaving Highland Park in a state of independence, which made putting together a schedule extremely challenging.

The Middlesex County Conference existed in those days with a membership of 13 schools. Eleven of those schools were quite large and football powerhouses, but South River and New Brunswick High Schools did not fit into that group competitively. Their larger opponents did not want the two smaller schools to leave the County Conference since they were relatively easy games for the larger schools to count on as a break from the more challenging competition.

Jay seized the opportunity to create a new conference that would allow Highland Park to have a dependable schedule each year, taking on opponents that were more equal to them in size and ability. Thus, in 1976 the Bicentennial League was born, taking its name in celebration of the nation's big birthday. The schools that comprised the fledgling league included North Brunswick, St. Peters, St. Pius, St. Thomas Aquinas, South Brunswick, and Highland Park.

When interviewed about the formation of the Bicentennial Conference by reporter Mark Plescia of the *Home News,* Dakelman stated, "Today, it is a necessity to be affiliated with a conference. If you're not in a conference, then you are left out."

Dakelman continued that a league format allowed for the creation of schedules and created healthy rivalries and fan interest by meeting the same teams each year. Regarding the relevance of conference play to the athletes, Dakelman noted, "Each game becomes important in league standings, and the kids get more recognition being on a conference team."

Miffed at the reaction of the Middlesex County Conference as well as other conferences at the inference that the Bicentennial Conference was comprised of "weaklings," Dakelman emphasized, "This conference will be a strong, competitive conference, and will have several outstanding teams that could compete in any league."

The Bicentennial Conference suited its purpose for a time, but soon problems in keeping the conference viable became insurmountable. St. Pius, always a tiny school, closed its doors forever. Not long after, St. Peter's High School gave up its football team and then also closed due to declining enrollment.

Jay knew that he needed to find a bigger and better solution to the perennial problem for Highland Park High School.

In 1977 a novice coach, Greg Ficarra, joined the football staff of South River High School under the leadership of Head Coach Bill Csatari, himself a legend. South River was the ideal school to work in if one was looking for a powerhouse football squad. Although not much bigger than Highland Park, South River produced such football legends as Joe Theisman of the Washington Redskins (now the Commanders), Drew Pearson of the Dallas Cowboys, and Kenny Jackson of the Philadelphia Eagles and Houston Oilers.

The legacy of football in South River stretched back to the 1930s when Alex Wojciechowicz played center for the Rams. Wojciechowicz is a member of the College Football Hall of Fame, where he was known as one of the "Seven Blocks of Granite" playing alongside Vince Lombardi for Fordham University. A two time All American, Wojciechowicz starred for 13 seasons in the NFL, playing both offense and defense for the Detroit Lions.

Ficarra loved coaching in South River, but full-time jobs in Physical Education were tough to come by in the '70s. South River was only able to hire Greg as a permanent sub. Therefore, when he was offered a permanent position in Edison Township, teaching elementary school and coaching at Edison High School, he grabbed the opportunity.

In 1980, Greg departed Edison and began teaching and coaching in Perth Amboy, a waterfront city that leads to Staten Island when one crosses the bridge over the New York border. In 1987, longtime Perth Amboy Athletic Director, Ray Cherneski, retired and, although young, Ficarra got the promotion.

In the late 80s there were several Athletic Directors in Middlesex County that had been in the job for decades. Charlie King of East Brunswick, Walt "Moe" Gasior of Carteret, Ron "Beanie" Osborne of J.F. Kennedy of Iselin, Joe Locascio of North Brunswick, Al Czech of South Plainfield, Norm Winter of Franklin, Bob Coward of Edison, Frank Petrillo of South Brunswick, Sam Lupo of Woodbridge and Pat Daly (the only female of the group) of New Brunswick had all been coaches with significant reputations over the years. But it was clear to Greg Ficarra that Jay Dakelman was the leader of the pack.

"I was definitely intimidated to be in the company of these people," Ficarra stated. "In fact, Coach Osborne had been my coach in high school, and I was never able to call him or Coach Dakelman by their first names."

The Athletic Directors Association of Middlesex County held two meetings a month. One was for the general membership; the other was for the Executive Committee. One day, Greg got confused about which meeting was occurring on a certain date and when he entered Jay's office at HPHS, he was aghast to see that he had crashed an Executive Committee Meeting.

Instead of chasing him from the meeting, the men welcomed Greg and urged him to stay. The seasoned Executive Committee knew that for many of them, retirement was looming large and new blood was needed desperately to keep their organization vibrant.

During that meeting, Jay and Greg were asked to put together a schedule for middle school basketball as sports were expanding rapidly in the lower grades.

"It was disarming to work with Jay. While we were working on the schedule, he guided me every step of the way . . . he was just so calm with his coaches, who kept coming into the office . . . he handled phone calls, he was brilliant at multi-tasking, but he never took his eyes off the schedule."

Ficarra soon became aware of Jay's burning desire to create a system of competition that was fair to every school involved.

"I remember one meeting," Ficarra said, "where Jay grabbed a piece of paper and wrote 'Competitive Balance' on it. This was the beginning of the discussion by what I refer to as the "Founding Fathers" of the Greater Middlesex Conference, one of the first mega-conferences in New Jersey.

"Since Jay had experience in forming conferences already, he understood what needed to be done. Jay brought his system to the GMC. He believed wholeheartedly in a different kind of system, which gave teams a fairer shot at making play-offs by receiving more points toward a championship."

Today, New Jersey high school athletics are based on "Super Conferences." These include the Hudson County Interscholastic Athletic League, the North Jersey Interscholastic Conference, the Northwest Jersey Athletic Conference, the Olympic Conference, the Shore Conference, the Skyland Conference, the Super Essex Conference, the Tri-County Conference, and the Union County Conference. Each of the Super Conferences is then divided into divisions that take into consideration size and ability to compete in that group.

For example, today The Greater Middlesex Conference consists of 34 private and public high schools located in the greater Middlesex County area. The league is broken up into five divisions: Gold, Silver, Red, White, and Blue. As enrollment changes in schools, their division may change to reflect school population growth or decline.

"The thing to understand with all of what we have today is that this was Jay's vision. His legacy lives on and has continued to grow as these conferences are evolving. But he was the driving force behind the development of the system we see today," Ficarra avers.

Another aspect of leadership of the "old guard" was their willingness to continue to grow and learn about sports.

"There are a lot of state and national conferences available to coaches and Athletic Directors. I enjoyed hanging out at night with the guys and learned so much from them," Greg reminisced. "For instance, one of the things that they talked about had to do with work ethic. After a competition, whether it was an away game or a home game, the AD was expected to be the last one in the building, win or lose. You stayed until everyone else was gone. It was your duty to lock up the building and make sure everyone was safely out.

"I remember going into some of the convention sessions and seeing Jay sitting in the front row, taking notes. I thought, 'Wow! Even with all that he knows, he is still ready to learn more.' It was Jay's work ethic that was so awesome. It was the way he carried himself—not what he said, it was what he did."

Lloyde Glicken of *The Star Ledger* interviewed Coach Dakelman in late December of 1990, shortly before Jay was to retire. Joe Policastro, Jay's protege and successor as AD, had planned an area in which Jay was to keep a desk and materials that he needed to conduct fundraising campaigns and his work with the NJSIAA.

"I want to see the play-offs changed," Jay told Glicken. "Now, maybe I'll get around and have a chance to convince people. People just don't want to change.

"I think the state should be divided into eight regions. A school can play in its own region against teams in its own group. Then, the eight champions from each group can play down to one champion in each group." Coach Dakelman favored the idea of abolishing a point system altogether and going to a three-game playoff for statewide group titles.

Jay noted that the biggest opposition to his idea meant that Thanksgiving Classics, which had long been traditional in the state, would have to be foregone to create a three-game championship round.

Gradually, however, the Thanksgiving Day Games have become a thing of the past. Many traditional rivalries, such as the Bloomfield-Montclair Game, once considered "inviolable," drawing 10,000 spectators on Turkey Day, have been abolished once Bloomfield moved into the Northern New Jersey Interscholastic League.

Jay continued to develop his plan for a system that he was devising to be equitable. "The parochial schools should be merged with the public schools so there would only be four groups; they should not be separate. We've melded the parochial with the public schools in many of our track championships. I don't think it hurt anything," he professed.

Jay further expressed his disdain for the power point system that the state was using currently. "The power points, in a sense, is a move back to the Colliton System. But at least now there is a chance to play for the championship on the field," he finished, referring to the institution of a post-season play-off series in which the title was determined in head-to-head competition.

Today, the state of New Jersey has finally adopted a plan similar to what Jay had been advocating for throughout his career. Although no system can ever be perfect due to the unexpected twists that a school can face in any given season, it is far fairer than the old Colliton System that robbed the Owls of the State Championship in 1959.

*The difference between a successful person and others is not a
lack of strength, not a lack of knowledge, but a lack of will.*
Vince Lombardi

CHAPTER 20

I DON'T KNOW ANYTHING

ABOUT TRACK!

Leon Kroll, Highland Park High School Class of 1955, recalled his earliest memories of Coach Dakelman. "I first met Jay in the mid-1940s when I was in the second or third grade. He was fresh out of the Army, and I was just fresh.

"He would come to Lafayette School once or twice a week to teach gym classes. I remember him as being the most enthusiastic and energetic teacher I had ever met. Jay was always screaming at us at the top of his lungs—to try harder or run faster or to work as a team.

"One time in 6th grade, he assembled the whole class and attempted to teach us close order drills, yelling commands out like a Marine Drill Sergeant, 'My mother can march better than that.'

"Six years later, Jay was still hollering. On cold, dark November afternoons, after we had run the same play 20 or 30 times, still not as perfectly or effortlessly or as automatically as he wanted, he would bark at us, 'My mother can run that play better than that!' or 'My grandmother can block better than you can!'"[1]

Although he claimed not to know anything about coaching track and he had never participated in the sport, Jay knew more than he thought he did. He quickly immersed himself in attending every clinic on the coaching of the sport that he could find, reading material from the latest athletic journals that were published, and consulting with coaches from successful high schools and colleges in the area.

Despite being a novice coach in Track and Field, having no track on which to practice and little equipment for his athletes to use, in 1947 the Owls of Highland Park managed to win the Central Jersey Group I and II Sectional and took fifth place overall at the State Meet, held at Rutgers Stadium. Jay had been very lucky to be assisted by Harry Winkler, a retired coach, who was enormously helpful in giving pointers to the novice head coach. Harry had been a middle-distance runner at St. Peter's College in his youth. Winkler and Jay quickly forged a bond based on mutual respect and love of sport.

In 1948, the Track team continued to build a dynasty. In an article called "Sun Slants," Tony Marano wrote, "Last Wednesday Highland Park's track team ended its regular season with a better than average showing. The trackmen will not compete until the State Meet on June 5. Though not in active competition, you can be sure that Coach Jay Dakelman will have his boys practicing day in and day out, as they have all season.

"Coach Dakelman has done a good job with track teams ever since he started coaching at the high school. He has done an excellent job when you consider the lack of facilities he has to cope with.

"The high school team does not have any track to practice on. The old faithful 'mud hole' and the 5th Avenue woods furnish the space for running events. Thanks to Rutgers College, the track team was able to avail itself of the facilities of the Rutgers track several times during the season to run timed events. However, this necessitates the usual arrangements and delays that always go with traveling with teams. With only two hurdles to use in his practice sessions, Coach D. was still able to turn out some good hurdlers."[2]

Highland Park repeated its win at the Central Jersey Group I and II Championship, incredibly without taking a single first place in any of the ten events.

Despite the loss of the seven talented seniors, Jay had 44 young men come out for the Track Team in the spring of 1949. Still assisted by Harry Winkler, Jay prepared his growing team for a busy dual meet season against six tough opponents including Somerville, Dunellen, Bound Brook, South River, Roselle Park, and Metuchen. The big meets included the Newark Board of Education Meet on May 7, the Long Branch Relays on May 14, the Middlesex County Meet on May 21, and the Central Jersey Sectional on May 28. The State Groups Meet followed on June 4.[3]

Incredibly, the Owls blew past all their dual meet competition in 1949, concluding with a 64 ½ -55 ½ victory over Metuchen. That meet was HP's ninth consecutive dual meet win over two seasons.[4]

In the first of the big meets of the 1949 season, New Brunswick managed to take home the Middlesex County crown, with Highland Park a close runner-up.

Would the Owls manage a threepeat of the Central Jersey Group I and II Championship in 1949, especially with Neptune chomping at their heels throughout the competition? With two events remaining on the day, Highland Park had a one-point edge. In the next to the last event of the meet, Walt Gandek of Highland Park took first place in the 100-yard dash, sewing up the title; Jay's third since becoming coach in a sport that he "knew nothing about."

The Shore Press reported that 18 records were shattered at the Central Jersey Sectional held that year at the legendary Asbury Park track. Walt Gandek and Dick Morse had shared the spotlight, smashing four records. Gandek had run the 100-yard dash in 10.2 and the 220-yard dash in 22.8. Morse sped over the High Hurdles in 16.2 and tied with Rodney Mott of Metuchen in the low hurdles with 25.8.[5] It had been a stellar championship season.

As the 1949 school year ended on a high from the success of the track team, there was another momentous occasion that took place on Father's Day, June 19. At 8:15 in the morning, Thelma presented Jay with their first-born daughter, whom they named Beth after Jay's late grandmother, Becki. If ever Jay felt like a winner, starting the family was the best trophy that he could add to his life.

Since there was nothing that Jay liked more than winning, as 1950 approached, he was salivating for the track season to begin so his team could go for a fourth straight Central Jersey Championship. Despite his growing fascination for Track and

Field and his intuitive ability to put kids in just the right events, Jay and the track team were hit hard when Harry Winkler died suddenly in late 1949. Moving forward without Winkler would be difficult and sad, but by now Jay had developed a strong foundation in the sport. He pledged to Harry's memory and devotion to the Owls that he would do his best to continue their winning tradition.

In the spring of 1950, a group of alumni trackmen from Highland Park came together and presented the Harry Winkler Memorial Trophy to the school. Each year, two smaller replicas of the trophy would be presented to the winner of the Mid City's half-mile run. The other would be presented by his teammates to the outstanding member of the Highland Park Track team. To qualify for the Winkler trophy, the Outstanding Member of the team had to exhibit the following qualities: sportsmanship, loyalty, reliability, leadership, team spirit, cooperation, character, and scholarship.[6] It is heartwarming to note that the award in Winkler's memory is still given at HPHS, 75 years after the coach's passing.

One of Jay's most notorious tactical moves at the beginning of each new year was to whine about the vacancies left by graduates from the previous year and other issues facing the team as a new season approached. By setting a melodramatic tone, his athletes were determined to prove to Coach how great they could be if they abided by his rules. Don't miss practice, give 150% of oneself, play fair, work for the good of the team, not self-glory (one of Jay's favorite aphorisms was always, "There is no 'I' in team). Coach D. gave Academy Award-winning performances of holding his head in his hands in near tears as he predicted doom and gloom, all the while plotting gleefully to take home yet another gleaming, faux gold figure of a runner perched atop the wooden base of the championship trophy.

By the time the Central Jersey Group I and II meet came around on May 28, 1950, the two defending champs, hurdler Dick Morse and sprinter Walt Gandek, were ready to roll. Other strong competitors were hurdlers Joe Edgar, Jim White, and George Brunson; jumpers Joe Sulfrian and Steve Lorik; pole vaulters Bob O'Grady, Jim Pepitone, and Jim Edgar; shot putters, Ned Mehrhof, John Billheimer, Patsy Iofreda, discus throwers John Billheimer, Dick Reiser, Bob Zeller, and javelin throwers Ernie and Billy Vanderveer and Bob Wagner.[7]

It was irritating as a coach, who was trying to converse with his athletes during a meet, that often Jay and his peers were called upon to time and judge places as the runners crossed the finish line. He questioned how fair the arrangement was since as a coach, it was difficult to take your eyes off your own competitors during competition. How could you pick fourth place when you were trying to see if your runner took first?

Jay could not understand why there were officials for football, basketball, and baseball but none for track and field. He took it upon himself to create an officials' association by recruiting Athletic Directors, parents, coaches, and former athletes to form the New Jersey Interscholastic Track and Field Officials Association. Jay enlisted the help of his close friend, Moe Gasior, the Athletic Director from Carteret; Moe's brother, Freddy; Moe's brother-in-law, John Little, Pete Donelon, a good pal of Jay's; and Bob Lozack, the Cross Country Coach at HP and Business teacher, to recruit men as the first Track and Field Officials Chapter in New Jersey.

The inaugural meeting of the Track and Field Officials Association was held in the faculty cafeteria at Highland Park High School. Jay took the helm as the organization's first president and Bob Lozack volunteered his services as Treasurer. Jay drafted a constitution for the fledgling organization which was ratified by the founders, a document which still serves as the framework of the organization today.

The New Jersey Track and Field Officials Association (NJTFOA) started as a single chapter but eventually spread across New Jersey. Today, there are seven large chapters including Northeast, Northwest, Central, Shore, Southern Bay Shore, Capital, and South. The officials from each district service the dual meets in their area and during the State Championship season, representatives from each district work at the many sites on competition days.

The NJTFOA has an Executive Committee that gathers several times a year to discuss issues that are evolving in the sport as times and needs change. For example, major issues have included what constitutes a legal uniform for athletes, can runners wear watches and other jewelry during their races, and the infractions for which an athlete can be disqualified. Jay, as the founder of the organization, served also as the first president of the Executive Committee.

Over the years, the rules have become more intricate as social issues have evolved. Health concerns dictated the need for some rules to be put in place. For example, as the AIDs epidemic spread, coaches, officials, and athletes had to be prepared for what to do if a competitor fell and sustained an injury that bled. Dehydration became a serious matter as climate change led to warmer spring and early summer days in which athletes need to drink plenty of fluids.

Due to Jay's long involvement in defining the rules for track in New Jersey, he was selected eventually as a representative from the Eastern District to serve on the National Federation of High School Athletics Rules Committee. This vital group meets each year in Kansas City to revisit every rule included in the Federation Rules of the sport. Jay served for several years on this committee, which was a great honor for him as well as for the state of NJ.

An example of how Jay's ideas impacted the national scene in Track and Field had to do with the structure of races in a meet. Jay felt that there was greater opportunity for teams with the best sprinters to score in competition, making it more likely for those teams to win meets. Therefore, in the 1980s he advocated for the addition of the 400-meter hurdle race for both girls and boys and the removal of the 4 X 100 m. dash in dual meets, except for relay meets.

As a result, NJ became the only state to run the 400 m. hurdles, while all the other states ran the 300 m. hurdles, feeling that the 400 was too grueling for the high school athlete. After seeing the phenomenal records being set in NJ by both girls and boys teams, eventually the Federation took out the 300 m. hurdles and instituted the 400 m. hurdles in the Federation National rulebook. This alteration to the structure of meets was just one of the innovations that Jay brought to a sport he "knew nothing about." Once again, it was his vision of fairness in a sport that led to his insistence on the addition of the tougher race.

One day, as he stood on the edge of the indoor track at the antiquated Jersey City Armory, Jay began chatting with Coach

Eugene "Red" Littler of Tenafly High School in Bergen County, NJ. Jay and Red made an odd couple as they stood complaining to each other about the miserable facility and the pace of the meet, which seemed to slog on forever.

Jay, as always battling his weight problem, stood next to tall and sinewy Red, who chewed on an unlit stogie, wearing his white cowboy hat and pointy, snakeskin boots, his perennial uniform of choice.

"We could do a better job than this at making this meet run more efficiently," Jay voiced his frustration to Red. They were developing a comfortable camaraderie as each meet took longer to finish.

"Let's do it!" Red replied enthusiastically.

Eugene "Red" Littler was born in Painesville, Ohio in 1918.[8] From a very early age Red was crazy about sports, particularly track. In high school, he was an undefeated sprinter and was named to the All-American High School team. When he graduated high school in 1938, the *Los Angeles Times* cited him as one of the three best sprinters in the United States that year.[9]

After a brief stint at Compton Junior College in California, his mile relay team set a National Junior College record, beating USC in head-to-head competition. At the time, USC was the nation's dominant track school.

After Junior College, Red transferred to the University of Nebraska where he ran for the famed coach, Ed Wier. In 1940, he set an NCAA indoor record for the 300-yard race, a record that was held for a decade. The following year, he shaved two seconds off the 440-yard race during the Sugar Bowl Meet in New Orleans.[10]

After graduating from Nebraska in 1942, Red joined the Navy and trained as a pilot.[11] He saw action in the Pacific during World War II and again during the Korean War. Including active reserves, Red had a distinguished 25-year career with the Navy and retired as a Lt. Commander in 1978.[12]

In 1954, Red began his 28-year career as a track, cross country, football, and basketball coach at Tenafly High School in Bergen County, NJ. He eventually became the Athletic Director and Vice Principal as well. During his career, he touched the lives of thousands of students.

His astonishing record as a track coach was 141-12-1, which included nine unbeaten teams. Under his reign, Red's teams won five State Outdoor and eight State Indoor Championships, nine Bergen County Titles, twelve league titles, and had two East US Mile Relay Championship squads.[13]

Jay and Red shared the honor of serving as the Referees for the Penn Relays High School Championships for over 25 years. The Penn Relays, held each year in April, is considered one of the most elite track meets in the world.

Together this unique pair of men, Red and Jay, who represented what Tom Brokaw dubbed "the greatest generation" came together to change forever the New Jersey State Championship system.

After their agreement to update the format of the State meet system, they took their proposal to Jim Growney, the Executive Director of the NJSIAA, to appoint them as the meet administrators for the State Championship Indoor and Outdoor meets, which the duo ran together for over 30 years, incorporating many imaginative innovations with them.

Over the years, Jay's friendships with the Rutgers Track and Field Coach, Les Wallach, proved to be extremely helpful as well as his relationship with Irwin Weiss, who eventually became the Athletic Director at Princeton University. Jay's relationship with Irwin would have a longstanding and positive influence on the New Jersey State High School Indoor Championship Programs in later years. One of the first things that Jay did to improve the Indoor Track State Meet was to contact his old friend, Irwin Weiss at Princeton University.

"Irwin," Jay said, "I've got an idea to propose to you. You know that the state has been holding our indoor meets at the Jersey City Armory, and it's just a mess. The meets start at 8:00 in the morning, and sometimes we don't get home until midnight. We have way outgrown that facility."

"I agree with you, Jay," said Irwin. "What are you thinking?

"We would like to move the State Indoor Championships to Jadwin Gym."

Jadwin Gym was the new athletic facility on the Princeton University Campus. The mother of Leander Stockwell Jadwin (Class of 1928) had donated $27 million dollars to the university in memory of her son, who had been killed in an automobile wreck shortly after his graduation from the University.[14]

Opened in 1969, the multipurpose athletic facility has a combined floor space of approximately 250,000 square feet, more total area than eight football fields.[15] The top floor has several basketball courts, and on the subfloors, there are six tennis courts, eleven international-sized squash courts, and a baseball/softball practice area with an artificial turf surface.

The 200-meter, six-lane track sits atop an indoor baseball field and there are three additional levels beneath that floor.

"Well, that's a fine idea. I'm sure Larry would love to have a first-hand look at the talent right at his home track," Irwin agreed. "Of course, it's going to take some inquiries and a lot of investigation to see if we can make it happen. I'll talk to Larry tomorrow and get him on board for starters."

The Larry to whom Irwin was referring was Larry Ellis, the first black head track coach at Princeton University, a position that he had held for 22 years.[16] The Head Track and Field Coach in the 1984 Olympics, Ellis's Tigers had captured eleven conference titles in track and eight in Cross Country during his tenure at Princeton University.

A graduate of DeWitt High School in New York, Ellis won the IC4A Cross Country Championship for NYU as a freshman. As a senior, he took second in the IC4A half mile and third in the AAU Championships.[17]

After graduating from NYU, Ellis entered the Army Artillery and served for seven months in Korea during the war, receiving an honorary discharge in 1953.[18]

After coaching at Jamaica High School for twelve years, building distinguished teams, in 1970 he was hired at Princeton University. Among the many great athletes whom he coached over the years, Olympic Gold Medalist and former world record holder in the long jump, Bob Beamon was one of his many stars.[19]

A charismatic leader, after the State Meet was moved to the luxurious Jadwin Gym in Princeton, Ellis was seen frequently chatting with the athletes, their coaches, and the many officials who enjoyed just being in the great man's presence. He was incredibly supportive of the New Jersey State Meet being held at Jadwin Gym.

The Indoor Meets at Jadwin Gym were extraordinary experiences for the youth of New Jersey. Just to say that they had run at the famous Ivy League Track was a privilege that many of the athletes never forgot. And there were many, many extraordinary races run by young men and women who went on to distinguish themselves in the Olympics and professional sports.

As each Indoor season ended, Jay and Red threw a party for the officials to celebrate another year of camaraderie and dedication. The men and women who spent long winter days atop shaky officials' stands, holding their watches and counting laps, (8 to a mile) deserved to celebrate their devotion to the sport. Platters of deli sandwiches, pickles, cole slaw, and macaroni salad, as well as adult beverages were brought into a room on a lower floor of the gym to be devoured by the exhausted officials as they wished each other well until the beginning of the spring season, just six weeks away.

There is no doubt that the fellowship and dedication the New Jersey Track and Field Officials Association enjoyed was due to the leadership and commitment of Jay Dakelman and Red Littler.

Today, in memory of the two visionaries, annual awards are given to two deserving track officials. The Gene ``Red" Littler Award is given to "The Official of the Year." It is presented to an NJTFOA official who has distinguished him/herself in officiating within an academic year. The Jay H. Dakelman Award goes to an official who has dedicated at least 25 years to the sport and has distinguished him/herself as a meet director or other prestigious position in the organization. In this way, the legacy of these two dedicated American educators is forever memorialized in a sport that they both loved.

We all have dreams. But in order to make dreams come into reality, it takes an awful lot of determination, dedication, self-discipline, and effort.
Jesse Owens

CHAPTER 21

MORE TRACK!

In 1958, after more than ten years of coaching without a home track or football field, Jaay was elated to find out that Superintendent E. H. Gilliland announced that the Highland Park Board of Education planned to initiate a much-needed building plan for the high school. The plan was to include classrooms, a new gym, and upgrades to many of the older classrooms. School authorities also decided to "develop the property in the rear of the school for football, baseball, track and tennis."[1] The plan was put before the township for a vote, which passed to the joy of the athletes and coaches at HPHS.

Germinating in Jay's mind was an idea for the "dream track" that was about to be constructed on the mud behind the high school. Why not build a track based on the blueprints of Rutgers Stadium? In fact, why not get the same kind of cinder that Rutgers had used in the creation of its renovated track?

And, with his many connections at Rutgers, Jay was able to do exactly that. The new track built in Highland Park was state-of-the-art when it opened in 1960. The material used for the actual running surface was called "En-Tout-Cas," which was a crushed brick material used for tennis courts as well. This unique product was imported from England and made for a very fast-running surface.[2]

Not long after the construction of the track, Jay took steps to fulfill another dream that he had to further catapult Highland Park's reputation in the sport that he now knew plenty about. He got together with Marshall Berman, one of his former athletes, who owned a successful cleaning business. Marshall wanted to give something back to the school that he loved and credited for his success.

The partnership between Berman and Coach Dakelman led to one of the most beloved and prestigious high school track meets in the history of the sport in New Jersey. The Highland Park Relays, instituted in 1961, was held on the second weekend of April, a week prior to the Penn Relays. Since the meet was an invitational, the schools which participated in the early days of the event were highly competitive.

However, the meet also fostered strong competition for novice runners, jumpers, and throwers as well, allowing for junior varsity entries in many events. The opportunity for the younger athletes to compete in a prestigious meet and bring home medals helped to make the Highland Park Relays even more popular with coaches, athletes, and spectators. The meet offered a unique combination of being a developmental opportunity for younger athletes while showcasing the talents of the experienced competitors.

The Highland Park Relays Games Committee did not invite only New Jersey schools to the meet. Competitive teams from

New York and Pennsylvania were welcomed as well, which made for an even more dynamic type of competition.

In every way, the Highland Park Relays was considered a class event. Most particularly, the awards that the winners received were some of the most coveted of any high school competition. All athletes who took first place in their events received watches, just as they did at the Penn Relays. The watches were a more practical sign of success than medals in that they could be worn proudly day after day so that students could remember their moments of glory at the meet.

The days of the Highland Park Relays were festive and exciting. The stands were filled with athletes attired in all colors of the rainbow. Proud parents, friends, and other relatives streamed into the stadium to cheer on the thrilling events of the day. The grounds around the beautiful, new track were filled with tents where competitors could rest, out of the sun's rays, when they were not performing on the track or in the field.

Many former athletes have stated repeatedly that the baseball teams of Highland Park tended to be mediocre. Conversely, the track team abounded with athletes clamoring to run, jump, or throw for Coach Dakelman. It turns out that there was a reason for the wealth of trackmen as opposed to baseball players.

Jerry Donini (Class of 1958) relayed this story about joining the track team. He stated, "In high school, my favorite sport starting out was basketball. Coach Dakelman had been my JV coach. In the basketball off-season of my sophomore year, Coach D. encouraged me to join the track team. I told him I wasn't interested in any sport other than basketball. He said, 'That's ok, come out for track to stay in good physical condition until basketball season starts again.'

"As it turned out, that was the best advice I could ever have gotten. I joined the track team and started working on the shot put and discus. Jay spent a great amount of time teaching me. He not only knew to a tee all the right components of form required to perform at your best but spent a good amount of his time teaching me. He had high requirements and set high standards, but at the same time was very supportive. I never had another coach like him. He was the greatest.

"I did very well in the shot put and earned multiple full scholarships to numerous universities. Yes, I had to do the work to get there, but I credit Coach Dakelman for being a great motivator and coach to make it happen. I only wish that when I went to college, he was still my coach. Very few people leave an indelible, positive mark on your memory throughout your life. Jay was one of those people."[3]

Another football player who told a similar story was Ted Kryzanowski, who loved baseball when he started high school. However, at the end of his freshman year, he was disillusioned with the way the team was coached and voiced his concerns to Coach D.

"Why don't you come out for track?" Jay cajoled.

Teddy gave it some thought and finally agreed. "It took some time for Coach to figure out what events would be best for me. Eventually, I became a high jumper and a long jumper."[4]

After high school Ted, a handsome, young man, was drafted into the Army and while in Vietnam, suffered a catastrophic injury in a battle in which many men in his unit were killed. Ted lost an arm on that dark day.

When he came home, he decided to attend an HPHS football game. He stopped at the ticket booth, bought a two-dollar seat, and started the trek to the field. As he was passing the back entrance of the school, the team barged through the gym doors, causing a riotous racket. Lost amid his brawny brutes, Jay could barely be seen. However, he spotted Teddy and left the team momentarily, extending his arms for an embrace. Knowing first-hand what the brave, young soldier had endured, Jay's love for Teddy was deeply felt.

"I'll never forget it," Kryzanowski pronounced when talking about his favorite memory of his coach. "Here he was, about to take the team on the field and he left them to say hello to me. It meant the world to me."[5]

Most amazingly, Ted explained, "I never knew about Jay's war experiences during World War II. It was not something that he ever talked about with us."[6]

There was the occasional athlete whom Jay chose to strong-arm into running for him. His own son, Mitchell, was one such case. At the time that Mitchell entered HPHS in the fall of 1967, he was a scrawny boy, weighing no more than 100 pounds and he stood about 5'8 in height. He was not football material.

However, Coach Dakelman had Mitch into his office early in the fall of his freshman year and said to him, "Mitchell, you obviously aren't coming out for football, but you are going to run Cross Country in the fall and track in the Winter and Spring season."

Mitchell, an easy-going young man, said, "Okay," and joined Bob Lozack's phenomenal Cross Country squad, which did very well. Mitch enjoyed the camaraderie of being part of a team and didn't mind the miles of running that he was expected to do every day. He liked running along the "banks of the Old Raritan" in Donaldson Park, which was Highland Park High School's home Cross Country course.

Going to track meets had been ingrained in Mitchell since childhood when Jay would bring him along to the Jersey City Armory to watch the races. He had also served as the football team mascot as a little boy, riding on the yellow buses with the boisterous teams who enjoyed beating most of their opponents.

Mitchell had an interesting hobby of which Jay approved wholeheartedly, especially since the entire football team got to enjoy his projects. Mitchell would abscond with rolls of adding machine tape from Grandpa Louie's basement and draw the highways of New Jersey in detail, mile by mile on the tape. He created facsimiles of the Garden State Parkway and the New Jersey Turnpike and would give the roll of tape to the first player in Row 1 of the bus. The other players would unwind the drawings carefully, pouring over the landmarks familiar to all of them. Mitchell would sit at the back of the bus, winding the rolls of tape carefully so as not to spoil his work. It was amazing how much the teens enjoyed and appreciated the drawings of Coach D's son.

Over the years, Mitchell learned to love running and continued at the University of Maryland, running Cross Country for Coach Dean and track for Coach Kovalidkedes.

The day after Mitchell had seen the family at the Penn Relays in the spring of 1975, he called his sister, Beth, to inform her that he was desperately trying to get in touch with their parents. He had been jogging that morning and suddenly heard a loud crack and fell to the ground. In fact, his femur had snapped in half just above the knee at a 90-degree angle and he had been taken to

Leland Memorial Hospital, the closest medical facility to the University. Leland Memorial was a small hospital run by 7th Day Adventists.

The physicians involved in Mitchell's case needed to do surgery immediately to put a pin in the young man's knee to immobilize it. Since Mitch was a senior and only a month from graduation, the news that he would be in traction for about six weeks was a devastating blow. Also, he had procured an internship at a radio station in Washington, D.C. that would now have to be foregone.

"I'll find Mom and Dad," Beth promised and took the phone number so that Thelma and Jay could contact the hospital with the insurance information and get updates on Mitchell's condition.

When Jay finally did answer the phone and Beth informed him of Mitchell's broken femur, Jay's response was, "Impossible. The femur is the strongest bone in the human body. He couldn't have broken his femur."

"Look, Dad," Beth countered, "I don't know anything about bones in the body. I'm just telling you what Mitch told me."

Thelma and Jay got right into Jay's old Buick and drove the four hours to College Park, Maryland, arriving about 9:00 that night. Mitch had the surgery, and his anxious parents awaited the results of testing that would show whether the break had been caused by a stress fracture or an unfortunate bout of cancer. Fortunately, disease was ruled out as the cause, but no definitive reason was ever decided upon for the break.

Luckily, all of Mitchell's professors waived his final exams, and the Dean of the School of Arts brought Mitchell's diploma to his hospital room following the formal university graduation. A well-known and popular figure on the Terrapin campus, everyone who was acquainted with Mitch felt terrible about his "bad break."

A Radio and Television major, Mitchell had a great fondness for old movies and vintage cartoons. Jay brought Mitch his projector and reels of films for his son to entertain the patients and nurses of Leland Memorial Hospital during his lengthy stay at the hospital. Despite being in traction and literally tied to his bed, Mitch would lean over to thread films into his projector and spend hours enjoying classic films.

One night at the end of June, Mitch called home at midnight and got his parents on the line. He was laughing, but the call wasn't very amusing to his distraught Mom and Dad.

"Tonight, they took me up to the operating room and put me in a body cast," Mitch explained. "The cast starts just under the armpits and goes to my ankles. Then, there is a bar between my legs to keep me totally immobile. I have one hole in the front and one hole in the back so I can go to the bathroom."

The idea of nursing Mitchell at home in the Dakelman house was daunting, to say the least, but on a beautiful summer Sunday, the rescue squad from Highland Park drove to College Park, Maryland and brought "the mummy" home, where he languished for another six weeks in the small family room of the house where a hospital bed had been brought in to accommodate Mitchell's situation.

It was amazing to watch Mitchell's attitude and good nature in his miserable predicament, and Thelma proved to be a patient nurse. Mitch continued to make jokes about his dilemma and counted the days until he would be cut out of the plaster prison in which his body was healing.

Finally, the day came and the cast, which was falling apart after so much use, was sawed off and Mitchell was given a pair of crutches to use to support his leg, which had shrunk significantly from the ordeal. He refused to use the crutches, didn't have physical therapy, but went back to his routine of running in Donaldson Park.

Miraculously, a couple of years later, the tenacious film buff ran the New York Marathon for the first time, completing the 26 miles in four hours and twenty minutes. Following the trauma of the injury that he had suffered, the entire family rejoiced in his total recovery and commitment to the sport that his father had dictated to him that he would run.

Mitchell's fortitude and devotion to the sport of Track and Field had been ingrained in him by a coach who had insisted that the 90-pound weakling take up a sport while in high school. Since he turned 18 years old, Mitch has been a devoted track official, serving as the Central Chapter's president, as well as president of the Executive Committee.

Over the years, Jay had some truly outstanding State Champions in a multitude of events, but one of the most exciting young men was Teddy Pisciotta, who was a remarkable hurdler. When Teddy received an invitation to the prestigious meet held in California, The Golden West Invitational, Jay jumped on the opportunity to take his star hurdler to the meet and set about raising money once again to pay for their flights, lodging and fees.

Initially, the Golden West Invitational was conceived as a postseason meet to showcase the most talented athletes in track and field in the nation.

"The GWI is a meet built on the idea of a 'go for broke competition' —no heats, no trials, no team score pressures," is how the meet is described on its website.[7] Athletes are invited from all over the nation to showcase the talented competitors.

Jay and Teddy relished their experience in California even though Teddy did not win his event. Jay was enormously proud to have Highland Park represented in a national meet. Neither Jay nor Teddy had ever been to California before, so the opportunity to represent Highland Park 3000 miles from home was extraordinary.

In 1968, Jay retired from coaching Track and Field due to his expanding duties as Athletic Director, a job to which he had been appointed several years before. Bus Lepine had advanced to being the Assistant Principal of the high school, and later served as the Business Administrator for the district. As the school continued to add more sports to the busy Athletic Department, the demands on Jay's time expanded exponentially.

When he accepted the job as Athletic Director, Jay still taught Physical Education several periods a day. The rest of the day was spent on the phone hiring buses, checking with officials to make sure that they were in place for the day's competition, working on schedules for the next year for each sport, and attending meetings, meetings, and more meetings. Many of the meetings called for Jay to travel to the New Jersey State Interscholastic Athletic Association headquarters in Robbinsville, NJ.

Usually, the meetings at NJSIAA had to do with the administration of the Indoor and Outdoor State Championship Meets. Each year, the NJSIAA had to revise the Rules and Regulations for those events, making sure that the deadlines for coaches to have their school's meet entries to the state office were accurate and rule changes between the National Federation Rules and the New Jersey Rules were clarified. Jay would go over the entry forms carefully and craft the program that would detail the schedule of the day's events, including the names and entry numbers of the athletes. Just one mistake in an athlete's number could throw everything off for the meet officials and coaches so perfection was necessary in recording all entry numbers.

The structure of the state meet system involved three weekends of track and field meets. The first weekend, which occurred during Memorial Day, was for the sectional championships. Eight meets were held across the state, which involved athletes from various regions to compete in four groups, each group based on the size of the male population in grades 10, 11, and 12.

The State Group Championships were held the following weekend. The top five athletes in each event competed against the top five from each of the other sections from the previous week. Using the scoring system devised by the National Federation of High School Sports, the team that scored the highest number of points for the day was deemed the State Championship Team for their group.

On the third weekend of the championship system, the top five competitors from each group competed against one another in The Meet of Champions, an extremely thrilling track and field competition, which was held at Rutgers Stadium in New Brunswick.

Over the years that Jay served as Meet Director for New Jersey, the job became more tedious and difficult. As the suburbs expanded in the state, the number of high schools eligible to enter the meet grew. Schools were larger and entered more athletes in each event, causing the length of the championship meets to become longer as well.

The biggest growth occurred when women's championships were added. Within several years of Womens Track and Field, it became necessary to institute separate sectional meets for the ladies in the first rung of the competition. Eventually, the first two weeks of the state competition had to be held at two sites on Friday and Saturday. These were extremely long and very hot days for the athletes and the officials to endure as New Jersey gets quite warm by early June.

Jay knew that he needed help in organizing the meet more efficiently and began to contemplate the idea of using computer technology to put the program together. He was fortunate to find an English teacher from South Jersey, Don Danser, who loved the sport and understood what was needed to improve the burden of meet administration. Don took over receiving the entries and creating the program. He and Jay worked well together, particularly in the subsequent weeks of the meet when programs had to be compiled within days of the sectional and group meets to be ready for the following week's competition.

Bringing in computer technology was a huge step forward in modernizing the antiquated system that had existed since the beginning of organized sports. In the coming years, there were many other innovations, such as the Fully Automatic Timing system, which took the stopwatches out of the hands of human beings and put them more effectively into a system recorded through computer technology. Using the F.A.T. ensured that the athletes were placed in the correct order of finish as opposed to the debates that ensued often on the finish line as to who took 3rd, 4th, or 5th in a race.

Always lauded as an innovator, Jay was prepared to leap into the next phase of keeping the meet contemporary and most importantly, fair to the athletes who competed. That was always his number one priority.

*Rather than focusing on the obstacle in your path, focus on
the bridge over the obstacle.*
Mary Lou Retton

CHAPTER 22

WOMEN IN SPORTS

Jay was determined to teach his little sister, Carol, how to play football in his parents' bedroom. He explained to her that the field was the large bed, and the goal posts were the four posters, two at each end of the bed. He would let her have his football and watch her crawl towards the wooden posts before diving onto her, nearly crushing her tiny body with his solid frame.

"Ma," Carol would scream in five-year-old frustration, "Jay won't let me make a touchdown!"

Even as a youngster, Jay believed to his core that women should have the same opportunities as men had when it came to athletic competition. He carried this belief with him through his entire career and began actively advocating for equality as early as the 1940s when he first started coaching track and field.

Going to Panzer College nurtured Jay's ideas regarding women's participation in sports. From the earliest days of the Newark Normal School of Physical Education and Hygiene, as the school was known originally, women took part in exercise and sport that would allow their bodies to become healthy and strong. The antiquated Victorian image of a woman being dainty, and frail began to fade as women embraced athleticism.

Due to the poor physical condition in which the army recruits reported for duty to serve in World War I, the government began to encourage schools to address the problem of physical fitness in the country's youth. Pathetically out of shape, the physicians in the United States began to take a serious look at the need for classes in Health and Physical Education from grades 1-12. Fortunately, once established, the need to include Health and Physical Education in the school curriculum has never wavered, despite its critics. Educators still recognize that without a physically fit and health-educated public, not even the smartest brainiac can succeed in life.

Back in the early teens of the 20th century, there were no institutions of higher learning that included teacher training in the field of Health and Physical Education. Thus, in 1917, Matthias Machery and Randall D. Warden, Directors of Physical Education for the city of Newark, started the Newark Normal School of Physical Education and Hygiene.[1]

At the end of 1920, the founders of the program turned it over to Henry Panzer, the Director of the Normal School at that time.[2] In 1925, the teachers' program moved to a site in East Orange, where the program went from a two-year course of studies to a three-year program.

In 1925, Panzer College purchased property at 139 Glenwood Avenue in East Orange. Until the school was able to construct its own gymnasium, the students shared a facility with Upsala College. The main building of the pretty, little campus can be seen on the opening pages of every *Olympia* yearbook published during the school's independent existence.

In 1928, the school added a fourth year of studies to its curriculum, which led to a Bachelor of Physical Education being offered. At this time, the school earned the name the Panzer College of Physical Education and Hygiene.[3]

Panzer College of Physical Education and Hygiene contributed greatly to the growing field of educators in the field. Aside from adding teachers to the profession, it "provided leadership for community groups—and gave service to individuals with special needs."[4]

Following Henry Panzer's sudden death in 1932, Dr. Margaret C. Brown, who had served as a teacher, registrar, and dean of the college since 1921, the Board of Trustees elected her as the President and Treasurer of the school. Under her superior tutelage, Panzer became recognized nationally as well as internationally as a college known for making great advancements in the profession. The fact that the Board of Trustees selected a woman to lead the school as it continued to develop shows how forward-thinking those associated with Panzer were from its earliest days. The wisdom of selecting Brown for the leadership post turned out to be brilliant. To this day, Dr. Margaret C. Brown is remembered and recognized in the field of Physical Education as a pioneer and prime motivator.

Through Brown's continuing efforts, New Jersey authorized the granting of the degree of Bachelor of Science in 1939, abandoning the old title of Bachelor of Physical Education.

By the time Jay committed to attend Panzer, having turned down the pre-med program at Purdue, much to the chagrin of his disappointed parents, the school was considered elite, due to Brown's tough leadership and demand for rigor in the classroom. Her expectations for students were set exceedingly high. For example, when not in Phys. Ed. class, students were expected to wear their Panzer blazers, nice slacks or skirts, and ties for men always. Dr. Brown believed that how one presented himself or herself to the world reflected his or her professional attitude as well as Panzer's reputation for producing the best teaching candidates in the field.

Dr. Brown, a Canadian by birth, earned both her Bachelor's and Master's Degrees at Rutgers—the State University of New Jersey and her Ph.D. at NYU.

As a proponent of the approach to Physical Education known as "movement education," which dated back to the 1880s, Dr. Brown co-authored a book with Betty Sommers, a Czech official with ties to rhythmic sports gymnastics, as it was known in the early 20th century.[5] Henry Panzer, who was a close friend as well as an associate of Dr. Brown, believed strongly in the theory of movement education as did she.

Movement education is instruction in the improvement of a person's motor skills through physical movement. Often part of physical therapy, the patient or student acquires a better understanding of how his/her body behaves when it is in motion with increased efficiency of movement in one's day to day activities through that understanding. The goal of movement education is for students to improve their overall health and physical movement by keying into how the body works.

As Jay continued his work in the field of Health and Physical Education, his philosophy diverged from that of Dr. Brown and Henry Panzer. In the 1970s, the world became obsessed with physical fitness, and as people took to jogging and working out to maintain their health and well-being, research deviated from pursuing movement alone as the cornerstone for the course of study in Health and Phys. Ed. With the boom in everything fitness-oriented, from the explosion of types of shoes available on the market to the flourishing of gyms, to Richard Simmons and *Dancing to the Oldies*, to Jane Fonda looking good at the age of fifty, the movement philosophy faded from relevance and popularity in colleges and universities.

The diversion from movement to fitness served for "heated discussions" between Jay and Dr. Brown regarding the way Physical Education should be taught. Clinging to her "old school" beliefs, Jay argued that the interest in physical fitness for life would instill in students the major justification for taking Health and Physical Education for twelve years of public-school education. By concentrating on activities that would benefit individuals for a lifetime, as well as including the importance of team sports in building confidence, camaraderie, and mutual respect between people with a personal stake in winning on the field of play, human beings would live longer, healthier, and more productive lives.

Over the years that Jay attended Panzer, he had an interesting relationship with Dr. Brown, one that grew to the point that Jay considered her a great mentor and dear friend. He continued to visit her regularly until her death at the age of 98 in August of 1990, only months before his own passing. He would take his three children to visit Dr. Brown when he visited in her later years, and when his youngest daughter, Rhonda, was contemplating becoming a Physical Education major in college, Dr. Brown offered her advice to one of New Jersey's first women state championship javelin throwers.

There is no question, however, that the heated debates that Dr. Brown and Jay enjoyed over the many years of their friendship, spurred Jay's imagination and contributed to the development of his vision for the importance of Health and Physical Education for all people, no matter their sex, age, or race.

By 1958, Panzer was struggling to stay afloat financially, and Montclair State College was considering the addition of a Health and Physical Education major to its growing teacher training programs. At the time, Panzer was the last of the private, single-purpose schools preparing Physical Education teachers in the country.

Thus, the two schools arranged for a merger, "bringing to the union its excellent progressional and academic standards, planned professional laboratory experiences, a curriculum of quality, traditions of 41 years, and supportive and influential alumni."[6]

According to USA Gym Legacy, "Without Margaret Brown, it is conceivable that women's gymnastics would not be the sport it is today. When Brown hit the gymnastics scene in the 1930s, the sport was run by men for men, but this soon changed thanks to her efforts and vision. Brown carried a catalogue of titles— delegate, manager, official, but what is most noteworthy is her contribution to help establish the US Women's Technical Committee based on her observations of the International Women's Gymnastics Committee. She served as the US gymnastics manager in three Olympics, judged internationally and administered both men's and women's gymnastics at the national level."[7]

At the time that Dr. Brown became involved in the Olympic movement, there was no women's committee in the sport of gymnastics. The AAU Men's Gymnastics Committee and the

American Olympic Committee oversaw both the men's and women's teams and competition.

In 1936, Brown represented the US as the Manager of the Olympic Team and World Championship judge. As a result of the insights that she gained while serving the team in Berlin, she was able to present recommendations to the 1936 American Olympic report as well as to Roy E. Moore, the Chairperson of the American Olympic Gymnastic Committee.[8] Shortly thereafter, a US Women's Technical Committee was established in the United States, and Dr. Margaret C. Brown served on this committee with distinction until 1960.

Her pioneering efforts to bring about the development of women's gymnastics in the United States were fulfilled when in 1969, she was invited to present the medals and report on the first DGWS National Intercollegiate Gymnastics Championships for Women at Springfield College. Her noteworthy efforts resulted in achieving her dream of women's athletics that she had harbored all her life.

When Jay began teaching at Highland Park High School, there were two other members of the Physical Education Department. Bus Lepine was the primary male instructor, and a diminutive firecracker from South Carolina, Maude Stockman, was the teacher for the girls' classes. By the early 1950s, a second woman, Marilyn Taigi, was added to the department and Jay dropped his duties as a Guidance Counselor and became full-time in Physical Education. Classes were divided so that one male instructor taught all the freshmen and junior boys and the other taught sophomores and seniors. The same division of the classes existed for the women.

The team of Phys. Ed. instructors wanted to showcase the many talents of young ladies in physical activities. Since the inception of the high school in 1936, one of the most popular clubs in existence was the Girl's Athletic Club, which met on a weekly basis for girls to enjoy playing field hockey, soccer, basketball, and softball after school.

With gym classes only 50 minutes long and seven minutes needed on either end for changing into one's maroon, skirted gym suit with the student's last name embroidered in three-inch letters across the back, only thirty minutes a class was allowed for play. Take into consideration that the first ten minutes of actual class time was devoted to the taking of attendance and calisthenics for warm-up, and the last ten minutes of class was taken up with showers and changing back into school clothes, students netted twenty minutes per class of actual play time.

Although the school was forty years from the establishment of actual interscholastic athletics, games took place between the Girls Athletic Clubs from New Brunswick and Highland Park starting in the late 1930s. The way in which these games usually worked was that the gym was sub-divided into three courts, allowing for five girls from each school to engage in a "game" per session. The situation was far from ideal, but at least the young women had an opportunity to engage in competitive sport, even if it was small.

Jay had heard about a special activity that Trenton High School had implemented to highlight women in sports. He suggested that Highland Park use the Trenton model and hold Girls' Sports Night every two years in which the female students of HPHS had time to shine in the gymnasium. Each gym class prepared a performance, including marching routines, calisthenics, or Modern Dance. Girls Sports Night occurred at the end of the second marking period, usually in February. Jay was the one who created the program of events from the beginning of Girls Sports Night.

The first Girls Sports Night took place in the "old gym" in 1952. Of the event Pat Burns Toth (Class of 1955) recalled, "Mrs. Stockman had us dancing. I remember that we did a "Falling Leaves routine."[9]

The two classes of Freshmen prepared marching routines, the Sophomores performed calisthenics routines, and the Juniors and Seniors created modern dances. The school was divided into two teams: the red and the gray. Since there were two sections of Physical Education for each grade level, the division of competition worked out evenly.

In the 1956 *Albadome*, the editors included this note, "To Mrs. Maude Stockman and Mrs. Marilyn Taigi, our gym teachers, we owe many thanks for their patient help and guidance toward a successful Girls Sports Night. The theme was 'Disneyland.' A varied program included marching, dancing, cheering, tumbling, and twirling. Barbara MacKinney did a wonderful job as Mistress of Ceremonies and general chairperson. The captain of the Red Team was Joice Anderson; of the Gray Team, Virginia Sullivan."[10]

In the Disney-themed Girls Sports Night, one sophomore class performed as "the Lady and the Tramp," competing against the other sophomore class who danced to "Siamese cats." The junior groups were teddy bears, another group performed as Robin Hood, and one group of seniors danced as sailors. Each number required the production of simple costumes and props if needed.

One of the most memorable numbers ever performed in a Girls Sports Night occurred in the 1956 program. The dancers wore black leotards and tights, with bright white gloves, hats, socks, and sneakers. The lights in the gym extinguished and the audience could see only the white articles of clothing moving to the music of "The Syncopated Clock." It was a stunning and memorable performance, and the group won its event on both nights.

The theme of the 1964 Girls Sports Night was the World's Fair, which was happening at the time in Long Island, New York. The freshmen girls marched to either "Stars and Stripes Forever" and "The Bridge Over the River Kwai ("Colonel Bogey's March"). Dressed in red kimonos, the Asian number was an enormous success during the competition against its "American" counterpart.

Margie Bernstein Metzgar (Class of '66) reminisced about Girls Sports Night, saying, "Girls Sports Night was a way for a girl like me, who was not particularly athletic, to participate in a fun group activity and get dressed up at the same time."[11]

While the girls performed for their parents, male students, and the community, the boy athletes assisted as "stage managers," moving tumbling mats, gymnastic equipment, and other props as needed onto and off the gymnasium floor.

Aside from his enthusiastic support of Girls Sports Night, Jay always had his eye out for exceptional female ability on the track. Dotty Eayres, remembered by her classmates as a tremendous athlete, was cited in the *Albadome*, along with her male counterpart, Steve Friedman as "Most Athletic."

"She was a muscular girl," reminisced Pat Burns Toth, one of Dotty's friends since they attended Lafayette Elementary

School together. "She was a great athlete. Mr. Dakelman took an interest in her and Marie Stout and got them involved in track."[12]

According to George Kish (Class of '55) husband of Dotty Eayres, "Coach Dakelman was able to get Dotty into the Olympic trials in Chicago. Her mother took her out there to run the hurdles. Unfortunately, Dotty did not qualify."[13]

Kish went on to explain that it was Dotty's dream to become a Physical Education teacher. "Mr. Dakelman helped Dotty get into Monmouth College for Physical Education. However, her parents wouldn't let her go to college, so she never got to fulfill that dream."[14]

In the early 1960s a beautiful, brunette, Rosemarie Heldrich, attended a track meet held in New Brunswick for children of the city. Part of a recreation program to keep students active during the summer months, children flocked to the event. Even though Rosemarie was a resident of Highland Park, her dad managed to get her into the meet.

Rosemarie's father, a banker in New Brunswick, urged the girl to run in the sprint races, although she preferred to run distance. As good fortune would have it, Les Wallach, the Rutgers track coach, and a close friend of Jay's, happened to be at the meet that day, watching the budding athletes and helping time races.

When Rosemarie beat all the boys in her age class, he put a phone call to Jay the next week. "This girl is a phenomenon," he told Jay. "It's a shame high schools don't have programs for the gals yet."

"That's okay," Jay said. "I have a plan for her. Thanks for letting me know."[15]

One afternoon, when Rosemarie was playing basketball in the Girls Athletic Club after school, she was standing near Coach Dakelman's office. He beckoned her to come speak to him.

"I hear that you are a talented runner," Jay began. "I'd like to offer you the opportunity to train with the boy's team. I can even find some races for you to compete in."

Rosemarie was stunned but extremely excited. She went home and told her dad, who was equally enthusiastic about the opportunity that Coach had just opened for his fleet-footed daughter.

The track team had begun practicing for the season when Rosemarie turned up one day to start working out with them. The young men were enthusiastic about her training with them and treated her as an equal, not as a mascot. They respected her seriousness and devotion to the sport, as well as her talent.

Since the Highland Park track was a cinder track, it was impossible to run on it in flat sneakers. The smooth soles of sneaks slid on the ashy surface and failed to grip as she ran. Mr. Heldrich began to scour local stores for spikes for girls, but there were none to available. Not one to be deterred, he paid a visit to Jay and asked him to help with a solution.

"Here's what we can do," Jay began. "After the war, I met a guy in Germany, a man named Adi Dassler. He has a shoe factory in Bavaria that makes the best athletic shoes in the world. I will write to him and see if he can make a pair of spikes especially for Rosemarie."

A few weeks later, the glorious spikes arrived at the Heldrich home. They were lipstick red, made of the softest leather that Rosemarie had ever felt. On the bottom of the shoes were the gleaming, one-inch spikes that she needed desperately to help her feet grip the track. They were the shoes of a serious athlete, not a girl who dabbled in running. She held the shoes to her and smelled the aroma of leather that she would relish each time she laced up the shoes for an event.

To think, she had a pair of shoes from Adi Das![16] Years ago when Jay had met Adi Dassler and had spoken about his teams one day in the future wearing Dassler's shoes, he never dreamed that the first pair purchased would be for a girl. Yes, Rosemarie Heldrich wore the first Adidas running shoes, purchased right from the master shoe smith himself!

Although races for girls were difficult to find, Jay encouraged Rosemarie to travel with the boy's team to every meet. At some meets, such as the annual meet at West Point, the coaches agreed to let Rosemarie run an exhibition race. She would take her position at the start, and the sound of the pistol propelled her out of the metal blocks. She ran the quarter mile on the old 440-yard tracks in 60 seconds, which for her time was impressive.[17]

Rosemarie was aware of how Coach Dakelman looked out for her. He would open the locker room for her so that she could change into her practice clothes privately. One day at practice, she got spiked badly by another runner on the turn of the track and bled heavily.

"We need to take care of that ankle right away," Coach Dakelman said to her. He led her into the gym and cleared out the boys' training room where a bubbling whirlpool tub sat. He filled the bottom of the tub with layers of ice and instructed Rosemarie to chill the offended ankle. Then, he kept the room locked so that the young woman could relax in private.

"He was always looking out for me," Rosemarie reminisced in a conversation about how Coach Dakelman encouraged her.

"I was a good student, mostly Bs," she said. "Montclair State was my first-choice school, but in those days, Montclair was considered the best state school and was extremely selective in whom they took. When Jay asked me where I wanted to go to school, as soon as I told him, he picked up the phone and called the track coach at Montclair State. After speaking with him for a few minutes, Jay hung up and said to me, 'Okay. You're in.'"[18]

Like Dotty Eayres before her, Jay believed that Rosemarie had Olympic potential, so he began to set up AAU meets for her in her Senior year of high school. He knew the importance of her being prepared to face the experienced competition that she would face if an Olympic trial ever happened, so he arranged a special race for her at Highland Park. Jay managed to get one of the girls who had already qualified for the Olympic team to go head-to-head with Rosemarie.

The night before the race, Rosemarie had to stay over at her grandmother's house. In the middle of the night, she did not feel well, and her temperature spiked. All night she tossed and fretted, perhaps due to nerves; maybe she just had a bug.

When she arrived at school the next day, Coach Dakelman could see how peaked she looked. She confessed that she had been ill during the night, but there was nothing they could do but go forward with the planned event. The Olympian blew Rosemarie away in the race and the Rosemarie felt humiliation, but not defeat.

Rosemarie continued to compete in AAU meets, which always started with what is known as the waterfall start. All the competitors in the race lined up on a curved line and when the starter's pistol rang out, the runners would cut in once they were a full stride ahead.

Rosemarie did qualify for the Olympic Trials at Randall's Island in New York. She was excited, nervous, and as she tied her bright red Adidas shoes onto her petite foot, she noticed for the first time that the start of this race was unlike the waterfall start to which she was accustomed. Here, at the Olympic trials, there were six runners, each assigned to a lane placed on the track. When the runners drew for lanes, she was lucky enough to draw the inside lane, Lane 1. However, when she looked up, all she could see was the other five girls, already so far ahead of her on the track that she could barely see the girl in Lane 6. Because she had no experience in starting a race this way, psychologically she was defeated even before the gun rang out. She lost the race and left the track feeling embarrassed and desolate.

Rosemarie did not give up her running career at this point. She did compete while at Montclair State and appeared at Madison Square Garden in an outstanding race. She has stayed involved in both education and running her entire life.

As a Speech teacher at Franklin High School in New Jersey, Rosemarie taught students who were classified as Special Education learners. Since she was associated with that needy population, she was asked by the school administration if she would like to coach the Special Education Track Team.

"At first, I really didn't want to coach," Rosemarie explained. "However, the Special Education team worked out with the regular track team and the coaches assisted my students. It turned out to be a very enjoyable experience for all of us."

Thus, Jay's desire to help a female student achieve her potential as a runner was passed along to another generation of students who might likewise have been passed over due to their differences.

Highland Park High School did get to brag about having an Olympian swimmer on the 1964 team, Suzie Pitt. Shortly after Pitt's 15th birthday, she set a new world record of 2:29.1 in the 200-meter butterfly, which was her specialty.[19] The extremely resolute and talented 16-year-old Pitt swam in the preliminary heats of the women's 4 X 100 meters' medley relay. Unfortunately, she did not have the opportunity to swim in the finals, in which her teammates did bring home the gold medals.

Upon her return to HPHS in the fall, Suzie addressed the student body in an exciting assembly where she detailed the difficulty of competing in worldwide competition. The entire school listened to Suzie's speech on her incredible experiences in Japan.

At the end of her Junior year in High School, she was selected as the New Jersey High School Athlete of the Year by members of the NJSIAA and a group of all-male sports writers. Her predecessor as the Award winner from the previous year had been Joe Theismann, the outstanding quarterback from rival high school, South River.[20]

Pitt went on to have a distinguished career in the sport of swimming, serving as the Head Coach of Swimming at Rutgers-the State University. After leaving Rutgers, she spent several years as the Director of Programs and Services at USA Swimming, the national governing body for swimming in the United States.

Although the football team was Jay's primary concern during the fall season, he always wanted the cheerleaders to look sharp and stand out in the crowd. He searched for unique uniforms for the young women and in the sixties, the girls wore short white skirts and turtlenecks with distinctive V-neck maroon and white button-down cardigans. Tams with white pom-poms on top completed the outfit. The girls looked adorable and crisp in their uniforms as they led the crowd in familiar cheers.

Heidi Schofiet, Class of 1991, recalled, "The times I remember most about Mr. D. were all the times I would go to him for help with things that the cheerleaders needed or wanted. He would listen to my entire story and usually would do whatever he could to get us what we needed as soon as possible. He always tried to help us out and he always supported our pep rallies."[21]

Jay had a close relationship with a jacket manufacturer in North Jersey, Hewitt Manufacturers. Each summer, the entire Dakelman family would travel to Hewitt headquarters to select new winter jackets. Jay produced the idea of a pristine white jacket to be worn solely by the Varsity cheerleaders. The only markings on the jacket, aside from the owner's name embroidered on the front, was the word OWLS in maroon spelled across the hood. Earning this beautiful and warm jacket was extremely prestigious and the girls had to work hard to achieve their varsity letter. In the frigid air of the Thanksgiving Classic against Metuchen, the cheerleaders were cozy and resembled snow bunnies as they donned their warm, white jackets.

In the early 1970s women's athletics was finally beginning to gain ground. Highland Park first added a basketball team and gymnastics team to the roster of sports. But Jay longed to add a Track and Field Team and began to advocate for its addition to the growing sports program at HPHS.

In the summer of her eighth-grade year, Rhonda, Jay's youngest daughter, told her father that she wanted to be a javelin thrower. Thrilled at the idea, the pair began to take nightly visits to Donaldson Park so that Jay could introduce Rhonda to the technicalities of javelin throwing. He patiently explained the approach to the throwing line, the steps required before planting the feet, and how to let the spear fly. Rhonda was thrilled with the feel of the javelin in her hands and loved spending time with her dad in this way.

Their collaborative efforts paid off. In Rhonda's first year at HPHS, the first Girls Track and Field Team was born, and Rhonda made the Varsity squad as a javelin thrower. Although Jay tried to convince her to throw the shot put and discus as well, Rhonda insisted that she just wanted to concentrate on the one event. Eventually, she won the New Jersey State Championship with a throw of 124 feet.

Following her four-year career in high school, Rhonda went on to Penn State University where she was a four-year letter winner on the Track and Field Team there. She majored in Physical Education due to her love of athletics and close ties to the Athletic Department at home.

After taking the silver medal in the 1977 Maccabiah Games in Israel, Rhonda graduated cum laude from Penn State and continued working on her Master's Degree at the University of Arizona, where she worked as an assistant coach with the men's track team.

"Working with the men's track and field team is interesting," said Rhonda. "They seem to respect my judgment. My job is to make sure that they do the drills that the head coach assigns in practice and to make suggestions. Recently, my duties have expanded to scheduling events and administration."[22]

Mike Bassoff, another graduate of Highland Park High School, happened to be an assistant coach at the University of Arizona at the same time Rhonda was there. He had served as a manager for Jay's teams while he was in high school. "Rhonda has no problems or any communication gap with the men's team," he observed. "She's a female Jay Dakelman. She looks, talks, and acts exactly like him. Her philosophy and the tone of her voice reminds me of my former coach," he continued.

"Rhonda is an important part of the team. She picks up the slack. There are too many events for the coach to cover and when he's occupied with one event, Rhonda's helping another part of the team."[23]

Just like so many other of Jay's proteges over the decades that he spent in education, Rhonda internalized the value of arduous work in becoming successful. She also reflected on Jay's assertion that equity among the sexes in athletics was an important value that needed to be nurtured, and the process of nurturing that seed started right within his own home.

Another idea that Jay brought to fruition was a developmental Girls Cross Country Meet held on Columbus Day each year starting in the early 1980s. Ray Zwigard, owner of Blue Ribbon Trophies and Medals in Somerset, NJ graciously sponsored the meet which became a favorite of coaches and spectators each fall, to say nothing of the young women who were thrilled to be running on the banks of the Raritan River in the scenic park.

Jay's daughter, Beth, the first woman starter at the New Jersey State Championship Meet, had learned meet administration skills from her father as well. She served as the Meet Director for the New Jersey State Central Section Cross

Country Championships for over 30 years. She also developed the format for the Blue Ribbon Invitational and served as its Meet Director for the entirety of its existence.

Two races were held at the Blue Ribbon Invitational. The first was the Varsity race in which coaches could enter their top seven athletes to compete. In the B Division race, coaches were allowed to enter as many teams as they wished, which was an extremely unique opportunity for schools that had an abundance of young athletes who wanted to be recognized in a prestigious meet.

Over its more than 20 years of existence, the Blue Ribbon Invitational remained a popular and respected meet. Many of Central Jersey's best Cross Country teams joined in the competition on those beautiful days in autumn.

There is no doubt that in every way that he could, Jay Dakelman aspired to bring women's athletics into the light of day. Whether it was dancing in the gymnasium, on the track, soccer field, or basketball court, Jay wanted every young woman to experience the joy of being on a team and striving to achieve her individual best. His obsession with involving women in sports would go a long way in gaining him national recognition.

His commitment to women's athletics was a testament to Jay's belief that physical fitness and the spirit of competition were essential for the development of a well-rounded and healthy human being.

I'm not here to make history . . . I'm here to make a difference.
Austin Gumbs

CHAPTER 23

GET RIGHT DOWN TO THE REAL

NITTY GRITTY

Over the years, Jay had a core staff that spent most of their teaching and coaching careers in Highland Park. Those who worked with him understood that there was magic in the riverside community that could not be found in other districts. A lot of that magic was generated by the formidable team of leaders that the school enjoyed from its inception forward.

The early days in which Jay worked with Bus Lepine and Maude Stockman were fun and exciting as the schools in Highland Park were swelling with "baby boomers." This triumvirate of leaders built a program that would put Highland Park on the map scholastically and athletically. The students followed their work ethic; they studied diligently, and they played sports using their heads as well as their hearts. The kids strove to bring honor to their school, coaches, parents, and community by winning championships in as many sports as possible.

Eventually, all three of the original trio studied for licenses in administration so that they could move "up the corporate ladder." Jay had a theory about why so many physical education teachers and coaches opted for school administration in the latter part of their careers.

"Since Physical Education classes are so large," he explained, "Phys. Ed. teachers learn early in their careers how to organize their students and maintain a structure that allows classes to function. Therefore, they can figure out the best plan for the organization of a school.

"Also, due to the size of the classes, Physical Education teachers are good at maintaining discipline in the classroom because if they don't, their classes will be chaotic, and nothing will get done.

Finally, as Phys. Ed. teachers age, instructing in the gym is not as easy as it is when one is young. Demonstrating techniques in sports becomes more challenging as we age, so many people opt to leave the gym floor to teach Health full time or become school administrators."

Maude Stockman eventually moved from her position as Department Chair of the Physical Education Department and gym teacher into the position of Assistant Principal. Bus Lepine left the classroom to become the school's Athletic Director, then Assistant Principal, to Assistant Superintendent to Acting Superintendent. He was exceptionally good as a business manager for the school district as well.

In honor of these two great pioneers at Highland Park High School, the baseball field was named the Austin E. Lepine Baseball Stadium, and the school gymnasium was named for Mrs. Stockman. These fitting honors were conducted during their lifetimes, so they got to enjoy the recognition of their dedication to the school.

Jay never aspired to leave the athletic scene. He did not want to become a disciplinarian or a member of the Central Office team. He was content to remain in his small office, located next to the gym, and was the site of the continuous flow of athletes, coaches, administrators, teachers, and Jay's "posse." However, in later years he frequently was asked to take charge of the principal's office when the principal had to leave the building for meetings or other business that needed his attention. Jay did enjoy making phone calls in the quiet domain of the principal's office when he had the opportunity.

In 1988, the Board of Education decided to honor Jay by naming the football field "The Jay Dakelman Field." He was thrilled to be honored in such a way, especially since he had taken so much pride in the creation of the sports complex as well as its recent renovation.

He loved to relate the tale of how one afternoon a little boy was riding across the newly seeded football field on his bicycle.

"Hey kid, get off the field!" he screamed at the youngster.

The arrogant boy turned around and yelled back, "Why? You don't own it!"

"Oh yes, I do!" Coach retorted, pointing to the sign noting The Jay Dakelman Field. "That's my name up there!"

Over the 47 years that Jay spent at Highland Park High School, he watched a parade of administrators come and go. He had a good relationship with most; butted heads with a few. However, two incredibly special men need to be acknowledged for their outstanding leadership skills, which enabled Jay to do the things that he needed to get done. During their time as administrators in the Highland Park School District, their leadership styles and love of educating youngsters served as a unique inspiration that catapulted the school system far beyond anything that could have been anticipated.

Jay's relationship with both men, Austin Gumbs and William (Bill) Donahue transcended the lines of collegiality; these three men became like brothers and served as the greatest leadership team in the history of the school.

Austin Gumbs, born on September 16, 1931, was a lifelong resident of Perth Amboy, New Jersey. Gumbs, with his mellifluous voice, majored in English and drama at Bowie State University in Maryland and returned home after graduation to fulfill his dream of teaching literature and directing the high school theater department.

Although Gumbs was born and raised in the United States, his parents, William Alexander Gumbs and Edith Gertrude Richardson, instilled a deep love of their island home of Anguilla in their children. Although Austin's parents immigrated to New Jersey in 1912, they kept the ties to Anguilla strong and visited frequently to see family and friends.

Gumbs acknowledged the debt that he owed to his parents and heritage for inculcating the values in him that would lead to a successful life. "A strong, independent thinking atmosphere pervaded our home," he stated. "We were forever reminded to respect ourselves as well as others. Our parents worked hard to support us, and I knew this was because of our traditional Anguillan upbringing. We were expected to strive to better ourselves and not to depend on others. Education was stressed with no other option permitted."[1]

One of the other core values instilled in Austin by his parents was his devotion to his strong faith in God. A lifelong member of St. Peter's Episcopal Church in Perth Amboy, Gumbs distinguished himself there as a renowned soloist, performing for hundreds of events over the 70 years that he was a member of the congregation.

However, the quality that truly defined the legacy that Austin Gumbs left upon Highland Park, Perth Amboy, and the world at large was his skill in leadership. As the first Black principal, appointed in 1971, and the first Black superintendent in the Highland Park School District (appointed in 1980), Austin led the high school and the district by being empathetic to his students, teachers, and the parents of the children whom he served. Of her father, Joycelyn Gumbs Alsup recalled, "He lived by the principle of 'Try to be understanding . . . not to be understood.'"[2]

Gumbs liked his students and staff to see him out and about the halls of the high school. His frequent visibility allowed him to develop relationships with all the people tied to the school. One of his favorite aphorisms was, "I am not here to make history . . . I am here to make a difference."[3] With his constant presence apparent, people were able to make connections and exchange quick conversations that often led to incredibly wonderful innovations being instituted in the building.

Austin never missed a Highland Park High School football game, and frequently attended track meets, basketball, and softball games. He loved supporting the school's choir and drama departments. He knew all the students in the four-year high school by name, making everyone feel like he or she was an essential part of the school community.

In 1972, Austin Gumbs made Perth Amboy history by being the first Black to be elected to the City Council. He spent much of his life dedicated to serving on municipal boards and committees to forward the advancement of the city. Later, he was elected to the Board of Education and held the position of President of that body for several years.[4]

The fact that Austin and Jay were the best of friends was well known. They could speak frankly to one another, even when sharing opposite opinions on a matter. (They really could see eye-to-eye since neither man was over five'5" in height).

On the Christmas Eve following Jay's death in 1991, the phone rang in the early evening at the Dakelman residence. Thelma answered the phone and was delighted to hear Austin's voice.

"I called to wish you a Happy Holiday," Austin said. "Every year, Jay would call me at 7:00 on Christmas Eve and say, 'Merry Christmas, Boss,' and now it is up to me to keep up with that tradition."

And so, he did for the rest of his life.

William Donahue was born on December 17, 1931, and grew up in the family home on South Third Avenue. In fact, his home was a block down from Jay's house. He was fiercely proud of being a Parkite all his life, although he did not attend Highland Park High School.

Being from a devout Irish family, Bill attended parochial school, including St. Peter's High School in New Brunswick. After completing his Bachelor's and Master's Degrees at Rutgers University, Bill entered the Air Force.

Bill married his sweetheart, Dotty, who hailed from Turners Falls, Massachusetts. Dotty was a nurse, and Bill was a navigator in the Air Force where he achieved the rank of First Lieutenant. Donahue saw active duty at the tail end of the Korean War.

Upon returning to Highland Park, Bill stepped into the career to which he had aspired: history teacher. Looking a tad like a leprechaun himself, Donahue stood no more than five' 6, with dark hair and brown eyes that twinkled when he laughed, which was often. An affable, kind, and understanding man, his students gravitated toward him because of his open demeanor. He was easy to talk to, made history fun for his learners, and was an all-around great guy.

Daughter Kerry Donahue Raslowsky said of her dad, "He was the best Dad any person could have. He was there for every one of our events. Since our mom worked as a nurse at night, we spent a lot of time with Dad after school. He was a jokester and kept us laughing all the time."[5]

Tumulty's Pub in New Brunswick has been a dining institution for over a century, and Bill enjoyed taking his three children to dinner there frequently while Mom worked.

"He could be a disciplinarian when he had to be," his son, Sean, stated, "but he did know how to be a jokester. He did a great impression of Donald Duck."[6]

After Austin Gumbs was promoted to the job of Superintendent of Schools in Highland Park, Donahue stepped into the principal's office. When asked if it was difficult to go to the high school where their father was the principal, all three Donahue children said no, it was just the opposite; it was a wonderful experience.

"I had a good group of friends," Sean explained, "but I did get bullied once in a while."

Kerri reminisced that every morning before leaving for the high school, which was a few blocks away on the north side of town, their dad would take a brief detour through Donaldson Park. He would drive by the river and around the circle in the park's center as if composing his thoughts and communing with nature would center him for the day.

Bill insisted that his children participate in co-curricular activities while getting their secondary education. Just as Jay did with his son, Mitchell, Bill had his second daughter, Erin, into his office shortly after she started high school.

"I want you to compete in at least one season of track while you're here," Donahue pointed at his willowy daughter.

Erin made up her mind that if she had to run, she was going to set about it in her first term at the school, so she joined the Cross County team. "It was very hard," she recalled. "The circumference of the school property was one mile, and on the first day of practice, as I came around the building on my first lap, I stopped at the front of the school and peered into my father's office window. I was exhausted and crying, and I wanted him to see how I was in agony. He saw me standing in front of the window and approached it. I looked directly at him, pleading. He took the rope that lowered the blinds and slowly closed them in my face."[7]

Kerri explained her father's vision of education, which was simple. "Kids first . . . it was always about what is best for the students."[8]

Just as Austin Gumbs had done before him, Bill Donahue attended every match, performance, and game that he could while he was the leader of the school. One could always count on seeing Mr. Gumbs, Mr. Donahue, and Mrs. Stockman standing together on the top row of the bleachers at every Highland Park football game, rooting for their favorite team. With that kind of support from his administrators, Jay was inspired to do even more to ensure that his athletes took home the state championships.

On Mother's Day 1985, Beth received an early morning phone call from her father. She knew immediately from the strained sound in his voice that something terrible had happened.

"Bill Donahue is dead," Jay uttered, his voice a whisper of agony.

"What?" Beth shrieked, disbelieving what she was hearing. Bill was only in his early fifties.

Jay explained that he had received a call at 3:00 a.m. from Dotty Donahue to come immediately to the Donahue home just a block up the street on South Third Avenue. A former student from the high school had stabbed Bill directly into his heart, and he died instantly. Obviously, the young man was deeply disturbed and captured immediately.

The shock of Mr. Donahue's death reverberated across the Highland Park community. In fact, the viewing occurred in the gymnasium of the school so that every student, parent, graduate, and resident of the town could come and say goodbye to a man who was admired and loved deeply by his community for being fair and an inspiration to all who knew him.

Bill's death made a serious dent in Jay's spirit; it was so shocking and unexpected. Losing a leader, the caliber of William

Donohue in such a senseless manner, uprooted the feeling of security and safety that HPHS had always offered. For a long time, nothing made sense.

However, for as long as the three dynamic men worked in tandem, Highland Park High School ran like a charm. There can be no substitute for great leadership. And it must be considered that the unusual triumvirate, a Black man, an Irish Catholic, and a Jew modeled for the world how people coming from diverse cultural backgrounds could share their vision for the power of education in the lives of the children whom they touched daily.

As with most popular coaches, former Highland Park High School graduates, such as Norman Arshan and Barry Levine, a sports reporter for *The Home News,* were frequent visitors in Jay's office. These devoted men helped raise money for expensive items like the lights that finally allowed Highland Park to play Friday night games. Like Jay's best friend, Pete Donelon, many of the visitors were pillars in the parents' organizations that made sure the athletes received the appropriate accolades and awards at the end of the seasons.

Since a large number of Highland Park graduates served in the township police, fire, and rescue departments, these important groups gave a lot to the athletic department as well. For example, the fire department generously provided blazers to senior football players each year so that they could look snazzy when they went on college visitations.

Another example of Jay's understanding of the hierarchy in the smooth running of the school was his axiom, "Always treat the custodians and secretaries with respect. Without them, the school does not function." He was insistent that the employees who worked behind the scenes be treated as the important cogs in the functioning machinery of school life that they are.

Central office secretaries Edith Kinney and Sally Watkin recalled the early morning greeting that they received from Jay as he breezed into the Main Office to sign in. Kinney said, "He would come up and talk to us about anything from the latest news in his career to the last book he read."[9]

Sally Watkin added, "When he would come back from a trip, he would make us feel as though we were there with all the vivid details that he gave."[10]

Theresa Ward, who worked in the Superintendent's Office remembered, "He was the prince of the Physical Education Department, so well read. I still have one of the gifts that he brought me from Italy, a little leather change purse."[11]

Once Bus Lepine and Maude Stockman moved into administration, Jay took over as Department Chair as well as Athletic Director. Over the years, the Physical Education Staff included Robert Kertes, Frank Cipot, Randy Vey, and Joseph Policastro. The women's staff consisted of Barbara Hirschman, Robin Quigley, Barbara Hagaman Howarth, B.J. Sklar Rego, Brooke Paskowitz, and Julie Klemowitz.

In a conversation with B.J., Julie, and Brooke, these women shared behind-the-scenes information about working for Jay Dakelman that others who admired and were awed by him never experienced firsthand.

Brooke described her initial introduction to Mr. Dakelman, which was when he came to observe her during her student teaching in Lawrenceville. Brooke happened to be teaching a unit on track when Jay arrived.

"The whole time he was there," she said, "he was busy inspecting the facilities at Lawrenceville. He walked around the track, looked at the lines for the start of the throwing and jumping areas. He didn't seem in the least bit interested in me.

"When the class was over, he came by and said thank you, but nothing else. He didn't say a word. Later, he sent Barbara Howarth down to observe me. Then I got a call that I had the job."[12]

All Jay needed to see was that Brooke was maintaining order in her classroom, and this he managed to do from a distance. Since Lawrenceville High School was located centrally in the state, he figured that while he was there, he would assess the facilities and see if they were capable of handling one of the sectional meets during the spring track season.

The women agreed that one of their least favorite things to do was call the Dakelman home on days that they needed to stay home from school.

"I always prayed that Mrs. Dakelman would answer the phone," Brooke said. "I was so scared to tell Jay that I was going to be out for the day. Nine times out of ten, though, he answered."[13]

And it wasn't that he ever chastised them for absences; it was just the feeling that they got when life got in the way of their jobs. Over the 47 years that Jay worked at Highland Park High School, he accumulated over six hundred sick days, rarely taking off. Once again, it was his strict work ethic that did the talking for him when it came to staying home from school.

Julie added another aspect of the discipline Jay gave to the department. The rule was that unless it was pouring rain, gym classes were held outside until Thanksgiving.

"It wasn't something we ever dared bring up with him, but some of those days were bitter cold," Brooke echoed.[14]

Of course, the students only had to deal with the chill one period of the day, but the teachers were outside, braving the cold five periods a day, coming in with noses running and windburned cheeks.

At home, Jay's demeanor was that of a pussycat. He was quiet and soft-spoken. However, in his office and on the field, a different version of Coach D. frequently appeared.

Brooke reminisced about her first year of teaching at HPHS. Being new, she did not comprehend the importance of the Thanksgiving Day rivalry between Highland Park and Metuchen. The beloved Goal Post Trophy was in contention each year, and rarely did Highland Park lose the game. Therefore, when Brooke bounced into the athletic office the Monday after Thanksgiving and sang out, "So how was everyone's Thanksgiving?" the men turned and scowled at her.

"Are you fucking kidding me?" Jay snarled.

They had lost the game to Metuchen.

"I never made that mistake again," Brooke sighed.[15]

Although many people thought that Jay was gruff, Brooke and Julie spoke about his tender side.

"I remember," Brooke said, "after I had a serious surgery, he came to the hospital to visit me, and he brought me flowers. He was wonderful and caring."

Julie concurred. "He really changed in his demeanor after his granddaughter, Shauna, was born."[16]

"He softened quite a bit after that," Brooke added, "and his face just glowed when he spoke about her."[17]

The ladies then recounted one afternoon when they decided to order Chinese food for lunch. They set up a card table in the back of the office. Julie and Brooke set the table with pretty placemats, napkins, and even put a candle in the middle of the table for a festive touch. As they sat enjoying their afternoon repast, Jay entered, shadowed by his buddy, Pete.

Jay looked at his department incredulously, not saying a word, and shrugged his shoulders. He continued to his desk where the phone was jangling for his attention.

There were days of fun and laughter in the Physical Education Department at HPHS because Jay allowed it to exist, even though each of his department members had important work to do with their students and athletes.

"Jay was very excited when we began to get girls teams," Julie stated.

Brooke agreed, "He made sure that every team had the best equipment that he could buy: the best uniforms, the best of everything. And he was incredibly supportive."

"Except," Julie added, "when it came to scheduling meets on Halloween."

"We told Jay to please not schedule any competitions for Halloween because even though we had high school kids, they still loved to go trick or treating," Brooke concurred.

It so happened that Julie had gotten her bus driver's license so that she could drive the school's van to away meets. One Halloween afternoon, the girls had gymnastics meet at Bridgewater-Raritan High School. Bridgewater is an affluent community and as the team bus whizzed down the streets toward their competition site, Julie suddenly jerked the van to the curb in front of some very impressive homes. She opened the door of the vehicle and said, "Okay girls, go ahead. Do a little trick or treating. We have a few minutes before we have to get to the school."[18]

Shocked at their good fortune, the athletes vacated the bus quickly and visited the nearby homes in their school uniforms instead of Halloween costumes. Loaded with candy, they exuberantly rejoined their coaches on the bus and continued to their match.

Considering that these coaches were the pioneers of women's athletics, they took on more than one coaching assignment. B.J.'s passion was tennis; however, she coached field hockey and basketball. Brooke coached gymnastics and softball, and Julie worked with the track and gymnastics team.

Frank Cipot, one of the male Phys. Ed. teachers who also grew up in Highland Park cited Jay as a major reason that he did so well in his position as Head Basketball coach. "When I was a kid, Mr. Dakelman was the legendary coach who was looked up to with awe and respect. When I became a teacher and assistant football coach with him, he became an instrumental part of my career. He taught me excellence through the demands of hard work. He would sometimes say, 'You only have success if you study and work harder than your opponent.' As a person, he was a very good friend and a wonderful man to work with."[19]

And then, of course, there is an assessment of Jay's prowess as the boss of the Athletic Department by Joe Policastro, who eventually succeeded Jay as Head Football Coach.

"The wins, the losses, the games, those things mattered to Jay when it came to coaching, but it was the kids that he really loved. What touched him was to have kids come back to the high school and say, 'I'm a doctor . . .' or 'a lawyer,' or 'a bricklayer,' or whatever, because of what I learned from you.

"He always listened. He was never too busy. You could call him at midnight or at 5:00 in the morning and ask, 'Hey, Jay, you up?' and he would say, 'Yeah, I'm listening.' Even when he yelled, he was listening."

Policastro admitted that if he had only one lesson that he learned from Jay, it was not about X's and O's. It is about knowing oneself. "Be an Athletic Director, like me, Joe," he told me, "but never give up coaching. Once you lose the kids, you lose everything that you love."[20]

The spirit, the will to win, and the will to excel are the things that endure.
Vince Lombardi

CHAPTER 24

1982 NATIONAL ATHLETIC DIRECTOR OF THE YEAR

When one is a winner, dozens of accolades come, and they are all wonderful and exciting. Over the years, Jay's personal collections of plaques and trophies covered every inch of the Dakelman's recreation room, not allowing for a single inch of wood paneling to show.

The Class of 1968 had dedicated the school yearbook, *The Albadome*, to Coach Dakelman, remembering him as one:

> . . . who has shown us that it is possible to attain any goal through dedication, perseverance, and sacrifice . . . who has developed the Athletic Department of HPHS into one of the finest in the area. . . who has demonstrated the importance of teamwork and sportsmanship. . . who is so respected by the Class of 1968 that we wish to have the *Albadome* dedicated to the "Coach of the Top 11 in '67" so that it may serve as a lasting record of our appreciation and respect to Mr. Jay Dakelman.[1]

At the end of the 1977 football season Jay relinquished the Head Coach's position to his protege, Joe Policastro, and dedicated himself to his Director of Athletics responsibilities with renewed fervor. With so many sports having been added over the years, the time it took to schedule competitions, hire officials, procure busses for away games, order equipment, manage the athletic budget and write out the necessary checks and vouchers required, put together coaching staff, check students' grades and health records, oversee fundraising efforts, and attend important Athletic Directors' meetings and conferences, there was barely enough time in a week to get everything done. The job had expanded so much that he no longer taught Physical Education; being the AD was a full time job.

Thus, it should not have been that big a surprise when on the evening of the 1977 fall sports banquet held in the high school gymnasium, a "sobbing Jay Dakelman announced that after 32 years, he was resigning as Head Football Coach."[2]

In his popular *Home News* column "The Barrelhouse," former HPHS stat man, Barry Levine wrote, "Combining the characteristics of an Oscar-winning Hollywood actor, high-priced Madison Avenue psychologist, General Patton's strategic acumen and El Exigente's demanding nature, the 57-year-old coach annually nursed the Owls victory to victory."[3]

After undergoing a dramatic open-heart surgery on April 21, 1977, at Cleveland Clinic Hospital in Ohio, Jay decided to return for one more year as head coach, finishing that season with a 9-1-1 record and a 35-12 thrashing of Dunellen to win the Central Jersey Group I Championship. After the game the Dunellen coach, who had been bragging in the newspapers as to how his team was going to destroy the Owls, was so infuriated, he sought

Jay out and pulled back his arm to punch the diminutive leader of the Owls. Everyone gasped in horror, knowing that one punch to the chest could kill Jay when the Dunellen coaches stepped in and pulled their leader away.

Jay thought the moment was hilarious and laughed all the way back to Highland Park where Thelma was preparing an impromptu victory party at home.

However, there was a dark cloud of reality in that moment of confrontation. Levine wrote, "A vicious competitor, the irascible Dakelman gained as much fame for his antics on the field as for his team's incredible won-lost record. It was not unusual for him to throw his hat to the turf, showing his displeasure over an official's call or seen attempting a field goal with a sideline marker."[4]

Jay admitted that following his quadruple bypass surgery, the doctors had suggested that it would be best for him to retire from coaching. But doing this proved to be impossible after facing death in the operating room. "Next to my family, there was nothing I love more than coaching football. I was fortunate because throughout the years my wife, Thelma, really put up with a lot," Jay confessed to the crowd at the sports banquet.

The red-eyed coach continued, "The toughest thing of all is ending my close relationship with the kids because I truly loved being with them. I love the kids and being around them because they keep you young. I enjoyed helping the kids leave Highland Park High School and become valuable members of their communities. That's probably the biggest thrill of all."[5]

Levine cited the clever tricks Dakelman kept up his sleeve as motivational tools over the years that he coached. "As a psychologist, there was none better. More than once, Owl players received sympathy cards prior to a big game supposedly signed by the other team. The entrance to the Owls' locker room always managed to get painted an opponent's colors prior to a crucial game. Although emphatically denying any knowledge of it, Dakelman, with the look of innocence befitting a choir boy, Dakelman would sit in his chair with a puzzled look as to how such a thing could happen. During one of his vehement halftime talks, somehow a chicken managed to get thrown into the locker room with a note saying, "The Owls are really chickens." Needless to say, that innocent opponent paid dearly."[6]

The most infamous trick that Jay ever pulled to excite his team occurred for the Thanksgiving Day game against Metuchen in 1971. Before the annual Pep Rally and Bonfire, the coaching staff had requested that each player bring a shopping bag with him for their final pre-game meeting of the year. At the end of the final session, the coaches collected the paper bags and placed them in the locker room.

Following the departure of the athletes, Jay and his staff got to work on their latest ploy. They lined up the helmets on the locker room benches and spray-painted each one with fluorescent pink paint. The effect was blinding.

In the morning, after a breakfast sponsored by the Parents of the Football Team, the young men entered the locker room and gasped at the unusual sight before them. As each boy headed for the bus, he received a bag, and the coaches instructed each player to keep the helmets hidden from the fans. No one was to see them until the Owls emerged from the locker room to play the game.

When the Owls took the field for pre-game warm-ups, the Metuchen coach asked Jay, "Hey, where are your helmets?" to which the wizened Coach D. replied, "We left them at the school. The managers went to get them."

Traditionally, after the marching band played "The Star-Spangled Banner," they formed two lines through which the team exploded onto the field. Only, this time, when the team came roaring onto the gridiron, the crowd rose to its feet, screaming with surprise and excitement when the fans eyeballed the neon helmets for the first time. They knew who had been behind this latest stunt to psyche out the opponent.

In retrospect, Jay commented that although the moment had been legendary in the history of HP football, the fluorescent helmets had nearly cost them the game, as it made the players easier to identify and follow during play. "Not to mention," he added, "what our re-conditioning bill was to put the helmets back to their original color."

Every afternoon and evening, as the Athletic Director, Jay's presence was required at home competitions: basketball games, wrestling matches, gymnastics competitions, and track meets. He always showed up for Cross Country matches in Donaldson Park as well. Jay's idea of being an effective Athletic Director was to be visible to athletes and coaches so that they knew they had his full support. Jay would consistently tell his coaches, "I am with you always, win or tie."

During his lengthy career, one theme was omnipresent in Jay's philosophy of the fundamental place that athletics should fall into a student's life. Always, always, Jay adhered to the rule "Scholastics first, Athletics second." Sports were a way in which youngsters developed their bodies to support their minds. Athletics and competition provided an outlet for the daily grind of studies. But, always, always, it was scholastics first.

In 1989, Senator Bill Bradley, himself a former basketball star at Princeton University, a Rhodes Scholar, and a long-time New York Knick, proposed a bill called the Student-Athletes' Right to Know Act, which would require schools receiving federal assistance to make public such graduation and retention statistics as an aid to student-athletes in selecting the school they would attend.[7]

Although Bradley's Act seemed to have the support of both college and high school administrations, two problems needed to be resolved in its implementation.

The first issue was that all universities would have to be consistent in the way the statistics would be compiled. For example, should students be counted as first-year students when they first started at a school, or should they be considered only after they completed their education? Should the retention rate be four years or simply upon making progress toward a degree?

The second question regarding the Act was who would keep track of all the data? Would the schools be responsible for tracking their information, or would a governmental agency be accountable?

When interviewed regarding the implementation of university reporting student retention statistics, Jay had clear opinions. "It is the obligation of the kid (the high school athlete) and the parents to find out what kind of a school the youngster would be attending. Is it a Rutgers or an Oklahoma?"[8]

Coach Dakelman, who had spent years early in his teaching career as a guidance counselor, and who had directed hundreds of students to the college where they were going to be most successful, felt that the Bradley bill was unnecessary.

"We always tell the athlete to ask what the graduation rate is," he stated. "The youngster should be asking what procedures there are for incoming freshmen. Is there a required study hall? Are there tutors? What support systems do they have for student athletes? Do they have an academic adviser? What do they do in the event a student is falling behind? There is a whole string of answers the student must know."[9]

Guaranteeing that every student-athlete who desired to further his or her college education was a passion of Jay's. In his earliest days as a coach, he recognized that he needed to stress the importance of getting a college education with his Black athletes as the surest way to improve their financial and social status. Since many of his Black students did not have the money needed for tuition, Jay insisted that being academically successful was the key to receiving hefty scholarship offers and finishing their degrees.

Jay spent many evenings at the homes of his athletes when college coaches came on recruitment calls. Ever watchful for details regarding a student's home life, Jay commented often about the dearth of reading materials in Black homes. "There are no books, magazines, or newspapers in their homes," he would state. "There is no legacy of literacy for these kids," he lamented. Jay, who was passionate about reading, recognized that valuing literacy started at home, and he was desperate to change the opportunities for his students of color. This was always a priority in his educational value system.

The second thing about which Jay was emphatic throughout his career was developing equality in sports opportunities for women. Having one daughter who was able to achieve a state championship, be a four-year letter winner at Penn State, and be a silver medalist in the Maccabiah Games in Israel, Jay's devotion to promoting women's athletics hit remarkably close to home.

Thus, when Jay was chosen as the Middlesex County Athletic Director of the Year in 1982, it was no surprise to his peers that he had been granted this honor. Winning the county award made Jay eligible for the state honor of Athletic Director of the year, which to his delight, he won handily.

Once he had been dubbed State of New Jersey Athletic Director of the Year, Jay was required to compose a detailed resume to be submitted to the Eastern Region contest for AD of the year. He filled in his stats for coaching, his accomplishments as a representative to the Track and Field committee of the National Federation of High School Athletics, and the list of presidencies that he had held in athletic, professional, and community organizations.

He wrote about his work as a member of the New Jersey Interscholastic Coaches Association, of which he was one of six founders. The organization instituted an annual North-South All-Star Football Game in 1978, played at Rutgers Stadium in New Brunswick. Jay had served as the first coach of the South team, which his talented athletes won. At least three of the young men who played for Jay in that game went onto the pros, including Irving Fryar and Jim Jeffcoat, both of whom went on to play in the NFL.

And, then he wrote about his passions as a leader in the athletic world: equity for women in sports and always, always, academics first.

As the New Jersey Director of Athletics, Jay and his family, friends, colleagues, and students, were thrilled to learn that he had been chosen as the Eastern Region Director of Athletics for the year. This new award meant that he was one of six regional ADs headed for Houston and the final judgment for National Athletic Director of the Year.

Before leaving for the final reckoning, Jay, who was an ardent collector of articles about his career and many teams, put together an album of his achievements that was "as thick as a telephone book."[10] Included in his magnum opus were his incredible statistics for coaching. In his 19 years as Head Football Coach, Jay's record was 138-34-2, a .802 overall winning record. His teams garnered thirteen sectional titles and posted four undefeated seasons. His track teams had won five State Group Titles, placed second on six occasions, and captured sixteen sectional titles.

The Highland Park High School Athletic Program had swelled from five to nineteen sports, and in the process of adding sports, developed one of the first comprehensive girls programs in Middlesex County. Of course, the growing programs meant more work for the Athletic Director, but Jay was content to do it. The more kids who participated in sports, the better.

On the county level, Jay had created the Athletic Directors, Coaches, Football coaches, and Track Officials into organizations that allowed them to function in meaningful ways for the advancement of sports.

Jay was one of the prime movers in the formation of the Garden State Conference in 1966 and subsequently, the Bicentennial Conference in 1976. Later, Jay and John Longo, the Athletic Director at South Brunswick High School, proposed the original plan for a county-wide athletic conference to the Middlesex County Superintendent of Schools. This was the original attempt at creating what has today evolved into Middlesex County's super-conference.

Taking over the state championship track meet system in 1960, Jay and his counterpart, Red Littler, developed an indoor track championship program that launched in 1963. From that time to 1982, 125,545 participants competed in the winter meets. Among the greatest of those athletes had been Renaldo Nehemiah and siblings, Carl, and Carol Lewis, who went on to gain international recognition in track and field.

Dakelman had served as the Referee for the Secondary Schools at the Penn Relays for 25 years and had traveled to Kansas City to participate on the National Federation of High School Track and Field Rules Committee.

Aside from his activities in interscholastic athletics, Dakelman donated much of his time to community affairs. A past president of the Highland Park Lions Club, he was a member of that group for over 30 years. He was also a member of the borough's recreation department for more than two decades and helped the Highland Park Police Department by administering physical tests for prospective candidates.

Jay had become a Mason after returning home from the war, and he and Thelma were active members in the Order of the Golden Chain, an organization that was an offshoot of the Masons. Together they served as patron and matron of Amity Link, their local chapter in the Order of the Golden Chain, whose primary mission was to fund a camp for underprivileged children.

The criteria that existed for winning the prestigious National Athletic Director of the Year Award were as follows: a person must have served as an athletic director for a minimum of ten years; have contributed to school and county programs; have accomplished other notable achievements on the state/ and or national level, as well as service to the community. There was no doubt[11] that Jay surpassed the requirements to win the award.[12]

Jay expressed his surprise at being a finalist in the competition to sportswriter Barry Levine. "I really have not realized the magnitude of this award and probably won't until I get to Houston on April 22. I didn't realize that the state sent my name to the regional selection committee and when I got the letter informing me, I was one of the finalists, I was really surprised.

"This award is a tribute to my school system and my administrators who allowed me to do things, my coaches and my wife, Thelma, who also let me do things in the athletic area without complaining," he concluded.[13]

Being at the convention in Texas was exciting for Thelma and Jay. When they arrived at their hotel, the couple found a telegram waiting for them from the coaching staff of HPHS. It read, "Jay, we are with you all the way —win or tie."

Of course, until the night of the banquet in which the winner of the prestigious award was to be revealed by the selection committee, Jay's stomach was in knots, although he gave a good impression of his being his low-key, unpretentious self.

When each of the men took his place on the stage to wait for the announcement of the winner, Jay stood in the center of the group. Poised in a handsome cream-colored suit, Jay's silver hair gleamed like a crown. Every other man on the platform was at least a foot taller than the five'5" Jay Howard Dakelman. He was clearly the runt of litter. One of the big guys wore a large, white Stetson, not unlike Jay's longtime friend, Red Littler. Jay smiled as that thought ran through his mind.

Then came the announcement: the winner of the 1982 National Athletic Director of the Year was Jay H. Dakelman.

Unexpectedly, tears sprang to Jay's eyes. He hadn't realized how much he had wanted this public acknowledgment of his life's work, his passions, his talent for leadership. There, in Houston, Texas, the smallest guy took home the biggest prize.

When the presenter stepped forward with the beautiful plaque proclaiming Jay as the National Athletic Director of the Year, he leaned over and whispered into Jay's ear, "Well, at least you didn't tie."

Yippee Ki Yay, cowboy!

The folks back at home were ecstatic when the announcement was made the next day about Coach Dakelman's achievement. Superintendent Austin Gumbs commented, "The entire Borough of Highland Park is extremely proud of the singular honor Mr. Dakelman has received. He was instrumental in bringing girls' athletics to the forefront on both the county and state levels. He is most deserving of this award for all he has accomplished in his years as the Director of Athletics."[14]

The response that Jay gave immediately after accepting the award was typical of his sardonic wit and passion for his position. He said, "I will be in the same office tomorrow morning at 7:30 as I always am. But I will never forget this trip to Houston and the award. And I will never forget the Highland Park students with whom I have dealt for the past 36 years. It is a thrill to see kids come up through the grades, watch their high school careers, and see what happens to them after graduation. Many have become doctors and lawyers, and others have come back to help our community. . . I am extremely proud of all of them and their accomplishments."[15]

Jay was the first Athletic Director from New Jersey to ever win the award, and to this day, is still the only Jerseyan to have been given this honor.

The awards, well, you hang up another plaque. It doesn't mean that much. The big thing is the kids, and their success is later. To think that you have contributed something to people, that's the most important thing.
Jay H. Dakelman

CHAPTER 25

THE LAST DANCE

The Owls were rematched against South River for the Central Jersey Group I Championship at the Bill Denny Stadium in South River on December 7, 1990. Playing on that field always brought unique challenges because the town of South River was brutally loyal to its football team. The town would shut down on game day so that every resident could attend and fill the stands with enough fans to make the stadium quake during the game. The game announcers were so pro-South River that they were infuriating and insulting to the visiting teams, which naturally heightened the tension between the weekly opponents.

South River came into this championship undefeated for this season. . . and Highland Park had only one loss, which had been against South River early in the 1990 season. If ever two teams were well matched for a championship battle, these two were ideal. Of course, South River had the hometown advantage, plus the motivation to beat the team that had captured the championship just a year ago on the Highland Park turf.

I stood in the bleachers, biting my leather gloves. This was Dad's last game before retirement after 47 years of bleeding maroon and gray for Highland Park High School. Even though he hadn't been the Head Coach in twelve years, his heart could not be separated from the game or the dedicated athletes who played it. Plus, his surrogate son, Joe Policastro was now the head coach.

As the fans had anticipated, the first half of the game was a bitter battle between the two sparring sides. Scoring was low, and although Highland Park had a great quarterback in Charles Archibald and two phenomenal backs in Tyrone Harrison and Bruce Presley, scoring was minimal. When the teams went into the locker rooms at halftime, South River held a slight edge over the Owls.

Rumors abounded that JoJo had asked his revered mentor to deliver the halftime speech. The locker room remained silent as the venerated coach inspired the team that was battling with everything, they had to win the game.

Coach Shawn Harrison confided to me in an interview that he had been perched at Jay's knee during the speech. "I was only a sophomore," Shawn said. "I did not even think that Jay knew my name at that time, but I listened to him speak and I was in awe. Of course, when we returned to the field, the team felt inspired and ready to finish off the Rams."

Although Shawn felt insignificant now, he came from one of HighlandPark's most important football families. His older brother, Raymond, had been a star, and his other brother, Tyrone, was a present HP hero. Later his sister gave birth to a baby boy, L.J. Smith, who had a distinguished career with the Philadelphia Eagles. Football was definitely coded into the Harrison DNA.

When the two squads resumed play after halftime, I was so jittery that Tom, my husband, could not stand next to me. "Please God," I begged, "don't let Dad's career end like this." My dreams of winning this final game dwindled with every tick of the clock. The Owls had been down at the goal line several times during the second half but just could not put the ball in.

With less than two minutes to play, South River had the ball and needed quarterback Nelson Bonea to ice the game by getting a first down. JoJo's hopes were sinking as Bonea took the ball from the center, 4th and 1 . . . but it didn't happen. The Rams failed to make the first down and suddenly, the momentum swung. JoJo confessed to me later that when South River lost the ball at the crucial point in the game, he knew that Highland Park would win.

Jay stepped up to Joe and said, "You idiot, can't you see that South River is well prepared for that play you are running? They practiced it all week. You must slant the line one way or the other and you can't pull both guards. Leave one in and they will get confused. I am telling you . . . do it."

And so, for the last time, JoJo followed his coach's advice, which with 20 seconds left on the clock, allowed the bullish Bruce Presley to plunge three yards across the goal line and score the miraculous winning touchdown. The Highland Park fans whooped with wild glee. They had beaten the Rams of South River for the state championship two years in a row.

The victory was, indeed, the perfect ending to Jay's career. It could not have been any better than if it had been a script written for *Friday Night Lights*.

Suddenly, a melee broke out in the center of the field. Accepting defeat on their home turf was impossible for the South

River fans. Screaming in anger, they streamed toward the Highland Park benches, fists raised.

Much to Shawn Harrison's astonishment, a South River fan lunged at Jay and threw him to the ground. Stunned, Coach Dakelman lay on the field for a moment until he regained his composure. Having just had open heart surgery for a second time in August, Jay knew that he was fragile.

After he made sure that he was okay, he looked up at Shawn and stretched out his hand. "Shawn," he said, "help me up."

In telling this story, Shawn added, "It was the first time that I ever heard Coach Dakelman call me by name. And it meant a lot." The coming together of those two hands was prophetic; thirty years later, Shawn Harrison would become the Head Football Coach of Highland Park High School.

Once on his feet, Shawn and Jay hurried to the buses which were gunning their motors, eager to leave South River before a riot started.

I heard from several witnesses that Dad had been punched so Tom and I searched the crowd to see if we could spot him. Before we could reach the buses, the caravan sped away, headed toward Highland Park.

"We've got to go up to the high school," I ordered Tom. "I've got to make sure that he is all right."

Exuberant fans meandered around the gym, celebrating the win. I spotted Dad in the middle of the gym and rushed to him. He was jumping up and down with the sheer joy of the moment, not seeming the worse for getting knocked down by an enraged South River fan.

"It was great!" he sputtered. "I was down on the field and some guy came at me. I went down, but I'm okay. And we beat them on their own turf. We beat them" There were many reasons, some of them very personal, for loving to beat South River.

He was more pumped up and excited than I had ever seen him. No victory had ever been so sweet; this final game meant so much. Jay's face was flushed; he was beaming with the exhilaration of the moment.

It was the last time that I would ever see the jubilation of victory on his face again.

Six weeks later, on January 28, 1991, Jay was gone.

AFTERWORD
LEGACY

The National Director of Athletics Convention took place in Los Angeles in December of 1990. As a former National Athletic Director of the Year, Jay enjoyed celebrity status at the convention and spent a good deal of time with colleagues and friends from all over the country, wishing him well in his retirement. Thelma spent the afternoons with other wives of ADs, sightseeing and shopping in the California sun. The trip was joyful and relaxing for both.

Jay made a terrible error on the plane ride home; he forgot to wear the elastic hose that prevented the formation of blood clots in those who have severe circulatory problems. As a result, he developed a golf ball-sized clot in his lower calf, and he had to be hospitalized immediately upon his return.

During his stay at Robert Wood Johnson Hospital in New Brunswick, Jay picked up pneumonia, his old nemesis. He spent a month on a ventilator, fighting for his life. His cardiologist, another former Highland Park athlete, Barnes Keller, assured the family that Jay would come through due to the strength of his recently repaired heart.

What no one anticipated, however, was that the blood clot would break loose and hit Jay's carotid artery. On the morning of

January 28, 1991, Jay succumbed to the clot, leaving all of those who knew and loved him, stunned and bereft.

It was an unbearable shock. He and Thelma had plans to travel, to enjoy their golden years together without the stress of a job that was so much more than a job to Dad.

In subsequent years, Rhonda, Mitchell, and I have discussed the fact that for our father, leaving Highland Park High School behind was impossible to bear, hastening his demise at the age of sixty-nine. My daughter, Shauna, was only five years old at the time of his death and therefore, her memories of "Poppy Jay" are sweet but vague. She remembers sitting on his lap, playing with the keys on his typewriter, watching *Flintstone* cartoons on the big screen TV in his office.

My siblings and I also talked about how Jay's war time experiences robbed him of vitality and spirit after the horrors that he had witnessed and faced again in the wee hours of the morning when sleep often eluded him. So many World War II veterans came home and swallowed their war experiences like bitter pills that choked them, making it impossible to share their stories with loved ones or even therapists. Who knows how our brave forces coped with returning to "normal" lives without processing the trauma of war?

Even though Jay Dakelman has been gone for over 30 years, just saying his name evokes stories from those he taught, coached, worked with, and loved. There are so many tributes to him that recall his memory on a yearly basis. For example, the Middlesex County Coaches Association celebrates dedicated athletes each spring at the Jay H. Dakelman Scholar-Athlete dinner, where scholarships are presented to deserving male and female students who are college or military-bound. The New

Jersey Track and Field Officials Association presents annual awards in memory of Jay and his friend, Gene Littler. The Jay H. Dakelman Lifetime Achievement Award honors those track and field officials who have devoted a minimum of 25 years to officiating the sport, and the Gene Littler Award is bestowed on the "Official of the Year" who has distinguished him or herself in a significant way each year.

Behind Highland Park High School the Jay Dakelman Track and Football Field is located, with a huge sign pronouncing the name. Just a few years ago, a well-deserved addition was made to Jay's name being associated with the field; the stadium was named in honor of Joe "JoJo" Policastro, Jay's beloved protege and successor as the Highland Park High School football coach. Jay and Joe are linked permanently with this indelible honor.

I received many letters of condolence after Dad died, but the one that resonated the most with me came from a man who told a story about his brother.

"I was not a very good student in gym class," he wrote, "and I don't think that Mr. Dakelman liked me very much. However, after I graduated, I noticed that my younger brother was starting to get involved with the wrong crowd and going down a bad path.

"I went over to the high school and visited your father in his office. I asked for his help in straightening my brother out, and he didn't hesitate for a moment to help. He managed to get my brother back on the right track, and I was forever grateful."

The renowned sportswriter, Gene Haley wrote this about Jay in one of his articles, "Mr. Dakelman was one of the most important people in athletics in Middlesex County. If there was something Mr. Dakelman wanted to do, he would do it. He was not just another guy joining in on the idea. He was the one in front, making things happen. He was the motivator."

Keith Cook, Class of 1991, who played in that memorable 1990 championship game against South River said, "Mr. Dakelman attracted a lot of college recruiters because he was so well-known and well-liked. He was dedicated to sports and Highland Park. I will always remember half-time of the South River game. We were down by fifteen points, and he came into the locker room and started talking to us. And then, with a few tears, he told us that we were a really good bunch of guys and that one of the reasons that he waited to retire until after football season was because he was so proud of us and he knew that we would excel."

John Broggi, Class of 1963, recalled, "Mr. Dakelman was responsible for making my love of sports grow to what it is now. He was my coach throughout high school. Even if there were students who weren't good at sports if they had an interest in athletics, Jay would find some way to use them, to get them involved, keeping stats or announcing, whatever it was, it was a hell of a lot more fun than sitting on the bench."

Dr. Mark Green, Class of 1964, remembered Jay fondly as his teacher and his dental patient. "Since I wasn't an athlete, I only had Mr. Dakelman as a Health and Physical Education teacher. However, when he became my patient, I knew that he was very proud of my accomplishments in becoming a dentist. I was always a little in awe when he was in my chair."

Stephanie Rehbein, Class of 1991 offered this story about Jay. "Mr. Dakelman was always there. Always willing to give advice and help out. There was something about him that inspired me to work hard and give my all. Whenever he went to the track meets (I don't think he ever missed one), he watched and yelled. The minute I saw him, I ran faster. I looked up to him and wanted to make him proud. A year ago, I had really bad shin splints. Mr. Dakelman found an article on how to get rid of them. He was always looking out for his athletes.

"Last year, the high school Athletic Department nominated me for a Walt Disney Doer and Dreamer award. Mr. Dakelman helped me prepare the entry form as well as the other requirements. To my surprise, I was one of the ten semifinalists from our state. The next step was an interview, which Mr. Dakelman personally drove me to. He made sure that everything was taken care of for me. When Mr. Dakelman was planning something, you never had to worry. He made sure that everything was completed and submitted on time. Mr. Dakelman was a man I respected a great deal."

Jack Simcsak, Class of 1966, a field goal kicker, and Owl quarterback, had many heart-warming stories to impart. "When I was in the sixth grade, my gym teacher, Mr. Leppert, was impressed with my ability to throw the football, and he told Jay about me.

"I went to practice on the first day of my freshman year, and Coach worked us so hard that when I came home, I told my mother, 'I quit,' and went up to bed. There was no way I was going to play to wake up feeling that bad every morning.

"When I didn't show up for practice the next day, the phone rang, and my mother answered it. She called me and told me to pick up the phone. It was Jay. 'You'd better get your ass down here right away!' he roared. You better believe I got dressed as fast as I could and ran all the way down to the high school."

In interviewing former athletes for this biography, the question that I was most interested in was Jay's ability to motivate youngsters to get the best performances from them. Jack Simcsak had a great story to share on this subject.

"The first three years that I was in high school, the great Rich Policastro was the quarterback and so I didn't have a lot of experience playing that position until my senior year. There had been another kid, Paul Rosenberg, who was in the class behind me and was supposed to take over as quarterback after Policastro graduated. However, Paul's family moved out of town, and I was 'it.'

"The summer before my senior season, Jay came to our house to speak to my parents about sending me to quarterback camp in Maine. I didn't think my parents were going to let me go, but after Jay's visit, they decided that it would be worth it, so I went.

"We lost the first game of the '65 season to South Plainfield, and I was feeling pretty bad about it. Walking back to the bus Jay was a little ahead of me; I was alone. As I passed by him, he muttered under his breath, just loud enough for me to hear, 'Sure wish Rosenberg hadn't moved.'

"When I heard him say this, I got so mad. I took my seat on the bus and fumed. 'I'll show him,'" I thought. "'Just wait until next week!' We didn't lose another game that season."

A classmate of mine, Dyanne Donovan Sebastian, told me that when her father was sick with cancer and couldn't see his son, Ricky, play in person, Jay came to the Donovan house with a movie projector and game film so that Mr. Donovan didn't miss a game. Comparable stories were related to me by Jack Simcsak and Jack Fertig, whose parents also received private screenings of their sons' games when they were ill. Jay never told anyone at home that he had done this wonderful, good deed for his football family.

Doug Milch, Class of '68 answered the question about motivation by saying, "Jay motivated me with his yelling. He could yell really loud and I never wanted to get yelled at by him. When I was a sophomore, I played like a sophomore. We lost our first game of the season to South Plainfield, 20-14 and at the following Monday practice we had a full scrimmage rather than our usual 'walk through.' Something got into me that day and I decided to try extra hard.

"The first team offense played against the second team defense, and I was in the defensive backfield at cornerback facing Jack Simscak, Billy Rausch, and Dave Myers. I was all over the field, making tackles and knocking down passes. And right before practice ended, Jay singled me out. 'Milch, good job today!' He had noticed! Then, further in the week he pulled me into his office and told me to be ready this weekend because he might put me in to play against South River."

David Ballou, Class of '92, recalled, "My memory of Jay Dakelman is that he was a man of great courage. His love of sports kept him on the practice field, consistently monitoring the progress of his high school football team. His great strength and personal courage inspired and drove the team to a ten-win state championship season. His experience with the game of football was unsurpassed. I recall a practice in which every time I snapped the football, it fell short or went over the head of the placeholder. With just a few words, he had my snaps perfect every time."

Jay was not only an expert strategist when it came to getting the most out of his students; he was great when it came to the facilities at Highland Park High School. He was the one who oversaw the building of the original cinder track in 1960, one of only two cinder tracks built on the East coast, a facility that was fourteen years overdue from the beginning of his tenure as Head Track Coach.

After the passage of Title IX, it became necessary to provide a locker room for the girls' team, equal to the facility that the boys' teams had. My sister, Rhonda, remembered Jay struggling with the dilemma of how to construct a locker room for the ladies without biting into the budget to renovate the track, which after twenty years was in serious need of improvement.

"The health classroom was very large," Rhonda described it, "and divided into two parts by an accordion door. The boys had Health class on one side and the girls had class on the other. Jay realized that if a solid wall was constructed between the girls' gym locker room and half of the health classroom, the problem could be solved. The girls' team locker room could go on one side of the health classroom and the boys' health classes could be taught in empty classrooms in the main part of the school. In this way, Jay found that he could kill two birds with one stone; he could use the money saved from not having to construct a new locker room and plans for the renovated track project could go forward. I remember that he was extremely proud of this solution."

I knew that this book would not be complete without interviewing Felix Lee, one the greatest players to ever compete for Highland Park. At first Felix, who lives in Ohio, was elusive, but when we finally made contact, he explained to me why contact was so difficult for him. "I never met my birth father," he began, "and my stepfather didn't like me very much, but I loved Coach Dakelman. He was like a father to me.

"I saw him for the first time in the spring of eighth grade," Felix explained. "He was watching our practice and afterward, he invited me and a few others to come to the high school and practice with the varsity team."

Aside from being a superior football player, Felix excelled in the sprints and throwing the shot put, winning state championships in four events.

"I was an average student, but your father gave me the idea about going to college. I hadn't thought about it before. He took me over to Rutgers for a college visit himself so that it wouldn't count as a college visitation trip. He said to me, 'Any fish can make it in a small pond. It takes a big fish to make it in a big pond.'"

Felix described his visit to Penn State to meet Joe Paterno, with whom Jay had a great relationship, having sent several players to play up in Happy Valley. Rhonda, who was a little ahead of Felix in school, and Thelma went on this trip to Penn State as well. It was a successful venture, and Rhonda decided that she was going to become a Nittany Lion at that time.

"On the way home from State College, Coach D. stopped at a seafood restaurant. I had never been in a restaurant before, and when the waitress handed me a menu, I didn't know what to do with it. . . and I certainly didn't know what to order.

"So I asked your dad, 'Do they have chicken?' and he said, 'Felix, you're in a seafood restaurant. Why don't you get the red snapper? It's the 'steak of fish.'

But, I got the chicken," he reminisced, then added, "Years later, I was at a seafood restaurant and decided to try the snapper because 'Coach Dakelman said that it was very good' . . . and it was . . ."

Felix went on to Ohio State where he played for the legendary coach, Woody Hayes. "Coach Hayes was much like your father. He even came to Highland Park to see me. He didn't like his athletes to have cars or girlfriends. He was all about control. He didn't want his team to talk to the press either. He was tough. He ran a tight schedule, and he was not against putting his hands on you."

Even now, fans remember Felix Lee with adoration for his spirit on the football field, the superior performances on the track, and his soft and sweet spirit which helped to make him an incredibly special young man.

Jay's long-lasting legacy, however, boils down to one thing: his commitment and love of helping youth meet their full potentials as human beings. Although he was offered several positions coaching on the college level, he turned them down because he knew that once a coach goes that route, home stability is sacrificed. It is rare for a college coach to spend his entire career at one school, and Jay did not want to uproot his children from Highland Park.

But there was more to his refrain from staying away from college ball. He knew that his niche was in identifying the position an athlete would perform at best and teaching him how to succeed in that post.

Jay's cardiologist, Barnes Keller, said of Jay, "Wherever he went, whatever he did, he looked after kids." Jack Simcsak reminisced, "I would give anything to be able to relive the feeling of playing in a Thanksgiving game against Metuchen or even to know how special it was to come back after graduation and see old teammates and friends at that game. Jay made playing the game of football so special that it was the catalyst for much of my success in life."

Former Physical Education teacher, Brooke Paskewich said, "I feel fortunate to have worked with him. He wanted to make his kids feel proud. Kids were his main concern. He was always on the phone trying to get a student into college. He always went that extra mile. Underneath his gruff exterior, you could always get a kind word. I never knew anyone as influential and knowledgeable as he was."

Charlie King, a former Athletic Director and Principal at East Brunswick High School worked closely with Jay on the formation of the Greater Middlesex Conference. He recalled, "Jay experienced most things that could happen to a person. I was very respectful of his talents and abilities . . . and he was the Wise Old Owl in many respects."

The final words on Jay Dakelman have to come from the man who knew him the best, Joe Policastro. "The wins, the losses, the games, those things mattered to him in coaching, but it was the kids that he really loved. What touched him was to have kids come back to the school and say, 'I'm a doctor,' or 'a lawyer,' or 'a bricklayer, or 'whatever because of what I learned from you.'"

Joe learned a lot from Jay Dakelman, "but the most important lesson was not about the X's and O's. It is about knowing oneself. He advised me to 'be an Athletic Director like me, Joe, only don't ever give up coaching. Once you lost the connection with the kids, you lose everything that you love.'"

After surviving the dangers and trauma of World War II, Jay overcame the deep scars in his heart and soul by putting his energy, intelligence, and empathy into molding young men and women into productive citizens. The best of "the greatest generation," he not only believed that all of humankind is equal, but he also fought to make equality a reality for every student with whom he came in contact.

With a gruff exterior, his humility and selflessness when honored for his achievements, Jay H. Dakelman demonstrated how a man can rise above adversity and become a beacon of light for others to follow.

The spectacular Albadome of Highland Park High School shortly after it opened in 1938.

1946, Jay is ready for his first job.

The Highland Park High School football coaching staff, 1946 (L. to R) Jay Dakelman, Dick Stedman, Bus Lepine, and Bill Mathaner

The famous professor, J.B. Nash at a Friday night camp dinner." Photo taken by Jay Dakelman.

Iconic photo of Jay and Bus, the Thanksgiving Classic against Metuchen, played at New Brunswick stadium, 1958. The Owls took home the Goal Post Trophy.

Watch out! Jay's about to throw his hat at this call!

Disgusted, Jay walks away from the ref.

"Give it to him, Jay," wrote colleague Bob Kertes on this photo of Jay
screaming at a ref.

Another iconic photo, Jay kicking a field marker, 1972.

Emulating Bear Bryant of Alabama in a houndstooth fedora, 1977.

Players from the 1946 Owls team, Jay's first squad.

Craig McGrath and Nate Stephenson speak at the 1965 Pep Rally for the
Metuchen game

J. Policastro
All State Quarterback
All State Group II
All County

The great Joseph "JoJo" Policastro, Jay's protege and best friend for life,
1960, JoJo's senior year. He was an All-State Quarterback.

The beautiful Rosemarie Heldrich, one of the first young ladies to run track
for HPHS. She wore red leather shoes, crafted for her especially by Adi
Dassler of Bavaria.

The 1964 Varsity team received their championship blazers from the HP Fire Chief. (L. to R. Glenn Meltzer, Joey Pancza, Gary Beno, Chief Zoltan Erdelyi, Sammy Tumolo, Richie Policastro, Casey Gunnell.

The 1964 Highland Park Owls.

Jay's daughter, Rhonda, was a champion javelin thrower on the first girls track team in Highland Park.

The 1966 HPHS cheerleaders in their iconic uniforms.

Jay with 1973 quarterback, J.J. Jaskowski.

Jay kneels with the unforgettable Felix Lee, not only a great football player,
but All State sprinter and shot putter.

Thelma and Jay at a game in 1977.

This is the awesome principal William Donahue.

Highland Park's first black principal and superintendent, the inimitable Austin Gumbs with Jay and Maude Stockman at a dinner honoring Jay in 1977.

1958 All State winning relay team.

1958 Jay showing off the new State Championship Track and Field hardware.

Phenomenal hurdler Teddy Pisciotta, who Jay escorted to the Golden West Invitational track meet in California, 1961.

Rosemarie Heldrich runs in her Adidas shoes in Madison Square Garden

The author, Beth Dakelman Moroney and friend, Johnny Ragone are co-
Meet Directors for the Cross Country Championships, 1976

ACKNOWLEDGEMENTS

Compiling the information to write this biography on the life of my father, Jay H. Dakelman, has been an odyssey filled with surprises. From the warmth and kindness of those whom I interviewed, I gained perspectives and stories about Jay's career that I had never heard before, and I am so grateful to all who shared their memories with me.

First, I would like to thank my Writers Clique "family," Ted Baker, Adam Smith, and Anne Quinn. Your enthusiasm for this project propelled me to cross the finish line with immense pride and ecstasy in fulfilling my dream of writing a biography on Jay's life. From the first moment that we began working together, I appreciated your encouragement and frank conversations. All writers should be as lucky as I am to have a "dream team" like you.

Thank you to former athletes Jerry Donini, Doug Milch, Jack Fertig, Shawn Harrison, Donnie Leftkowitz, Glenn Meltzer, Jack Simscak, Steve Riese, Joey Pancza, Kenny Germann, and Teddy Krzyzanowsk. To Craig McGrath, thank you for reviewing the manuscript and making sure that the military information about World War II made sense; I enjoyed our conversations more than I can say.

Special thanks to my classmates, David and Linda Camporese who donated Highland Park High School family memorabilia to my research that you should have been able to share with your beautiful son. This gesture of kindness meant the world to me.

To Michael Dow, son of Dad's best friend, Jimmy and his beautiful wife, Dotty, I appreciate sharing childhood memories of our families bonding at Christmas time and your mother's delicious holiday cookies.

To Julie Klemowicz, B.J. Sklar Rego, and Brooke Paskowich, you regaled me at our reunion lunch with stories that were just so "Jay" that you brought his spirit back to me in a powerful way. It was great to see the three of you together again.

Leon Kroll gave me tales of Jay's early antics on the field and in the classroom during his first days in Highland Park that were beyond hilarious and helped to fill in the gaps from the 1940s and early 1950s.

Speaking to Pat Burns Toth and George Kish, husband of Dotty Ayres, was a joy beyond measure. They recounted stories about Jay's early commitment to furthering the careers of women athletes. I spent an incredibly special day with Rosemarie Heldrich Kiser who made me scream out loud in Panera's when she imparted the information about her red Adidas shoes that came from Adi Dassler himself. I knew that Dad had met Dassler in Bavaria, but I never heard that her special running shoes were the fruit of Dad's visit to the earliest Adidas factory.

To Greg Ficarra, thank you for filling me in on Jay's ability to multi-task and mentor young Athletic Directors. I know that you and so many other ADs from the Greater Middlesex County Conference respected Jay's dedication to all athletes receiving fair treatment on and off the playing field.

Thank you to Michael Lassiter, Principal of Highland Park High School, for permitting me to research the archives at the school library when I needed to be there. I am grateful to Joyce Puccio, Media Librarian at HPHS, for assisting me in finding and collating material that was useful to completing this story.

To my childhood friends, Margie Bernstein Metzgar and Bobbie Zimmerman Olson, it was great to reminisce about your visions of coming into the lion's den and saying hi to the pussy cat in the armchair who everyone else in the world saw as a man of mythical proportions. Recalling the taxi service that Jay provided for our four years of high school with my "best friend, Betsy Lake Schack" gave us a good deal of opportunities to laugh. To this day I cannot believe that Jay chauffeured Betsy, Ruth, Harriet, Roni, and me to school every day for four years in the green monster of a Buick that he drove for a decade.

Reminiscing with the families of the two greatest teachers and administrators I ever knew, Austin Gumbs and William Donahue, was a joy beyond measure. Their humanity, humor, and humility places them in the highest tier of educators whom I have ever known. Deepest thanks to Joycelyn Gumbs Alsup, Sean Donahue, Kerry Donahue Raslowsky, and Erin Donahue Serge for giving me further insight to these greatest of men. They are missed on an eternal basis among those of us from Highland Park.

To Felix Lee, thanks for giving Jay some of the best moments that he ever had with one of his stars. You are just so special to the Dakelman family and always will be. We love you.

To Joseph Policastro, you will always be JoJo to me, my brother from another mother; you were the boy and the man who spent more time than anyone else on this planet with Jay and I know that your relationship with him was one of the most important of your life. I could not have written this tribute to Jay without your support and input. There simply are not enough words to tell you how important you are to the Dakelman family.

Rhonda, I always love "channeling my inner Jay" with you. Your memory is impeccable, and because you are an athlete and coach, a true chip off the old block, your contributions and recollections were vital to reconstructing the story of Dad's coaching days. It is a good thing that we speak the same language.

Without maintaining the trove of photographic slides, the negatives of pictures that Jay took during World War II, and the enormous collection of crumbling newspaper articles and scrapbooks, I would not have been able to write about the early days of track and field in Highland Park. Mitchell, you have a way of surprising me like no one else can. Thank you for being my brother and one of my best friends.

To my family, Shauna, Jon, and Lily, thank you for your encouragement and handholding that you did throughout the ordeal of putting the puzzle pieces together to create a coherent story.

And finally, to my husband, Tom, who met his father-in-law for the first time in true Dakelman tradition at a 1981 Middlesex County Track and Field Championship in South River, thank you for listening to me moan over the last five years as I struggled to put this book together. Jay and I were co-starters at that County meet, and his performance that day gave you a glimpse into what life would be like if you hooked up with me permanently. I guess he did not scare you too much. And then, of course, there was the fact that Jay had season tickets to the Giants did not hurt either. Jay even chose our wedding date because on November 22, 1981, "the Giants were away." Ha! Ha! Welcome to the Dakelman family where all momentous events are scheduled based on the dates of meets, matches, and games.

Although she is no longer with us, thanks to my special mother, Thelma, the songbird, for the sacrifices that she made to accommodate Dad's schedule over the years. I am sure that he wasn't at all embarrassed when she took out her needlepoint to work on while at the Giants-Dallas game in 1979.

Before I close these remarks, the person to whom I owe the most in writing *The Bridge to Victory* is Jay Dakelman. Although he left us long ago, I felt his uncanny presence behind me throughout this journey. There were too many times that coincidences occurred for him not to have been part of the game plan.

Here is one example of those coincidences. As I mentioned multiple times in the book, Jay was fastidious about taking photographs. During the time that I was conducting research on J.B. Nash, I found it odd that Jay had not taken any photographs of his NYU professor during summer camp for his Master's Degree. On the morning of Super Bowl Sunday in 2021, I was bemoaning that fact to Tom.

When my brother arrived later that day to watch the Super Bowl with us, he had a photo album tucked under his arm. "Here's another album I found," he said as he thrust the book at me. "It's from Dad's college days."

As I perused the scrapbook, I noticed that at the end were photos from NYU camp, and there, on the last page, is a photo of J.B. Nash having dinner with his students. Add that strange coincidence to the fact that Jay departed from us the day after the

Super Bowl in 1991 and sent me the photo of Nash on Super Bowl Sunday.

How could I ignore the fact that you were with me through every phase of this journey, Dad? Although I am so proud to have completed this tribute to your extraordinary life, I will miss the connection that we shared during this amazing journey. Your rock-steady patriotism and the sacrifices that you made in youth are appreciated forever by those who knew and loved you. However, the most important lesson that you taught by modeling it throughout your life was your vision of equality for every person, male or female, no matter what color or creed. Thank you for being the beacon of light who settled for nothing less than victory in all fields of play.

BIBLIOGRAPHY

Albadomes, Highland Park High School Yearbooks, 1936-1991.

Albin, Ed. "Figg Paces Owls," *The Home News, 1977.*

Allena, Dave. "Raritan Valley Teams Fighting for Sectional Crowns," *The Home News,* November 6, 1977.

"Austin 'Bus' Lepine," Rutgers Athletics Hall of Fame. scarletknights.com.

baseball-reference.com/register/player/fcgi?id=lepine001aus

Bank, Irv. "Carteret in Third Try for Group III Laurels," *The Home News,* n.d., 1976.

Bank, Irv. "Carteret Snubbed on County Team," *The Home News,* n.d., 1976.

Bank, Irv. "Central Jersey Group IV Playoff Could Pit Capraro vs.

Capraro," *The Home News,* n.d.

Bank, Irv. "Cohen Disappointed in Times: 'Greatest Thing for Dakelman," *The Home News,* July 31, 1977, p. B8.

Bank, Irv. "Just What Does Running Up Lop-sided Scores Prove?" *The Home News,* n.d., 1977.

Bank, Irv. "Playoff Games Bring End to Area Football Season," *The Home News,* August 26, 1976.

Bank, Irv. "Recine Feels Cleats May Be the Reason," *The Home News,* n.d., 1976.

Bank, Irv. "Tigers Over Chiefs," *Home News,* n.d., 1976.

Beck, Alfred M., Abe Bortz, Charles W. Lynch, Lida Mayo, and Ralph F. Weld. *The Corps of Engineers: The War Against Germany.:* Center of Military History, United States Army. Washington, D.C.: 1985.

Blasko, Andrea. "Dakelman Accepts Award with Grace," December 1990.

Brennan, Sean. "Courage, Dedication Inspires Jay Dakelman,*"* *The Highland Fling,"* June 10, 1977.

Brennan, Sean. "Dakelman Retires as Grid Coach," *The Highland Fling,* December 23, 1977, p. 1.

Bruns, John and Tom Hester. "Colleges Would List Athletes' Grad Rate, *The Home News,* June 18, 1989.

Cancro, Bob. "Owls Blitz Monroe, 30-8," *The Home News,* Dec. 12, 1976, B4.

Cancro, Bob. "Owls Go On Rampage Against West Windsor, 20-7," *The Home News,* n.d., 1977.

"County Athletes Impress: Jim Fielding and Dave Evans Double Winners; Owls, Bulldogs in Good Team Showings," *The Home News,* May 1948.

Denman, Elliott. "The Press Box: Felix the Future Buckeye," *The Star Ledger,* 1976.

"Evans Scores Wins in 100 and 220 Runs, Owls Place Third in State Track Meet," *The Home News,* June 1948.

Glicken, Lloyde. "All-State Eleven Honored Jan. 27," *The Star Ledger,* January 1977.

Glicken, Lloyde. "Dakelman Displays Class On and Off Field," *The Star Ledger,* August 22, 1977, p.32.

Glicken, Lloyde. "Dakelman hands AD Reins to Policastro: Finishes Long, Successful Career at Highland Park," *The Star Ledger,* December 31, 1990, p. 48.

Glicken, Lloyde. "Dakelman Picked as Top Coach," *The Star Ledger,* n.d. 1976.

Glicken, Lloyd. "Dakelman Wants Numbers Game Sacked in Football Playoff System," *The Star Ledger, nd.*

Glicken, Lloyde. "Jay Dakelman, 69, Highland Park Coach," *The Star Ledger,* January 30, 1991.

Glicken, Lloyde. "Verducci Reunited with DeRogatis," *The Star Ledger,* December 26, 1976.

Guetti, Mike. "Scholastic Football Fans Faced with Difficult Choice," *The Home News,* 1976.

Haley, Gene. "Highland Park's Gridiron Reunion Best of the Bunch," *The Home News,* July 31, 1989, p. E10.

Haley, Gene. "Highland Park Rally Tops Bulldogs, 15-8," *The Home News,* Nov. 25, 1977, p.26.

Haas, Robert, Lt.-Col. *86th Engineer Heavy Ponton Battalion History: 9 July 1941-9 July 1945.* Munich: J.G. Weiss, August 1945.

Hechler, Ken, U.S. House of Representatives. *The Bridge at Remagen: The Amazing Story of March 7, 1945.*

Heilman, Don. "Dakelman Retires as Coach," *The Home News,* December 1977, p.1.

Heilman, Don. "Likens Hayes to Dakelman: Lee Enjoys Playing for Ohio State," *The Home News,* November 27, 1977, p. B8.

Heilman, Don. "Scholastic Game of the Week: Highland Park, South Brunswick Coaches Say Defense Will Decide," *The Home News,* 1977.

Heilman, Don. "Without Dakelman Sidelines Won't Be the Same," *The Home News,* December 1977, p. B1.

Heilman, Don. "Vikings, Owls Battle to 0-0 Tie," *The Home News,* October 23, 1977.

Heilman, Don. "Game of the Week: Owls vs. Rams," *The Home News,* Nov. 4, 1977.

Henn, Bob. "Middlesex All-Stars Are Well Balanced," *New York Sunday News,* December 12, 1976.

"Highland Park and Colonia Dominate 'Big 33'," *The Home News,* 1976.

"Highland Park Coasts 20-7," *The Star Ledger,* n.d., 1977.

Highland Park High School Football Program 1999.

"Highland Park Triumphs, 27-6," *The Star Ledger,* 1976.

"Home News Top Ten: Nine Ranked Teams in C.J. Playoffs,"* The Home News,* n.d., 1977.

"How the Army's Amazing Bailey Bridge is Built," *The War Illustrated,* January 19, 1945.

How the Weather Affected the War, The Weather Channel.

"Hundreds bid goodbye to Park's 'wise old owl' by Lily T'ang Ling. *Highland Park Herald,* February 1, 1991, pp. 1-2.

"In Memoriam" tandfonline.com. (Obituary for J.B. Nash).

Johnson, Bob. "Highland Park Keeps Central Jersey Track Title," *Asbury Park Press,* n.d., *1948.*

Journal of Health, Physical Education, Recreation. Vol. 36, No. 9, 1965.

Kolva, Jeanne and Joanne Pisciotta. Highland Park: Borough of Homes. Charleston, S.C.: Arcadia, 2005.

Kolva, Jeanne. Images of America: Highland Park in the 20th Century. Charleston, S.C.: Arcadia, 2012.

Kolva, Jeanne and Joanne Pisciotta. Images of America: Highland Park. Charleston, S.C.: Arcadia, 1999.

Konick, Jr. Emery, "Friends to Honor Dakelman," The Home News, 1976.

legacy.com/us/obituaries/mycentraljersey/name/margaret-lepine-obituary?id=24694431

Levine, Barry. "Dakelman Ends Career," The News Tribune, December 9, 1977, p. 24.

Levine, Barry. "Dakelman Hurdled Obstacles to Produce Winning Team," The Home News, Sept. 18, 1976.

Levine, Barry. "Final Minute Touchdown Foils Metuchen Gridders," News Tribune, November 28, 1977.

Levine, Barry. "Highland Park Blanks Rams to Clinch Bicentennial Title," The Home News, November 7, 1976.

Levine, Barry. "Junior Connection Shines," The Home News, November 14, 1976, p. B8.

Levine, Barry. "Keansburg Crushes Owls' Title Hopes, Victory Streak," The Home News, n.d., 1976.

Levine, Barry. "Owls Follow Dakelman's Instructions," The Home News, n.d., 1976.

Levine, Barry. "Owls Hooting Over Fourth Win," The Home News, n.d.

Levine, Barry. "Owls Overcome Adversity, St. Thomas," The Home News, Sept. 25, 1976, p.9.

Levine, Barry. "Owls Overwhelm North Brunswick," The Home News, October 3, 1976.

Levine, Barry. "Owls Shoot for Perfection in Group I Title Game," *The Home News,* n.d., 1976.

Levine, Barry. "Dakelman Tapped as Best Athletic Director in U.S." *The Home News,* April 26, 1982, p. 12.

Levine, Barry. "Undefeated Highland Park Defenses Metuchen, 14-6, *The Home News,* n.d.

Mahoney, John. "Owls Blank Bruins, 15-0," *The Home News,* n.d., 1977.

Marano, Tony. "Sun Slants: Track Forgotten Sport," *The Star Ledger,* May 1948.

Markowitz, Arnold. "Highland Park Coach Puts Crying Towel Away," *The Star Ledger,* Nov. 1964.

Markowitz, Arnold. "Highland Park —Perfectionism," *The Star Ledger,* October 1964.

McGlaughlin, Joe. "Highland Park May Still Get That Practice Field and Continue Its Remarkable Record,"1956.

"Middlesex Player of Week: Highland Park's Harrison Does So Many Things Well," *The Home News,* 1976.

"Middle Street Synagogue." en.m.wikipedia.org.

Miller, Al. "Owls Nip Bulldogs 18-14; Finish Unbeaten," *The Home News* November 27, 1964, p.29.

montclair.on.worldcat.org/search

Neill, Ted. "The Capital of Ruins —Nine Facts About the Battle for St. Lo."

Militaryhistorynow.com, 12 March 2019.

New York City Dept. of Education (1948). Extending Education Through Camping. The School Camp Experiment. NY: Life Camps.

"19 Records Set in Central N.J. School Meet," *The Home News,* May 28, 1950.

Novich, Dr. Max M. "A Contender for Hall of Fame," *The Jewish News,* July 5, 1979, p. 35.

"Once Upon a Time in the Vest," from *Sports Articles of the Day.* Vol. 4, No. 5. June 1964 AAU Meet at Rutgers.

O'Rourke, Pete. "Buckeyes Land Lee," *The Home News,* n.d., 1977.

O'Rourke, Pete. "Dakelman to Receive Key," *The Home News,* February 1976.

"Owls, Cards, Raiders Top Bicentennial Team," *The Home News,* n.d., 1976.

Ozier, Lance W. Ed.D. "Camp as Educator: Lessons Learned from History." American Camp Association Camping Magazine.

Pall, Tom. "In 19th Season: Dakelman Looks for Magic Potion," *The Home News,* September 23, 1977.

Pall, Tom. "Dakelman: My Most Memorable," *The Home News,* December 7, 1977.

Pall, Tom. "Highland Park-Windsor Battle to Feature Defense," *The Home News,* 1977.

Pall, Tom. "Owls Start BAC Defense by Defeating St. Thomas. *Home News.* September 24, 1977.

Pall, Tom. "Owls Branch Out Behind FB Figg," *The Home News,* October 24, 1976,

Pall, Tom. "Owls Trounce Monroe," *The Home News,* October 8, 1977.

Pall, Tom. "Parkites Prevail, 7-0," *The Home News,* September 1977.

Pall, Tom. "Six Area Teams Vie for Championships," *The Home News,* Nov. 30, 1977.

Pall, Tom. "South River Stops Highland Park," *The Home News,* November 6, 1977.

Pall, Tom. "Unbeaten Owls Roll Past St. Peter's," *The Home News,* October 31, 1976, p. B7.

Pall, Tom. "Will Highland Park Try to Surprise Dunellen?" *The Home News,* December 5, 1977.

Patella, John. "H. Park Loses Its Best Coach," *The Home News,* January 31, 1991.

Paul, Gordon. "Figg, Riese Lead Highland Park," *The Star Ledger,* December 7, 1977.

Perone, Joe. "Penalties Hurt Green Brook," *The Star Ledger,* n.d., 1976.

Picker, Doug. "All Middlesex: Hawkes, Kovacs, Fallon," *The Home News,* n.d., 1976.

Picker, Doug. "8-0 Highland Park to Face Green Brook," *The Home News,* n.d., 1976.

Plescia, Mark. "Conferences Going Through Those Changes," *The Home News,* n.d., 1976.

Puccio, John. "Owls Rout Dunellen," *The Home News,* December 7, 1977.

"Riese Leads Owls Past St. Peter's," *The Home News,* October 24, 1977.

Rubin, Kimberly. "Jay Howard Dakelman," *The Highland Fling,* March 14, 1991, pp. 4-5.

scarletknights.com/honors/rutgers-athletics-hall-of-fame/austin-bus-lepine/136.

Shapiro, Les. "Highland Park Blanks St. Peters," *The Home News,* October 1949.

Sullivan, Jim. "Highland Park Wins Track Title, *Asbury Park Press,* May 29, 1949.

"Track Victory to Somerville," *The Courier News,* April 22, 1948.

Travers, Bill. Notice of Selection as Coach of the Daily News Coach of the Year, Western Union Mailgram, Dec. 3, 1976.

Turi, Gemma. "Women's Sports," *The Home News*, n.d., B10.

Usagymlegacy.com

Van Leer, Laurel. "His Love of Sports Lifelong," *The Home News,* January 31, 1991.

Zardetto, Ray. "Dunellen's Season Ends on Sour Note," *Courier News,* Dec. 5, 1977.

ENDNOTES

CHAPTER 1

[1] Olympia. Panzer yearbook, 1943, p. 2.

[2] "RMS Queen Elizabeth." En.m.wikipedia.org

[3] Robert Haas, Lt. Col. 86th engineer Heavy Pontoon Battalion History: 9 July 1941 to 9 July 1945. Munich: J.G. Weiss, August 1945, p.19.

[4] Haas, 19.

CHAPTER 2

[1] Robert Haas, Lt. Col. 86th engineer Heavy Pontoon Battalion History: 9 July 1941 to 9 July 1945. Munich: J.G. Weiss, August 1945, p.19.

[2] Haas, 22.

[3] Haas, 22.

[4] Alfred M. Beck, Abe Bortz, Charles W. Lynch, Lida Mayo, and Ralph F. Weld. The Corps of Engineers: The War Against Germany. Center of Military History, United States Army, Washington, D.C., 1985, p.vii.

[5] Haas, 20.

[6] "Middle Street Synagogue." en.m.wikipedia.org

[7] Information about the families with whom Jay bonded is taken from photographs that Jay took during his time in the Cotswolds. There are numerous photos of various pharmacies in the area.

[8] Tortworth Castle information taken from photographs that Jay took.

[9] Haas, 23.

[10] Haas, 23.

[11] Haas, 24.

[12] Haas, 24.

[13] Haas, 25.

[14] Haas, 25.

CHAPTER 3

[1] Robert Haas, Lt. Col. <u>86th engineer Heavy Pontoon Battalion History: 9 July 1941 to 9 July 1945.</u> Munich: J.G. Weiss, August 1945, p.29.

[2] Haas, p.29.

[3] Haas, p. 30.

[4] Haas, p. 30.

[5] Haas, p. 30.

[6] The story of "Frenchie" is taken from Jay's photo albums.

[7] Ted Neill. "The Capital of Ruins—--Nine Facts About the Battle of St. Lo." Militaryhistorynow.com, 12 March 2019.

[8] Neill.

[9] Neill.

[10] Neill.

[11] Neill.

[12] Neill.

[13] Haas, p.31.

[14] Neill.

[15] Haas, p. 31.

[16] Neill.

[17] Neill.

[18] Haas, p. 32.

[19] Haas, p. 32

CHAPTER 4

[1] Jay loathed General Eisenhower for the rest of his life after the blunders that the General made during the war. Most particularly, Jay never forgave Eisenhower's delay of taking Berlin when he had the opportunity to do so. Instead, Eisenhower opted to wait for the arrival of the Russians so that the two conquering armies could appear to be in alignment for the most glorious

moment of the war. Jay felt that this decision led ultimately to the division of East and West Berlin.

[2] "The Liberation of Paris." nationalww2museum.org, August 25, 2023.

[3] "The Liberation of Paris."

[4] "The Liberation of Paris."

[5] "The Liberation of Paris."

[6] "The Liberation of Paris."

[7] Robert Haas, Lt. Col. 86th engineer Heavy Pontoon Battalion History: 9 July 1941 to 9 July 1945. Munich: J.G. Weiss, August 1945, p.32.

[8] "The Liberation of Paris."

[9] The information about Jay's sightseeing during his brief furlough in Paris is taken from the captions underneath the photographs in his albums.

[10] Haas, p. 32.

[11] Haas, p. 32.

[12] "Bailey Bridges." en.m.wikipedia.org

[13] "Bailey Bridges."

[14] "Bailey Bridges."

[15] Haas, p. 33.

CHAPTER 5

[1] Robert Haas, Lt. Col. 86th engineer Heavy Pontoon Battalion History: 9 July 1941 to 9 July 1945. Munich: J.G. Weiss, August 1945, p. 34.

[2] Haas, p. 34.

[3] Haas, p. 34.

[4] Haas, p. 34.

[5] "How Weather Affected the War." *The Weather Channel.*

[6] "How Weather Affected the War." *The Weather Channel.*

[7] Haas, p. 35.

[8] Haas, p. 36.

[9] Haas, p. 36.

[10] Haas, p. 36

[11] Haas, p. 36.

[12] Massacre at Malmedy

[13] Haas, p. 37.

14 Haas, p. 37.

CHAPTER 6

1 Although when Jay started his war-time correspondence with Thelma Jacoby, neither of them had an idea of how those letters would change the course of their lives, Thelma saved each missive for the rest of her life. Fortunately, the letters remain in pristine condition, having been preserved in a plastic bag for almost 80 years. She also saved several empty bottles of Parisian perfume which Jay referred to in his letters. These relics of their early relationship are treasured to this day by the Dakelman family.

2 Note: Jay had been promoted from the rank of Private to Corporal.

3 Robert Haas, Lt. Col. 86th engineer Heavy Pontoon Battalion History: 9 July 1941 to 9 July 1945. Munich: J.G. Weiss, August 1945, p.38.

4 Haas, p. 39,

5 Haas, p. 39.

6 Haas, p. 39.

7 Haas, p. 40.

8 Haas, p. 40

9 Haas, p. 40

CHAPTER 7

1 Robert Haas, Lt. Col. 86th engineer Heavy Pontoon Battalion History: 9 July 1941 to 9 July 1945. Munich: J.G. Weiss, August 1945, p.41.

2 Haas, p. 41.

3 The Bridge at Remagen. Directed by John Guillermin, United Artists, 1969.

4 Haas, p. 41.

5 Alfred M. Beck, Abe Bortz, Charles W. Lynch, Lida Mayo, and Ralph F. Weld. The Corps of Engineers: The War Against Germany. Washington, D.C.: Center of Military History, 1985, p. 505.

6 Alfred Beck, et. al., p. 505.

7 Haas, p. 42.

8 Haas, p. 42.

9 Haas, p. 43.

[10] Information taken from the captions of photographs taken by Corporal Jay Dakelman at the Battle of Remagen.

[11] Haas, p. 43.

[12] Alfred Beck, et. al., p. 521.

[13] Alfred Beck, et. al. p. 555.

CHAPTER 8

[1] Robert Haas, Lt. Col. <u>86th engineer Heavy Pontoon Battalion History: 9 July 1941 to 9 July 1945.</u> Munich: J.G. Weiss, August 1945, p.43.

[2] Haas, p. 44.

[3] Haas, p. 45.

[4] Haas, p. 45.

[5] Haas, p. 45.

[6] Hass, p. 45.

CHAPTER 9

[1] Robert Haas, Lt. Col. <u>86th engineer Heavy Pontoon Battalion History: 9 July 1941 to 9 July 1945.</u> Munich: J.G. Weiss, August 1945, p.45.

[2] The story of Jay's experiences in Buchenwald were relayed to the author over the years in which they were able to talk about it. Details of the experience did not come easily from Jay, but little by little he described the horror that he and the men of the 86th witnessed in the two camps that they liberated. He imparted these stories to me long before I ever saw photographs or film that confirmed what Jay had said.

Towards the end of his life, Jay did speak to several high school classes about his experiences during World War II, but he concentrated mostly on the accomplishments of the 86th as the heroic bridge builders and engineers that they were during the war. Never once did he speak of the atrocities that he had witnessed in the camps.

[3] "Buchenwald," <u>Holocaust Encyclopedia.</u> encyclopediaushmm.org

[4] "Buchenwald."

[5] Ilse Koch. simple.m.wikipedia.org

[6] Ilse Koch.

Chapter 10

[1] Whenever I go out to speak on my father's experiences during the war, whether it is to a school, religious or community organization, I bring the relics mentioned in this chapter with me. By far, the one that gets the greatest reaction is the swastika. The Nazi symbol of horror still raises the hackles on the arms of those who understand the meaning of the barbarism that it represents.

[2] Robert Haas, Lt. Col. 86th engineer Heavy Pontoon Battalion History: 9 July 1941 to 9 July 1945. Munich: J.G. Weiss, August 1945, p.45.

[3] Haas, p. 47.

[4] Haas, p. 47.

[5] Haas, p. 47.

[6] Haas, p. 48.

[7] Haas, p. 48.

Chapter 11

[1] Robert Haas, Lt. Col. 86th engineer Heavy Ponton Battalion History: 9 July 1941 to 9 July 1945. Munich: J.G. Weiss, August 1945, p.52.

[2] All information about Camp Cleveland is taken from Jay's photographs. He made copious notes about the people and places he had been during the war in the three thick albums that he compiled after the war. His near perfect memory made it easy for him to document each photo. Since the Eisenhower Library, where much of the information on the European front had been stored after the war burned down in the 1950s, many of Jay's photos could be rare.

At the tail end of the third album are photographs of some Yankee baseball games that Jay attended upon his return to the United States. The pictures of America's favorite pastime seem to be a fitting coda to Jay's tribulations during the war. He is home. He is safe. He is watching Yankee baseball. It doesn't get any better than that.

Chapter 12

[1] "In Memoriam" tandfonline.com. (Obituary for J. B. Nash).

[2] "In Memoriam" tandfonline.com.

CHAPTER 13

[1] Albadome, 1947.

CHAPTER 14

[1] Jean Kolva. Images of America: Highland Park in the 20th Century. Charleston, South Carolina: Arcadia, 2012, p. 53.
[2] Kolva, p. 53.
[3] Kolva, p. 54.
[4] Interview with Leon Kroll, January 2023.
[5] Kolva, p. 58.
[6] Kolva, p. 65.
[7] Jay often made this comment to the author.
[8] Interview with Joe Policastro, February 2022.
[9] Interview with Shawn Harrison, September 2023.

CHAPTER 15

[1] Footnotes 1-9 are all taken from a lengthy interview with Joe Policastro that took place in February of 2022.
[2] Footnotes 10-19 are all taken from the 1960 Highland Park High School Yearbook, *The Albadome 20-23.*
[3] Interview with Joe Policastro, February 2022.

CHAPTER 16

[1] Arnold Markowitz. "Highland Park Coach Puts Crying Towel Away," The Star Ledger, November 1964.
[2] Markowitz.
[3] Markowitz.
[4] Markowitz.
[5] Markowitz.
[6] Markowitz.
[7] Interview with Joe Pancza, February 2023.
[8] Markowitz.

[9] Interview with Joe Pancza.

[10] Al Miller. "Owls Nip Bulldogs 18-14; Finish Unbeaten," *The Home News*, November 27, 1964.

[11] Miller.

[12] Interview with Joe Pancza.

[13] Interview with Jack Fertig, January 2023.

CHAPTER 17

[1] Mark Plescia. "Conferences Going Through Those Changes, The Home News,
N.d., 1976.

[2] Plescia.

[3] Plescia.

[4] Interview with Felix Lee, January 2023.

[5] Interview with Felix Lee.

[6] Interview with Felix Lee.

[7] Barry Levine. "Jimenez Ineligible," *The Home News*, Sept. 1976.

[8] Barry Levine. "Owls Overcome Adversity, St. Thomas," *The Home News*, September 25, 1976.

[9] Levine, "Owls Overcome Adversity, St. Thomas."

[10] Levine, "Owls Overcome Adversity, St. Thomas."

[11] Levine, "Owls Overcome Adversity, St. Thomas."

[12] Barry Levine. "Dakelman Hurdled Obstacles to Produce Winning Team," *The Home News*, September 19, 1976.

[13] Levine, "Dakelman Hurdled Obstacles."

[14] Levine, "Dakelman Hurdled Obstacles."

[15] Barry Levine. "Owls Overwhelm North Brunswick," *The Home News*, November 3, 1976.

[16] Levine, "Owls Overwhelm North Brunswick."

[17] Levine, "Owls Overwhelm North Brunswick."

[18] Levine, "Owls Overwhelm North Brunswick."

[19] Levine, "Owls Overwhelm North Brunswick."

[20] Levine, "Owls Overwhelm North Brunswick."

[21] Levine, "Owls Overwhelm North Brunswick."

[22] Levine, "Owls Overwhelm North Brunswick."

[23] Levine, "Owls Overwhelm North Brunswick."

[24] Levine, "Owls Overwhelm North Brunswick."

[25] Levine, "Owls Overwhelm North Brunswick."

[26] Levine, "Owls Overwhelm North Brunswick."

[27] Barry Levine. "Owls Hooting Over Fourth Win." The Home News, 25, 1976.

[28] Levine, "Owls Hooting Over Fourth Win."

[29] Levine, "Owls Hooting Over Fourth Win."

[30] Levine, "Owls Hooting Over Fourth Win."

[31] Levine, "Owls Hooting Over Fourth Win."

[32] Tom Pall. "Owls Branch Out Behind FB Figg," *The Home News*, October 24, 1976.

[33] Pall, "Owls Branch Out Behind FB Figg."

[34] Pall, "Owls Branch Out Behind FB Figg."

[35] Tom Pall. "Unbeaten Owls Roll Past St. Peter's," The Home News, October 31, 1976, p. B7.

[36] Pall, "Unbeaten Owls Roll Past St. Peter's."

[37] Barry Levine. "Highland Park Blanks Rams to Clinch Bicentennial Title," *The Home News,* November 6, 1976.

[38] Levine, "Highland Park Blanks Rams."

[39] Levine, "Highland Park Blanks Rams."

[40] Levine, "Highland Park Blanks Rams."

[41] "St. Pius Defeated," *The Home News*, November 14, 1976.

[42] "St. Pius Defeated."

[43] Irv Bank. "Central Jersey Group IV Playoff Could Pit Capraro vs. Capraro," *The Home News*, November 1976.

[44] Irv. Bank. "Central Jersey Group IV Playoff."

[45] Barry Levine. "Owls Follow Dakelman's Instructions to a TD," *The Home News*, n.d.

[46] Levine, "Owls Follow Dakelman's Instructions to a TD."

[47] Barry Levine, "Owls Follow Dakelman's Instructions to a TD."

[48] Levine, "Undefeated Highland Park Defenses Metuchen, 14-6."

[49] Levine, "Undefeated Highland Park Defenses Metuchen, 14-6."

[50] Levine, "Undefeated Highland Park Defenses Metuchen, 14-6."

[51] Levine, "Undefeated Highland Park Defenses Metuchen, 14-6."

[52] Doug Picker. "8-0 Highland Park to Face Green Brook," *The Home News*, n.d.

[53] Doug Picker, "8-0 Highland Park to Face Green Brook."

CHAPTER 18

[1] Letter from former athlete, David Malatesta.

[2] Interview with Joe Policastro.

[3] Interview with Joe Policastro.

[4] Interview with Joe Policastro."

[5] Barry Levine. "Keansburg Crushes Owls' Title Hopes, Victory Streak, *The Home News,* December 1976, B4.

[6] Barry Levine, "Keansburg Crushes Owls."

[7] Barry Levine, "Keansburg Crushes Owls."

[8] Barry Levine, "Keansburg Crushes Owls."

[9] Barry Levine, "Keansburg Crushes Owls."

[10] Lloyde Glicken. "All-State Eleven Honored January 27," *The Star Ledger*, n.d.

[11] Lloyde Glicken, "All-State Eleven Honored January 27."

[12] *Daily News Telegram,* December 3, 1976.

[13] Telegram from Frank Burns, Head Football Coach Rutgers University.

[14] Letter From Bob, Athletic Director at Piscataway High School, Panzer Classmate of Jay's.

[15] Letter From Gene Felker, Director of the Annual Football Clinic in Atlantic City.

[16] Letter from Mark Berkowitz, former student HPHS.

[17] Elliott Denman. "The Press Box: Felix the Future Buckeye" *The Star Ledger,* 1976.

CHAPTER 19

[1] Charlie Bloom. *Highland Park Football Reunion Booklet.*

[2] Charlie Bloom. *Highland Park Football Reunion Booklet.*

[3] Charlie Bloom. *Highland Park Football Reunion Booklet.*

[4] Mark Plescia. "Conferences Going Through Those Changes," *The Home News,* n.d.

[5] Plescia, "Conferences Going Through Those Changes."

CHAPTER 20

[1] Interview with Leon Kroll, former student and athlete.

[2] Tony Marano. "Sun Slants: Track Forgotten Sport, *The Star Ledger,* May 1948.

[3] Article on the Central Jersey Meet from *The Asbury Park Press,* no title or date recorded.

[4] "Zebras, Jefferson Top Group IV Contenders in Shore Track Meet," *Asbury Park Press,* n.d.

[5] Bob Johnson. "Highland Park Keeps Central Jersey Track Title," *Asbury Park Press,* June 1948.

[6] "Morse Sets Two Repeats at C.J. Sectional," *Asbury Park Press,* n.d.

[7] "Winckler Memorial Trophy Presented to Highland Park, *The Home News,* 1949.

[8] "Highland Park Wins Central Jersey Track Championship," *The Home News,* 1950.

[9] "Eugene C. 'Red' Littler, September 3, 2008. Starherald.com

[10] "Eugene C. 'Red' Littler, September 3, 2008. Starherald.com

[11] "Eugene C. 'Red' Littler, September 3, 2008. Starherald.com

[12] "Eugene C. 'Red' Littler, September 3, 2008. Starherald.com

[13] "Eugene C. 'Red' Littler, September 3, 2008. Starherald.com

[14] "Eugene C. 'Red' Littler, September 3, 2008. Starherald.com

[15] "Eugene C. 'Red' Littler, September 3, 2008. Starherald.com

[16] "Eugene C. 'Red' Littler, September 3, 2008. Starherald.com

[17] "Larry Ellis- Princeton Trailblazer."

[18] "Larry Ellis- Princeton Trailblazer."

[19] "Larry Ellis- Princeton Trailblazer."

CHAPTER 21

[1] Joe McGlaughlin. "Highland Park May Still Get That Practice Field and Continue Its Remarkable Track Record," 1956.

[2] "Once Upon a Time in the Vest," from *Sports Articles of the Day.* Vol.4, No. 5, June 1964, AAU Meet at Rutgers.

[3] Interview with Jerry Donini, former HPHS athlete.

[4] Interview with Ted Kryzinowski, former HPHS athlete.

[5] Interview with Kryzinowski.

[6] Interview with Kryzinowski.

[7] Goldenwestinvitational.org

CHAPTER 22

[1] *Olympia 1936,* Panzer College Yearbook.

[2] *Olympia 1936.*

[3] *Olympia 1936.*

[4] *Olympia 1936.*

[5] "Margaret Brown, Retired Educator Dies." *The New York Times,* August 3, 1990.

[6] "Panzer College Merges with Montclair State," montclair.edu, Exercise Science
And Physiology.

[7] "Margaret Brown, Retired Educator Dies."

[8] "Margaret Brown, Retired Educator Dies."

[9] Interview with Pat Burns Toth, HPHS alumna.

[10] *Albadome 1956,* "Girls Sports Night."

[11] Interview with Marjorie Bernstein Metzgar, HPHS alumna.

[12] Interview with Pat Burns Toth.

[13] Interview with George Kish, HPHS alum.

[14] Interview with George Kish.

[15] Interview with Rosemarie Heldrich, HPHS alumna.

[16] Interview with Rosemarie Heldrich, HPHS alumna.

[17] Interview with Rosemarie Heldrich, HPHS alumna.

[18] "Susan Pitt, HPHS Olympic Swimmer," Wikipedia.

[19] "Susan Pitt, HPHS Olympic Swimmer," Wikipedia.

[20] "Susan Pitt, HPHS Olympic Swimmer," Wikipedia.

[21] Quote from Heidi Schofiet, *Highland Park Fling,* January 1991.

[22] Gemma Turi. "Women's Sports," *The Home News,* n.d., B10.

[23] Gemma Turi. "Women's Sports."

CHAPTER 23

[1] "Austin Gumbs," obituary. *The Home News Tribune,* February 19, 2017.

[2] Interview with Joycelyn Gumbs Alsup.

[3] "Austin Gumbs," obituary.

[4] "Austin Gumbs," obituary.

[5] Interview with Kerry Donahue Raslowsky, HPHS alumna.

[6] Interview with Sean Donahue, HPHS alum.

[7] Interview with Erin Donahue Sorge, HPHS alumna.

[8] Interview with Erin Donahue Sorge.

[9] *The Fling,* January 1991.

[10] *The Fling,* January 1991.

[11] Interview with Theresa Ward.

[12] Interview with Brooke Paskewich

[13] Interview with Brooke Paskewich

[14] Interview with Brooke Paskewich

[15] Interview with Brooke Paskewich

[16] Interview with Julie Klemowitz

[17] Interview with Brooke Paskowich

[18] Interview with Julie Klemowitz.

[19] *The Fling,* January 1991.

[20] Interview with Joe Policastro.

CHAPTER 24

[1] *Albadome 1968.*

[2] Barry Levine. "Dakelman Ends Career," *The News Tribune,* December 9, 1977, p. 24.

[3] Barry Levine, "Dakelman Ends Career."

[4] Barry Levine, "Dakelman Ends Career."

[5] Barry Levine, "Dakelman Ends Career."

[6] Barry Levine, "Dakelman Ends Career."

[7] John Bruns and Tom Hester. "Colleges Would List Athletes' Grad Rate," *The Home News Tribune,* June 18, 1989.

[8] John Bruns and Tom Hester. "Colleges Would List Athletes' Grad Rate," *The Home News Tribune,* June 18, 1989.

[9] John Bruns and Tom Hester. "Colleges Would List Athletes' Grad Rate," *The Home News Tribune,* June 18, 1989.

[10] John Bruns and Tom Hester. "Colleges Would List Athletes' Grad Rate," *The Home News Tribune,* June 18, 1989.

[11] John Bruns and Tom Hester. "Colleges Would List Athletes' Grad Rate," *The Home News Tribune,* June 18, 1989.

[12] John Bruns and Tom Hester. "Colleges Would List Athletes' Grad Rate," *The Home News Tribune,* June 18, 1989.

[13] Barry Levine. "Dakelman Tapped as Best Athletic Director in U.S." *The Home News,* April 26, 1982, p. 12.

[14] Barry Levine, "Dakelman Tapped as Best Athletic Director in U.S."

[15] Barry Levine, "Dakelman Tapped as Best Athletic Director in U.S."

www.ingramcontent.com/pod-product-compliance
Lightning Source LLC
Chambersburg PA
CBHW070901120626
46546CB00001B/93